IN THE singular phantasmagoria that was the mind of Samuel Taylor Coleridge—that fabulous mixture of visions and fact, metaphysics and Unitarianism, domestic sentiment and social emotionalism, chaotic fragments and rounded wholes—there are many caverns to be explored. Scholars and poets find them enticing labyrinths and emerge from exploration intoxicated with Coleridge's originality and learning, which, interpreted, so well illuminate his complex poetry.

In *The Road to Xanadu* one such explorer, John Livingston Lowes, traced out the routes and roots of *The Ancient Mariner* and *Kubla Khan;* but he left the mystery of *Christabel* untouched, because, he confessed, he had come upon nothing to explain it. Mr. Nethercot now charts the road to Tryermaine (not really so far off the road to Xanadu) and penetrates the preternatural background of the great, unfinished poem, *Christabel*.

Adventuring into a strange half-world of lamias, serpents, vampires, and demons of the air, Mr. Nethercot finds, behind Coleridge's depiction of Geraldine—the first and most subtle of all vampirical creatures in English literature—the poet's doctrine of penance and vicarious atonement. This theory he traces through the maze of Coleridge's readings in witchcraft, medical demonology, the occult, and the transmigration of souls.

The history of the poem is reviewed, previous commentaries and interpretations are discussed, and the influence of Gothic fiction upon its form is fully considered. Other parts of the book deal with the local and natural background of the poem, the use of names, the conception of the "guardian spirit," and the sources of many interesting incidents and details in the poem. The author offers original speculations concerning Coleridge's literary theories and probable intentions.

The Road to Tryermaine

THE UNIVERSITY OF CHICAGO PRESS, CHICAGO

THE BAKER & TAYLOR COMPANY, NEW YORK; THE CAMBRIDGE UNIVERSITY
PRESS, LONDON; THE MARUZEN-KABUSHIKI-KAISHA, TOKYO, OSAKA,
KYOTO, FUKUOKA, SENDAI; THE COMMERCIAL PRESS, LIMITED, SHANGHAI

The Road to Tryermaine

*A Study of the History, Background, and
Purposes of Coleridge's "Christabel"*

BY
ARTHUR H. NETHERCOT

THE UNIVERSITY OF CHICAGO PRESS · CHICAGO

FOREWORD

IN THE singular phantasmagoria that was the mind of Samuel Taylor Coleridge—that almost fabulous mixture of visions and fact, metaphysics and Unitarianism, domestic sentiment and social emotionalism, chaotic fragments and perfectly rounded wholes—there are many subterranean caverns to be explored. Some of these, like the course of Alph, the sacred river, may remain forever measureless to man; but others, like the route to Xanadu, if not exactly charted on any map which would meet the approval of a twentieth-century geodetic survey, have at least had their general directions and relative positions plotted, as a medieval cartographer might have tentatively set down his illustrated warning, "Hic Anthropophagi." Tartary and Cathay, the south polar regions and the rotting Pacific at the equator, are at the same time both more familiar and also more mysterious places since John Livingston Lowes traced their nebulous boundaries as he pursued the great Khan, Kublai, and the glittering-eyed old mariner on the road to Xanadu.[1]

But Professor Lowes has regretfully confessed that he was forced to leave one major tract still *terra incognita* on his chart. The road to Xanadu may now be marked for safe travel by those armchair voyagers who are willing to lend themselves to the spell of his rare blend of scholarship and imagination; but the mountain path from Langdale Hall to Tryermaine and back is still untrodden, although the journey of Bard Bracy to the castle of Lord Roland de Vaux to inform that nobleman of his daughter Geraldine's safety, and the account of what occurred there as well as at the home of Sir Leoline, bade fair to be as strange a tale as ever Coleridge or any other Gothic romancer ever spun. But, wrote Professor Lowes in an early footnote to

---

[1] John Livingston Lowes, *The Road to Xanadu A Study in the Ways of the Imagination* (Boston and New York, 1927; rev. 1930). All references will be to the revised edition.

v

his book: "I have not included 'Christabel,' for the reason that 'Christabel' has failed completely to include itself. Wherever the mysterious tracts from which it rose may lie, they are off the road which leads to 'The Ancient Mariner' and 'Kubla Khan.' And we are following only where known facts lead. I wish I did know in what distant deeps or skies the secret lurks; but the elusive clue is yet to capture."[2]

In the present study I have endeavored to hunt down that "elusive clue" and even to capture the quarry that left it. In the process I have been forced to the conclusion that, dim as the spoor may seem to those who have not parted the thickets and examined the humus in precisely the right places and under exactly the right light, the "mysterious tracts" from which "Christabel" arose are not really so far off the road to Xanadu as Professor Lowes believed. In fact, the roads frequently coincide for fairly long stretches; and if one path chances to wander off from the other, it will later return to it again, to cross it or to accompany it in comradely fashion for another interval. Again and again Lowes was on the very brink of making the discovery which would have placed Tryermaine, like the south polar sea, on his route to Tartary; but he or his guardian spirit invariably turned his gaze in another direction, so that more obvious objects drew his attention and he was saved from slipping into the hidden valley which would have revealed a whole new vista to him.

His escape is the more remarkable, too, because before him had gone at least one other explorer who came even closer to the plunge than he. If Lowes skirted the brink of the mystery, then Ernest Hartley Coleridge, in his edition of "Christabel" for the Royal Society of Literature in 1907,[3] had one foot partly over the edge and could scarcely have avoided glimpsing the contours of the valley beneath. But something—whether near-sightedness or indolence I cannot say—made him withdraw be-

---

[2] *Ibid.*, p. 4 n.

[3] *Christabel by Samuel Taylor Coleridge Illustrated by a Facsimile of the Manuscript and by Textual and Other Notes by Ernest Hartley Coleridge* (London, 1907); referred to hereafter as "E.H.C." This important work is, unfortunately, miserably edited and proofread.

fore he had made anything more than a casual survey of the
prospect, and so he too lost his opportunity to solve a mystery
which had perplexed the literary world for over a century. To
both him and Professor Lowes, however, I owe a large debt for
their aid in breaking ground. A considerable amount of the
material in my study has been used or suggested by them,
though without their always recognizing its significance. In
justice to myself, nevertheless, I should add that my own basic
theories were derived from a study of the poem itself before I
discovered how close my predecessors had come to the same
views.[4]

At the same time, I wish to avoid any countercharge of dogma-
tizing on my own part in the following pages. I believe that the
facts and speculations which I shall set forth have more than a
modicum of truth in them. To my mind the details of material
and idea which I have gleaned in retracing Lowes's path and in
striking off into new byways of my own all blend into a unified
picture whose groundwork and outlines are clear, even though
it has not received the finishing strokes which would have con-
jured up the whole story. But I have no wish to maintain that
S. T. C.'s mind and imagination worked in such and such a
fashion and no otherwise. I do not claim to be able to point to
each phrase and circumstance in "Christabel" and cite absolute chapter and verse for its origin. In examining and winnow-
ing certain aspects of Coleridge's life and reading during the
period when he was composing his three greatest poems, I hope
only to convince the reader that the genesis of the plot, the
characters, the descriptions, the purpose, etc., might well be
thus and so. Before and during the years when "The Rime of
the Ancient Mariner", "Kubla Khan", and "Christabel" were
taking shape, their author was doing an enormous amount of
erudite and recondite reading. He was also living. It is at least

[4] Donald R. Tuttle, "*Christabel* Sources in Percy's *Reliques* and the Gothic Romances,"
PMLA, LIII (June, 1938), 445–74, has also conducted a limited exploration, but, although not completely accepting Lowes's assertions concerning the relationship (or lack
of relationship) between the sources of "Christabel" and those of the other two poems,
has too hastily concluded that the "chief sources" of the first were simply the minor
sources of the other two: Percy and a few Gothic novels. As I shall try to show, Coleridge used these works, but in a far less fundamental way than Mr. Tuttle assumes.

an odd coincidence, if no more, that echoes of this reading and this living should recur so frequently in his writing, if some such process as that which Professor Lowes ascribes to the mysterious "hooked atoms" of memory were not going on. Generous allowance, of course, must be made for coincidence; but it can scarcely be the whole story. I say this in spite of Coleridge's own warning, issued in his preface to the poem in 1816 for the purpose of precluding any "charges of plagiarism or servile imitation" which might be leveled against either Scott, Byron, or himself: "For there is amongst us a set of critics, who seem to hold, that every possible thought and image is traditional; who have no notion that there are such things as fountains in the world, small as well as great; and who would therefore charitably derive every rill they behold flowing, from a perforation made in some other man's tank."[5]

Fountains, however, must have their sources too, though they spring from nature rather than artifice. The following study, therefore, should furnish the background for a more intelligent and, I hope, illuminating interpretation of "Christabel" than has hitherto been possible.

September 8, 1939

[5] E.H.C., pp. 57–58.

TABLE OF CONTENTS

BOOK I. THE HISTORY OF THE POEM

BOOK II. THE CENTRAL MYSTERY

BOOK III. SUBSIDIARY ELEMENTS

BOOK IV. THE INTERPRETATION

INDEX

BOOK I

THE HISTORY OF THE POEM

I

CAETERA DESUNT

SPECULATION over the unfinished works of authors has always been rife and frequently been idle. The *logomachia* has been long and furious about how Dickens would have solved *Edwin Drood*, what Thackeray planned to do with *Denis Duval*, and why Stevenson's *Weir of Hermiston* would have been his greatest novel—if he had completed it. Sir Arthur Quiller-Couch actually had the brazenness to fill out Stevenson's fragmentary *St. Ives*, and George Chapman became the amanuensis for Marlowe's ghost in *Hero and Leander*. But, great as has been the wonder as to Coleridge's intentions in "Christabel", few have had the temerity to suggest a continuation into what might have been, or even an explanation of what was; and none of these few has ever found any general approval for his ideas. Part of the reason, perhaps, is not too hard to find: Coleridge himself threw out so many conflicting hints about the poem, its genesis, its wholeness of conception, its purpose, and his intentions toward completing it that its readers have been dazed and baffled as to the truth and have often questioned whether even the poet really knew how to extricate himself and his characters from the eerie plight in which he had entangled them. The history of the poem is not one of the least mysterious and tantalizing aspects of the whole matter.

During the entire period of the *Lyrical Ballads*, the story of that "lovely lady", the sweet and innocent Christabel, exposed to the unnamable designs of the diabolic but fascinating Geraldine, haunted him with what he called its "true wild weird spirit".[1] Yet even the evidence concerning the time when he began the composition of the poem is filled with contradictions. His avid memory probably did not start storing away

[1] [Thomas Allsop,] *Letters, Conversations and Recollections of S. T. Coleridge* (London, 1836), I, 94.

much of the material which was later to be fused by his imagination until he commenced to borrow books from the Bristol circulating library in 1795.[2] The actual writing, however, did not begin till 1797 or, more probably, 1798. Many years later, in a letter to Byron, Coleridge himself stated dogmatically: "The *Christabel*, which you have mentioned in so obliging a manner, was composed by me in the year 1797—I should say that the plan of the whole poem was formed and the first book and half the second were finished" in that year.[3] In his preface the following year, when the poem was published for the first time, he wisely modified his assertion about "half the second", which obviously was not composed (at least in its finally printed form) until he had moved up into the Lake District in 1800: "The first part of the following poem was written in the year one thousand seven hundred and ninety seven, at Stowey, in the county of Somerset."[4] This statement was echoed in 1838 by his friend, physician, and biographer, Dr. James Gillman.[5] Coleridge's memory for dates and other such uncompromising facts, however, was not so alert as it was for the picturesque, the strange, and the sensuous. In other words, there is not an iota of contemporary evidence to place the poem in 1797, which would mean that it was begun before "The Ancient Mariner", whereas there is plenty, including other testimony from the author himself, which would date it the next year.[6]

No strictly contemporary clue hinting at the emergence of such a poem as "Christabel" occurs before January 31, 1798, a

[2] Paul Kaufman, "The Reading of Southey and Coleridge: The Record of Their Borrowings from the Bristol Library, 1793–98," *Modern Philology*, XXI (February, 1924), 317–20, gives the titles and dates of the borrowings.

[3] Letter of October 22, 1815, in Earl Leslie Griggs, *Unpublished Letters of Samuel Taylor Coleridge Including Certain Letters Republished from Original Sources* (London, 1932), II, 146; referred to hereafter as "Griggs".

[4] E.H.C., p. 57 n.

[5] James Gillman, *The Life of Samuel Taylor Coleridge* (London, 1838), pp. 280–81.

[6] E.H.C. (pp. 1–5) gives a partial discussion of this matter. Coleridge makes a similar mistake in regard to the date of "Kubla Khan"; see *The Poems of Samuel Taylor Coleridge Including Poems and Versions of Poems Herein Published for the First Time, Edited with Textual and Bibliographical Notes by Ernest Hartley Coleridge* (London, 1935), p. 295 n. This work will hereafter be referred to simply as *"Poems"*.

date which marks the first of a series of entries in Dorothy Wordsworth's journal, wherein certain lines and phrases issue which were to appear later (or perhaps had already appeared) in the poem itself.[7] The earliest of these, in fact, was also set down in a tentative metrified form in Coleridge's own note-book, the famous "Gutch memorandum book" of which Lowes has made such yeoman use.[8] Confirming these dates is the poet's own statement in the well-known passage in chapter xiv of his *Biographia Literaria*, in which, after discussing the relation-ship which he and Wordsworth planned to maintain between the supernatural and the humanly sympathetic in poetry, he added: "With this view I wrote 'The Ancient Mariner,' and was preparing among other poems, the 'Dark Ladie,' and the 'Christobel,' [*sic*] in which I should have more nearly realized my ideal, than I had done in my first attempt."[9] This allusion clear-ly implies that the unfinished poems followed the finished one. "The Ancient Mariner" was apparently completed on March 23, if the assertion in Dorothy Wordsworth's journal to the effect that Coleridge brought his "ballad" to Alfoxden "fin-ished" on that day may be applied, as it generally is, to this poem.[10] By summer, however, a large section of "Christabel" had been achieved, for Wordsworth's description of the pleas-ures of that season spent among the Quantocks shows that

---

[7] William Knight, *Journals of Dorothy Wordsworth* (London, 1897), I, 6, 13, 14, etc., under dates of January 31, March 7, March 31, etc.

[8] First printed and discussed by Alois Brandl, "S. T. Coleridges Notizbuch aus den Jahren 1795–1798," in Herrig's *Archiv für das Studium der neueren Sprachen und Litera-turen*, XCVII (1896), 333–72; to some extent annotated and corrected by Lowes, chaps. i–iii; referred to hereafter as "*Archiv*". The manuscript is now in the British Museum, Add. MSS, 27901.

[9] Coleridge, *Biographia Literaria; or Biographical Sketches of My Literary Life and Opinions* (London, 1817), II, 2–3. "The Dark Ladie" was another poem which he was always hoping to finish, or so he promised William Sotheby's daughter on July 13, 1802. See his letter to Southey, in *Letters of Samuel Taylor Coleridge Edited by Ernest Hartley Coleridge* (London, 1895), I, 375. This work will be referred to hereafter simply as "*Letters*".

[10] *Journals of Dorothy Wordsworth*, I, 14. On the other hand, on February 18 Cole-ridge himself wrote a letter to Joseph Cottle in which he remarked: "I have finished my ballad—it is 340 lines." This length would certainly not fit the "Mariner", and Griggs (I, 100) suggests that it might apply to the first part of "Christabel", which runs to 331 lines.

Coleridge had already begun his practice of reciting the poem aloud to his friends:

> . . . . beloved Friend!
> When looking back, thou seest, in clearer view
> Than any liveliest sight of yesterday,
> That summer, under whose indulgent skies,
> Upon smooth Quantock's airy ridge we roved
> Unchecked, or loitered 'mid her sylvan combs,
> Thou in bewitching words, with happy heart,
> Didst chaunt the vision of that Ancient Man,
> The bright-eyed Mariner, and rueful woes
> Didst utter of the Lady Christabel. . . . .[11]

If a somewhat vague allusion in a letter of Coleridge to his brother George may be applied to "Christabel", the first part of the poem was certainly completed by May 14: "I have written a Poem lately which I think even the Major (who is no admirer of the art) would like."[12]

The poet always loved to share his creations with others, and "Christabel" lent itself admirably to his habit of regaling his friends with recitations. The first indubitable proof of the existence of the poem transpires as a result of this custom, for when his subsidization by his patrons, Josiah and Thomas Wedgwood, sons of the famous potter, made possible a trip to Germany in 1799,[13] he enlightened many hours among the Harz Mountains in this fashion. Dr. Clement Carlyon, one of the party of seven who made the trip and ascended the Brocken together, afterward described these occasions somewhat ironically in his reminiscences: "He frequently recited his own poetry, and not unfrequently led us further into the labyrinth of his metaphysical elucidations, either of particular passages, or of the original conception of any of his productions, than we were able to follow him."[14] How much Coleridge really divulged of the secret of the "original conception" of "Christabel", Carlyon does not record, though he seems to have been very close to the

---

[11] *The Prelude*, Book XIV, ll. 392–401. Since this passage was written at least by 1805, it is much more reliable than Coleridge's recollections in 1815 and 1816.

[12] Griggs, I, 105. The "Major" was James Coleridge, another brother.

[13] *Letters*, I, 234–35 and n.; II, 611 and n.

[14] Clement Carlyon, *Early Years and Late Reflections* (London, 1836), p. 134.

heart of the mystery. But his taste did not incline toward the Gothic, and he preferred the more trifling verses which the poet also enjoyed declaiming. Unfortunately, therefore, if Coleridge actually told his friends his intentions, Carlyon was too obtuse or too impervious to be impressed. All he remembered was a scrap or two: "At the conclusion of . . . . the first stanza . . . . , he would perhaps comment at full length upon such a line as—

Tu whit!—Tu whoo!

that we might not fall into the mistake of supposing originality to be its sole merit. In fact, he very seldom went right on to the end of any piece of poetry—to pause and analyse was his delight. What he told us fellow travellers respecting *Christabel*, he has since repeated in print, in words which, if not the very same, are equally Coleridgean."[15] All of which sounds very much as if the good doctor were trying to cover up his youthful negligence with an assumption of omniscience.

Upon Coleridge's return to England, he began the thirty-five-year-long series of promises and reassurances about the poem which kept its admirers in a state of suspended hope until almost the day of his death. Robert Southey was collecting copy for the 1800 edition of his *Annual Anthology* and attempted to persuade his friend, just reconciled after the pantisocracy debacle, to seal their bond with a full-grown and matured "Christabel". Coleridge, in an optimistic and helpful mood, agreed, and on October 15, 1799, undertook to make a start, but dissented from Southey's belief that it would be a suitable opening poem for the volume.[16] By November 10 he was endeavoring to make his explanation of why he was convinced that the poem should not be given such a prominent position atone for the obvious fact that as yet he had written nothing more upon it: "In my last letter I said I would give you my reasons for thinking 'Christabel,' *were* it finished, and finished as spiritedly as it commences, yet still an improper opening poem. My reason is, it cannot be expected to please all. *Those* who dislike it will deem it extravagant ravings, and go on

---

[15] *Ibid.*, pp. 138–39.   [16] *Letters*, I, 310.

through the rest of the collection with the feeling of disgust, and it is not impossible that were it liked by any it would still not harmonise with the *real-life* poems that follow. It ought, I think, to be the last."[17] But, whether or not Southey agreed with him, he could not overcome his inhibitions, and inspiration still failed him, so that on December 9 he admitted sadly: "I am afraid that I have scarce poetic enthusiasm enough to finish 'Christabel'. . . . ."[18] That was the end of Southey's hopeful project, although his friend solaced him with some other contributions.

Only a total change of environment and atmosphere was able to shake Coleridge out of his lethargy or impotence. Early in 1800 he paid his first visit to Wordsworth in Grasmere and left some of his papers in the charge of Charles Lamb at Pentonville. Among these was an imperfect copy of "Christabel" which so much aroused Lamb's interest and curiosity that in the middle of April he wrote its author requesting the missing lines; but Coleridge paid no attention, so that in the summer Lamb wrote again, repeating his wish.[19] Similarly on May 1 Southey requested Coleridge from Lisbon: "Write to me, and some long letters; and send me your *Christabell* and your *Three Graves*, and finish them on purpose to send them." But by the end of July Coleridge had not answered.[20] The reason for his impolite silence was apparently that he was at last at work—or seriously trying to work—on the second instalment. His later statement in his preface that he wrote the "second part, after my return from Germany, in the year one thousand eight hundred, at Keswick, Cumberland,"[21] can this time be accepted because it is corroborated by plenty of other evidence. The actual composition was begun at Greta Hall, probably in the latter part of August. At any rate, on Sunday, the thirty-first

[17] *Ibid.*, p. 313.   [18] *Ibid.*, p. 317.

[19] E. V. Lucas, *The Letters of Charles Lamb to Which Are Added Those of His Sister, Mary Lamb* (London, 1935), I, 186, 194; E.H.C., pp. 37–38.

[20] Maurice H. Fitzgerald, *Robert Southey's Letters A Selection* (London, etc., 1912), pp. 26, 37.

[21] E.H.C., p. 57 n.

of that month, Dorothy Wordsworth put down in her diary: "Coleridge reading a part of *Christabel*. Talked much about the mountains, etc., etc."[22] For it is only in the second part of the poem that the locale becomes at all specific; and the mountains of Cumberland were to play a large role in the setting. Moreover, Wordworth's plan to bring out a second edition of the *Lyrical Ballads* spurred his temperamental colleague with new energy, and it was with the full intention of overcoming the recalcitrant material in time for this volume that Coleridge attacked his task once more.

The most circumstantial and illuminating account of what occurred at this time is contained in his letter to Josiah Wedgwood on November 1: "But immediately on my arrival in this country I undertook to finish a poem which I had begun, entitled Christabel, for a second volume of the Lyrical Ballads. I tried to perform my promise; but the deep unutterable Disgust, which I had suffered in the translation of that accursed Wallenstein, seemed to have stricken me with barrenness, and nothing would come of it. I desisted with a deeper dejection than I am willing to remember. The wind from the Skiddaw and Borrowdale was often as loud as wind need be—and many a walk in the clouds on the mountains did I take; but all would not do—till one day I dined out at the house of a neighbouring clergyman, and somehow or other drank so much wine, that I found some effort and dexterity necessary to balance myself on the hither edge of sobriety. The next day, my verse making faculties returned to me, and I proceeded successfully—till my poem grew so long and in Wordsworth's opinion so impressive, that he rejected it from his volume as disproportionate both in size and merit, and as discordant in its character. . . . . ."[23] Thus as, by the author's own frank admission, an "anodyne" is irretrievably connected with the writing of "Kubla Khan", so the aroma of a prodigality of wine must cling forever to the second portion of "Christabel".

So confident were the two men that this time all would go

---

[22] *Journals of Dorothy Wordsworth*, I, 47.   [23] Griggs, I, 158–59.

well that the completed part of the poem was actually sent to the printer, Joseph Cottle's partner, Nathaniel Biggs, who apparently began to set up the type. At least, on September 15 Wordsworth wrote to him: "It is my particular request that, if no part of the poem of Christabel is already printed off, the poems which I now send should be inserted before Christabel. This I wish to be done even if the press for Christabel be composed. I had no notion that the printing of Christabel would be begun till you had received further intelligence from Mr. Coleridge. . . . ."[24] Again, on October 10, Wordsworth wrote to the same effect,[25] but he was apparently too late to stop composition, for on December 2 Coleridge himself requested his friend, the young chemist, Humphry Davy, who may have acted as a sort of intermediary for the manuscript, to have "all that is printed of 'Christabel' " forwarded to him by post.[26] What information these proof sheets might have afforded if any of them had survived is another mere matter of speculation.

For even in the midst of his fresh enthusiasm Coleridge had experienced a new revulsion. On September 17 he apologized to another of their mutual friends, J. W. Tobin: "The delay in Copy has been owing in part to me, as the writer of Christabel. Every line has been produced by me with labor-pangs. I abandon Poetry altogether—I leave the higher and deeper kinds to Wordsworth, the delightful, popular and simply dignified to Southey; and reserve for myself the honorable attempt to make others feel and understand their writings, as they deserve to be felt and understood."[27] In the same mood he wrote to Davy a few days later, comparing "Christabel" and Wordsworth's poetry: "I assure you I think very differently of 'Christabel.' I would rather have written 'Ruth,' and 'Nature's Lady,' than a million such poems. But why do I calumniate my own spirit by saying 'I would rather'? God knows it is as

[24] W. Hale White, *A Description of the Wordsworth & Coleridge Manuscripts in the Possession of Mr. T. Norton Longman* (London, 1897), pp. 14–15.

[25] *Ibid.*, pp. 26–28.   [26] *Letters*, I, 342.

[27] Lowes, pp. 304, 570–71; see also E.H.C., pp. 39–40, who uses the spelling "Christobel".

delightful to me that they *are* written. I *know* that at present, and I *hope* that it will be so; so my mind has disciplined itself into a willing exertion of its powers, without any reference to their comparative value."[28] But this humility, coupled with the resolve to act as the mere interpreter of the works of his friends, was fortunately not to last. By the end of the month he was bold enough to supplement a draft by Wordsworth for the preface to the new edition by writing of "the assistance of a Friend who contributed largely to the first volume, and who has now furnished me with the ~~long and beautiful~~ [*sic*] Poem of Christabel, without which I should not have ventured to present a second volume to the public. . . . ."[29] This statement was made in good faith, but in one of his optimistic moods. Temporarily, however, everything was going remarkably well. On Saturday, October 4, he brought his manuscript to Grasmere, for Dorothy Wordsworth wrote: "Exceedingly delighted with the second part of *Christabel*." The next morning she added: "Coleridge read *Christabel* a second time; we had increasing pleasure." But that day and the next must have heard a lively discussion in the cottage, for on Monday appears the sudden and unexplained entry: "Determined not to print *Christabel* with the L. B."[30] This decision was confirmed by Wordsworth himself by October 10, or before, when he ordered the printer to cancel the page of the preface which announced the inclusion of "Christabel", and added: "It is my wish and determination that (whatever the expense may be, which I hereby take upon myself) such pages of the Poem of Christabel as have been printed (if any such there be) be cancelled."[31]

The explanation of this abrupt alteration in plan, however, was quite different from what might have been prophesied. Coleridge's letter to Wedgwood contained the clue. His poetic

[28] Letter to Davy, October 9, 1800, *Letters*, I, 337. "Nature's Lady" is apparently a rejected title for "Three Years She Grew in Sun and Shower".

[29] White, p. 19.

[30] *Journals of Dorothy Wordsworth*, I, 51–52.

[31] White, pp. 26–28. Nevertheless, some copies of the book with the original preface were run off and issued; see John Edwin Wells, "*Lyrical Ballads*, 1800: Cancel Leaves," *PMLA*, LIII (1938), 207.

frenzy had come upon him with such a rush that he had been unable to keep it in bounds. The poem, to Wordsworth's mind, had grown so long and impressive that it would have been out of place among the *Lyrical Ballads*. Here is one of the most curious and perplexing elements in the whole history of "Christabel". For the two parts of the poem, together with their "Conclusions", as finally printed, total only 677 lines! "The Conclusion to Part I", in the opinion of Ernest Hartley Coleridge, was probably written in this same October, and not in 1798 like the rest of this section, as references in Coleridge's own letters and notebook as well as in Dorothy Wordsworth's journal would indicate.[32] Moreover, "The Conclusion to Part II", once more according to E. H. C., was probably written about the same time and was really intended to belong to "Christabel", rather than having been casually attached to it later, as many critics have held.[33] The same editor hazards another speculation: "I am all but convinced that the lines entitled 'The Knight's Tomb' ('Where is the grave of Sir Arthur O'Kellyn?'), which Scott quoted from memory in *Ivanhoe* (cap. viii), were also composed, not as 'an experiment for a metre', but in the metre, and for the continuation, of *Christabel*."[34]

Even if this rather unlikely hypothesis be admitted and all the extra parts counted in, a great hiatus still remains between the extant poem and the original as here described. Two of Coleridge's letters in October, in fact, actually specify lengths for his composition which are twice that which remains. On October 9 he wrote to Davy: "The 'Christabel' was running up to 1,300 lines, and was so much admired by Wordsworth, that he thought it indelicate to print two volumes with his name, in which so much of another man's work was included;

---

[32] E.H.C., pp. 17–20, 38.

[33] *Ibid.*, pp. 31–32, 44. It first appears in a letter of Coleridge to Southey, May 6, 1801 (*Letters*, I, 355–56), with no suggestion of any association with "Christabel". Instead, Coleridge states that his son Hartley prompted it, and adds: "A very metaphysical account of fathers calling their children rogues, rascals, little varlets, etc." See below, p. 164, n. 1.

[34] E.H.C., p. 32; see *Poems*, p. 432.

and, which was of more consequence, the poem was in direct
opposition to the very purpose for which the lyrical ballads
were published, viz., an experiment to see how far those passions
which alone give any value to extraordinary incidents were
capable of interesting, in and for themselves, in the incidents
of common life. We mean to publish the 'Christabel,' therefore,
with a long blank-verse poem of Wordsworth's, entitled 'The
Pedlar.' "[35] The throes of creation were still upon him, however, for a few days later he informed Thomas Poole: "The
truth is, the endeavor to finish Christabel, (which has swelled
into a Poem of 1,400 lines) for the second Volume of the Lyrical
Ballads threw my business terribly back. . . . ."[36] More data
to the same effect may be gleaned from his letter to Byron in
1815, for there only he tells definitely of a now vanished third
part: "I should say that the plan of the whole poem was
formed and the first book and half the second were finished [in
1797!]—and it was not till after my return from Germany in
the year 1800 that I resumed it—and finished the second and a
part of the third book. That is all that Mr. W. Scott can have
seen."[37] If that is all that Scott can have seen then, there must
have been more for others to see later. The conclusion seems
perfectly clear: Coleridge actually composed a "Christabel"
which, fragmentary as it was, was nevertheless more than twice
as long as the version which was finally printed. What happened to the remainder, and why? The problem is not made any
easier by a further sentence in the same letter to Byron: "A
Lady is now transcribing the Christabel, in the form and as far
as it existed before my voyage to the Mediterranean."[38] This
lady was Mrs. Wordsworth's sister, Sarah Hutchinson, and her
copy was apparently the one which formed the basis for the
1816 edition.[39] Yet Coleridge's voyage to the Mediterranean,
where he spent ten months as secretary to the governor of

[35] *Letters*, I, 337 and n. "The Pedlar" was an early title for "The Excursion".

[36] Letter about October 14, 1800, in Griggs, I, 156.

[37] Letter of October 22, 1815, in Griggs, II, 146.

[38] *Ibid.*, p. 147.   [39] E.H.C., p. 54.

Malta, was taken in 1804. Thus he implies not only that Miss Hutchinson's manuscript contained the completed part of the third book but also that a different version of "Christabel" was in existence after 1804. Was this version made at Malta, as is here implied, or is it still another, worked on in 1807? For Dorothy Wordsworth in a letter late in that year told her friend Mrs. Thomas Clarkson, wife of Coleridge's friend the slave liberator, the latest tidings of the poet: "The best news contained in his letter was that he had been going on with *Christabel*, and had written almost as much as we have already seen. . . . ."[40] Yet none of the recorded manuscripts contains, or ever contained, anything but a few minor variations from the text printed in 1816. Is it any wonder that critics and editors have torn their hair and confessed their utter mystification and defeat?[41]

In 1800 and 1801 Coleridge was still confident that it was within his power to accomplish the five books which he had projected, and the plans for an independent publication went on apace. It therefore seems likely that the poem expanded to far more than the 1,400 lines mentioned in the letter to Poole, in spite of the opposition of a few of his friends, such as Charles Lamb, who earnestly exhorted him to leave the first part alone. Of this episode, Lamb observed to Gillman many years later: "I was very angry with Coleridge, when I first heard that he had written a second canto, and that he intended to finish it; but when I read the beautiful apostrophe to the two friends, it calmed me."[42] By March 16, 1801, Coleridge was so sanguine, not merely about the tale but also about two prose essays that

[40] William Knight, *Letters of the Wordsworth Family from 1785 to 1855* (Boston and London, 1907), I, 324.

[41] Yet, airily waving aside all this incontrovertible evidence, Frances Winwar confidently dogmatizes that "Christabel" "at its longest never exceeded six hundred and seventy-seven lines. . . . ." This statement is of a piece with her belief that Wordsworth, by his exclusion of the fragment from the *Lyrical Ballads*, whatever his motive, "killed Coleridge as a poet." See *Farewell the Banner "*. . . . *Three Persons and One Soul* . . . . " *Coleridge, Wordsworth and Dorothy* (New York, 1938), pp. 290, 292.

[42] Gillman, pp. 302-3. The "apostrophe" may be found in ll. 408 ff.; these lines, describing the reconciliation between two friends (Coleridge and Southey, of course), were quoted and called "the best and sweetest lines I ever wrote" in a letter Coleridge sent to Poole on February 13, 1813 (*Letters*, II, 609).

he contemplated, that he informed Poole: "I shall therefore take a week's respite, and make 'Christabel' ready for the press; which I shall publish by itself, in order to get rid of all my engagements with Longman. . . . . I shall . . . . immediately publish my 'Christabel,' with two essays annexed to it, on the 'Preternatural' and on 'Metre.' "[43] Wordsworth became imbued with the same enthusiastic confidence and told the same correspondent on April 9: "*Christabel* is to be printed at the Bulmerian press, with vignettes, &c., &c. I long to have the book in my hand, it will be such a beauty."[44] But the Bulmerian vision also evaporated. In 1803, however, there were still some surviving hopes to put the poem into print. In fact, a remark by Charles Lamb, who was engaged at this time in revising the third edition of Coleridge's *Poems* for the press, suggests that the publishing of "Christabel" in one of the anthologies was even being considered: "Another volume will clear off all your Anthologic Morning-Postian Epistolary Miscellanies; but pray don't put 'Christabel' therein; don't let that sweet maid come forth attended with Lady Holland's mob at her heels. Let there be a separate volume of Tales, choice Tales, 'Ancient Mariners,' &c."[45]

One other attempt by some hopeful publishers was made a month later, but this time the author himself took a haughty attitude. In a letter to his wife on April 4, 1803, he apprised her: "To-day I dine again with Sotheby. He had informed me that ten gentlemen who have met me at his house desired him to solicit me to finish the 'Christabel,' and to permit them to publish it for me; and they engaged that it should be in paper, printing, and decorations the most magnificent thing that had hitherto appeared. Of course I declined it. The lovely lady shan't come to that pass! Many times rather would I have it printed at Soulby's on the true ballad paper."[46] But by this

[43] *Letters*, I, 349. See also his letter of January 7 (Griggs, I, 167).

[44] E.H.C., p. 44.

[45] Letter of Lamb to Coleridge, May 27, 1803, in Lamb, *Letters*, I, 350.

[46] *Letters*, I, 421–22; this version of the letter differs in some minor respects (such as the phrase "ten gentlemen" rather than "the gentlemen") from that given later in E.H.C., pp. 45–46.

time the poem had entered on the next stage of its almost fabulous history—that of private circulation and special readings.

Public curiosity about the tale had waxed so great that the knowledge of its existence had passed far beyond the borders of the small original circle of intimates and publishers. In October, 1800, Dr. John Stoddart, a friend of Coleridge's school-fellow Robert Allen, had paid a visit to Grasmere and had carried away with him a manuscript of "Christabel" as a trophy. About two years later he was the guest of Walter Scott at Lasswade, near Edinburgh. A turn in the conversation brought Coleridge's name into the discussion, and Stoddart used the occasion to give a "casual recitation" of "Christabel" from his manuscript.[47] The poem made a tremendous impression on Scott, as a succession of later repercussions proves. First of all, he commenced reciting it himself, and in his 1815 letter to Byron, Coleridge asserted: "Before I went to Malta, I heard from Lady Beaumont, I know not whether more gratified or more surprized, that Mr. Scott had recited the Christabel and experienced no common admiration."[48] Lady Beaumont was the wife of another of Coleridge's patrons, Sir George Beaumont, and she too had received a copy of "Christabel", sent to her before March 17, 1804, through John Richman.[49] Whether Scott used her copy or Stoddart's is not clear, but it was probably Stoddart's.

Southey, however, was the first to comment on the similarities between *The Lay of the Last Minstrel*, published in 1805, and "Christabel". On March 5, 1805, he announced in a letter to C. W. W. Wynn: "The beginning of the story is too like Coleridge's *Christobell*, which he had seen; the very line 'Jesu Maria, shield her well!' is caught from it. When you see the *Christobell* you will not doubt that Scott has imitated it; I do not think designedly, but the echo was in his ear, not for emula-

---

[47] John Gibson Lockhart, *Memoirs of the Life of Sir Walter Scott, Bart.* (Boston, 1881), II, 162; E.H.C., p. 44.

[48] Griggs, II, 146–47.   [49] *Ibid.*, I, 313.

tion, but *propter amorem.*"[50] Scott himself admitted as much, for, according to Lockhart, Stoddart's reading had so "fixed the music of that noble fragment in his memory" that he determined to throw a Scotch story "into somewhat of a similar cadence".[51] When the matter was called to Coleridge's attention, however, he magnanimously remarked that, although he "did not overhugely admire the 'Lay of the Last Minstrel' ", he "saw no likeness whatever to the 'Christabel,' much less any improper resemblance."[52] Nevertheless, when *The Lady of the Lake* was printed in 1810, he himself hinted to Wordsworth that the character of Allan-bane was apparently modeled after Bard Bracy.[53] Despite this private querulousness, however, when a critic whose name has not survived wrote him in December, 1811, and "offered to review W. Scott's poem to his injury", Coleridge replied with a long discussion of Scott's alleged plagiarism, especially in *The Lay*, and exculpated his rival from any dishonest intentions.[54] Nevertheless, he took particular pains in his 1816 preface to forestall any accusations that the reading public might make of influence in the opposite direction, since both Scott's and Byron's verse narratives had appeared in print before his: "I am confident, however, that as far as the present poem is concerned, the celebrated poets whose writings I might be suspected of having imitated, either in particular passages, or in the tone and the spirit of the whole, would be among the first to vindicate me from the charge. . . . ."[55] The other poets, of course, were only too happy to acknowledge his priority. In the preface to the 1830 edition of his poems Scott stated frankly that he was "bound to make the acknowledgment due from the pupil to his master", and before 1810 he had told Francis Jeffrey, editor of *The Edinburgh Review*, that the

[50] E.H.C., p. 45; *Southey's Letters*, p. 97.

[51] Lockhart, II, 162.

[52] Letter to Southey, December 14, 1807, in *Letters*, II, 523.

[53] Letter to Wordsworth in E.H.C., p. 46. This is apparently the letter, with notes, printed in Griggs, II, 39; but Griggs applies Coleridge's comment, "A miserable copy of the Bard," to Gray's poem of that name.

[54] Griggs, II, 61–67. [55] E.H.C., p. 58.

meter of "Christabel" had suggested and determined that of
The Lay.[56] Certainly Scott did all that he could to make amends
for any unintentional harm he had caused, when, early in
June, 1815, he himself recited "Christabel" to Lord Byron in
the drawing-room of John Murray, publisher of *The Quarterly
Review*.[57]

In fact, the story never palled, for ten years later he was still
reciting it for the delectation and education of his friends at
Abbotsford, as the following anecdote by Captain Basil Hall
indicates: "In the evening we had a great feast indeed. Sir
Walter asked us if we had ever read Christabel, and upon some
of us admitting with shame that we had never even seen it,
he offered to read it, and took a chair in the midst of all the
party in the library. He read the poem from end to end with a
wonderful pathos and variety of expression—in some parts his
voice was deep and sonorous, at others loud and animated, but
all most carefully appropriate, and very sweetly modulated. In
his hands, at all events, Christabel justified Lord Byron's often-
quizzed character of it—'a wild and singularly original and
beautiful poem.' "[58]

Long before its publication, however, various other people
knew it also. For instance, on May 1, 1809, Wordsworth had
read it aloud, along with his own "White Doe", to the John
Wilson who was to add to his fame as "Christopher North" and
who had become an intimate friend of the whole Lake circle
shortly after he had moved to his home on Lake Windermere
in the preceding year.[59] According to Dorothy Wordsworth's
account of the occasion to De Quincey, Wilson had been
"much delighted" with both. Amusingly enough, this reading
had been preceded a day or two earlier by a joint reading of the

---

[56] *Ibid.*, p. 45; Lockhart, II, 162; and *Edinburgh Review*, XXVIII (August, 1817),
510 n. In the last-mentioned, Jeffrey says that the four or five lines Scott once recited to
him were all he knew of the poem till after it was published.

[57] E.H.C., p. 46.

[58] Extract from the journal of Captain Basil Hall, December 30, 1824, in Lockhart,
VII, 66.

[59] Letter of Dorothy Wordsworth, *Letters of the Wordsworth Family*, I, 433.

poem by Dorothy and her sister-in-law, Sarah Hutchinson, to little Johnny Wordsworth, Christopher's son. Johnny "was excessively interested, especially with the first part, but he asked 'why she [Christabel] could not say her prayers in her own room,' and it was his opinion that she ought to have gone 'directly to her father's room to tell him that she had met with the Lady under the old oak tree and all about it.' "[60] Thus out of the mouths of babes—!

In a very different category, the clever but unscrupulous snob, William Hazlitt, had evidently also heard the poem or read it in manuscript, for when he came to slash and damn it in one of his reviews he made his major attack pivot on a line which had been removed before the poem was printed. As will be seen later, he was smart enough to realize the importance of the line in giving a clue to the meaning and original intention, but his mind was so perverted and malicious as to misinterpret it completely. As for the means of his access to the story, he afterward married Sarah Stoddart, who had a copy which she may have got directly from that of Sarah Hutchinson or from that which her brother John had made earlier.[61]

But the most celebrated and sensational of all the occasions on which "Christabel" was recited aloud occurred at Geneva, Switzerland, on an evening in the middle of July, 1816, not long after its publication, but probably before Byron, the reciter, had received a copy. The story concerns Shelley particularly, but also involves the rest of the party, which was practically self-exiled from England—Mary Godwin, Claire Clairmont, and Byron's personal physician and secretary, the Scotchman Dr. John Polidori. First recounted as an "Extract of a Letter from Geneva, with Anecdotes of Lord Byron, &c." in *The New Monthly Magazine*, the tale runs: "Among other things which the lady, from whom I procured these anecdotes, related to me, she mentioned the outline of a ghost story by Lord Byron. It appears that one evening Lord Byron, Mr. P. B. Shelly [*sic*], the two ladies and the gentleman before

[60] *Ibid.*, p. 430.   [61] E.H.C., pp. 44, 49, 54, 67 n., 76 n.

alluded to, after having perused a German work, which was entitled Phantasmagoriana, began relating ghost stories; when his lordship having recited the beginning of Christabel, then unpublished, the whole took so strong a hold of Mr. Shelly's mind, that he suddenly started up and ran out of the room. The physician and Lord Byron followed, and discovered him leaning against a mantelpiece with cold drops of perspiration trickling down his face." Solicitously they gave him "something to refresh him", but not till then, with admirable restraint, did they inquire "into the cause of his alarm". Shelley's wild imagination, they found, had again run away with him, for, as he had listened to the unfolding description of the Lady Geraldine, he had suddenly had a terrifying vision of eyes in the bosom of one of the Godwin girls. Apparently to his heated brain her nipples had become eyes in her breasts, and he had been "obliged to leave the room in order to destroy the impression". For he had already heard such a story told about a lady in the neighborhood where he lived, and his imagination, with all its youthful Gothic propensities, had been unable to rid itself of the picture. The aftermath of the affair was that Byron, Polidori, and Mary Godwin agreed to engage in a written competition of supernatural tales, and that *Frankenstein* and Polidori's *The Vampyre* resulted.[62] It may be worth noting that "Monk" Lewis had joined Byron's party just before this time.

The excitement and wonder that "Christabel" had aroused in literary circles even before publication culminated in April, 1814, when an unindentified versifier, signing himself "V.", published a continuation and conclusion to the story in *The European Magazine*[63] in spite of the fact that most of his readers could certainly not have read the beginning. This incident perhaps whetted Byron's interest in Coleridge's work. At any

[62] *New Monthly Magazine and Universal Register*, XI (April 1, 1819), 195; also quoted by Montague Summers, *The Vampire, His Kith and Kin* (London, 1928), p. 281; see also John Addington Symonds, *Shelley* ("English Men of Letters") (New York, n.d.), p. 90.

[63] "Christobell," *European Magazine, and London Review*, LXVII (April, 1815), 35-36. E.H.C. (p. 105 n.) suggests James Hogg as a possible author, but I am skeptical.

rate, although Byron did not succeed in getting Murray to bring out a selected edition of Coleridge, with a special preface to "The Rime of the Ancient Mariner" on the employment of the supernatural in poetry,[64] he did persuade that publisher to print the fragmentary "Christabel", together with the even more fragmentary "Kubla Khan" and the twenty-six couplets of "The Pains of Sleep", on May 25, 1816.[65] Scott's reading of the poem aloud at Murray's the year before had apparently convinced Byron of its remarkable qualities; and Coleridge had sent him a copy soon after his letter of October 22, 1815, in which he gave Byron a very frank account of himself and the history of this particular work.[66]

So at last, eighteen years after its inception, "Christabel" was surrendered to the mercies of the reading public. The public was not very merciful. As late as 1828 Coleridge's young disciple, John Sterling (the later subject of Carlyle's famous biography), could write—though not with entire accuracy—in *The Athenaeum* that the poem was still "the only one of his writings which is ever treated with unmingled contempt. . . . ."[67] Few indeed were Coleridge's friends at first among the reviewers. *The Critical Review* and *The European Magazine* were almost alone in showing any appreciation or understanding.[68] Cole-

[64] Letter of Coleridge to Byron, March 30, 1815, in Griggs, II, 133.

[65] E.H.C., p. 47. On September 22, 1816, Coleridge wrote to Rest Fenner: "Excepting the fragment of the Christabel (and even this was a bargain made for me during my illness), I have had no concern with any publisher . . . ." (Griggs, II, 185). On April 26, 1816, Lamb wrote to Wordsworth: "Coleridge is printing Xtabel, by Lord Byron's recommendation to Murray, with what he calls a vision, 'Kubla Khan' . . . ." (Lamb, *Letters*, II, 190), and on June 1 asked Matilda Betham if she had seen "Christabel" since its publication (*ibid.*, p. 193). Lucas (*ibid.*, p. 192 n.) suggests that these allusions controvert the opinion attributed to Lamb in Fanny Godwin's letter to Mary Shelley, July 20, 1816: "Lamb says *Christabel* ought never to have been published; and that no one understood it . . . ." (see Edward Dowden, *The Life of Percy Bysshe Shelley*, London, 1887, II, 41). She goes on to add that Coleridge is "writing fast a continuation. . . . ."

[66] E.H.C., pp. 46–47; Griggs, II, 146–48.

[67] *Essays and Tales of John Sterling* (London, 1848), I, 101.

[68] For May and November, 1816, respectively. For extracts from the reviews and notices of the poem, see E.H.C., Appen. I. Gillman (pp. 304–7) quotes from another favorable review, which is both anonymous and unlocated.

ridge, however, had probably known what to expect. Almost any work which had enjoyed such an advance "press" could expect to be mauled by the envious and the hypercritical; but this work was not only by one of the Lakers: it had also been sponsored by the unspeakable Byron, who had just been driven out of England by an uprising of all the respectable and noble-minded people in the country! Mrs. Coleridge knew what to prepare for, when she wrote concerning her husband to Thomas Poole the day before publication: "You will also be sorry for another thing respecting him—Oh! when will he give his friends any-thing but pain? he has been so unwise as to publish his frag-ments of 'Christabel' and 'Koula-Khan' [*sic*] Murray is the pub-lisher, & the price is 4ˢ 6ᵈ—we were all sadly vexed when we read the advertizement of these things."[69] Matters had come to a pretty pass when even the poet's wife (however estranged from him), while realizing only too well the family's need for money, could write so unsympathetically of his doings.

Yet this hostile critical reception did not destroy public inter-est. Rather, it sharpened it. Admirers continued to multiply, and the demand for a completion of the story grew stronger.[70] But, although a new stage in the history of "Christabel" might have been expected to begin at this point, it was another case of "Plus ça change, plus c'est la même chose." In his preface he had held out the hope that he would "be able to embody in verse the three parts yet to come, in the course of the present year."[71] There is no reason to doubt that he himself would have been even more pleased than his admirers if he had been able to redeem his perennial promises; but at the same time the need for money put upon him a continual pressure, which also amounted almost to an inhibition. He confessed to De Quincey

[69] Stephen Potter, *Minnow among Tritons (Mrs. S. T. Coleridge's Letters to Thomas Poole 1799–1834)* (London, 1934), p. 48.

[70] In a letter of July 22, 1817, for instance, Coleridge told Poole how John Hookham Frere had advised him to finish the poem (*Letters*, II, 674).

[71] E.H.C., p. 57 n. He had also written Murray in May, 1816, that he wished ex-ceedingly to finish the poem (Griggs, II, 169), and on February 27, 1817, he assured Murray that the copyright of the poem, "when completed," would be "reserved for your refusal or acceptance" (*Letters*, II, 699).

in 1821: "Meantime, the Christabel, which I should never have consented to publish, a mere fragment as it was, but for his [Hartley's] goading wants, the £80 received from it going to make up the last sum, fell almost dead-born from the Press. . . . ."[72] So, when the family continued in need after the publication, he reminded his wife that "the probable advantages of finishing the Christabel" would be much more than the £20 necessary at that moment.[73] Twice, therefore, he evolved plans to go to the seashore to write, hoping that a change in environment would provoke new inspiration, as it had when he had left Somersetshire for the Lakes. Of the first project, he wrote only a little over a month after the publication: "By the Sea side I hope to finish my Christabel: and if this and Tranquillity with exercise and change of air should give me confidence in myself, I shall probably attempt to realize a Plan" to write a fortnightly or monthly letter on German literature.[74] Just a year later he is broaching a similar plan to his wife.[75]

All was in vain. True, in November, 1816, he made some minor changes and additions in a copy of the first edition which he presented to David Hinves, the confidential servant of William Stewart Rose, who had entertained him at Muddiford; and these alterations were printed in 1828.[76] But as the actuality dwindled, his visions grew more and more grandiose. About the year 1820 he told his friend Thomas Allsop: "If I should finish 'Christabel,' I shall certainly extend it and give new characters, and a greater number of incidents. This the 'reading public' require, and this is the reason that Sir Walter Scott's poems, though so loosely written, are pleasing and interest us by their picturesqueness. If a genial recurrence of the ray divine should

[72] Letter of August 9, 1821, in Griggs, II, 295.

[73] Letter of August 24, 1817, ibid., p. 207.

[74] Letter to Boosey, August 31, 1816, ibid., p. 175.

[75] Letter of August 24, 1817, ibid., p. 207: "My health makes it almost necessary for me to be at the seaside for 6 weeks, as the difference of the expense will not be above 20£, and the probable advantages in finishing the Christabel much more."

[76] E.H.C., pp. 50, 55.

occur for a few weeks, I shall certainly attempt it."[77] Thus he attempted to buoy up his spirits. In the editions of 1828 and 1829 he allowed the statement of his original preface, to the effect that he trusted that he could complete the remaining three books "in the course of the present year", to stand. Only in 1834, the year of his death, did it disappear.[78] Just the year before, in his *Table Talk*, he had begun to imply his doubts of finishing to his intimate circle, when he admitted, "I fear I could not carry on with equal success the execution of the idea," although at the same time he insisted, "I could write as good verses now as ever I did, if I were perfectly free from vexations, and were in the *ad libitum* hearing of fine music, which has a sensible effect in harmonising my thoughts, and in animating and, as it were, lubricating, my inventive faculty."[79] The scene is a sad and dispiriting one, but Coleridge put up a brave front to the end.

Among all this welter of dates, contradictions, disappointments, and delusions, what indication is there that the poet had any really concrete plan for finishing his story? Here contradiction and uncertainty still prevail. If Allsop is to be trusted, Coleridge told him, about 1820, when discussing the possibility of completing "Christabel" according to the model of Scott: "I had the whole of the two cantos in my mind before I began it; certainly the first canto is more perfect, has more of the true wild weird spirit than the last."[80] There is no suggestion here that he had thought beyond this point. Wordsworth, moreover, was very skeptical about his collaborator's having designed a complete plot in advance. In a conversation with Coleridge's

---

[77] Allsop, I, 94. In January, 1821, he again told Allsop: "Of my Poetic Works I would fain finish the 'Christabel' " (*ibid.*, p. 156). Allsop, a young man, had incurred Coleridge's gratitude for his praise of "Christabel" against the reviews in the *Edinburgh*, *Quarterly*, etc. See Coleridge's letter to him, December 2, 1818, in *Letters*, II, 696–98.

[78] E.H.C., p. 58 n.

[79] *Table Talk*, July 6, 1833, in *The Table Talk and Omniana of Samuel Taylor Coleridge* (London, 1909), p. 241.

[80] Allsop, I, 94.

nephew, Justice John Taylor Coleridge, in 1836, he asserted that he "had no idea how 'Christabelle' was to have been finished, and he did not think my uncle had ever conceived, in his own mind, any definite plan for it; that the poem had been composed while they were in habits of daily intercourse, and almost in his presence, and when there was the most unreserved intercourse between them as to all their literary projects and productions, and he had never heard from him any plan for finishing it. Not that he doubted my uncle's *sincerity* in his subsequent assertions to the contrary; because, he said, schemes of this sort passed rapidly and vividly through his mind, and so impressed him, that he often fancied he had arranged things, which really and upon trial proved to be mere embryos. I omitted to ask him, what seems obvious enough now, whether, in conversing about it, he had never asked my uncle how it would end. The answer would have settled the question. He regretted that the story had not been made to end the same night in which it begun. There was difficulty and danger in bringing such a personage as the witch to the daylight, and to the breakfast-table; and unless the poem was to have been long enough to give time for creating a second interest, there was a great probability of the conclusion being flat after such a commencement."[81] Charles Lamb, too, another of Coleridge's most intimate associates during the period of composition, told Gillman that he had been "very angry" when he learned that even a second part had been written in an attempt to fulfil the first.[82] On the other hand, Coleridge himself asseverated in his letter to Byron in 1815: "I should say that the plan of the whole poem was formed and the first Book and half the second were finished" during the first flush of creation.[83] He was still sticking to this conviction in 1833, when he made his significant remark in *Table Talk*: "The reason of my not finishing *Christabel* is not, that I don't know

[81] Christopher Wordsworth, *Memoirs of William Wordsworth, Poet-Laureate, D.C.L.* (London, 1851), II, 306–7.

[82] Gillman, p. 302.

[83] Griggs, II, 146–47.

how to do it—for I have, as I always had, the whole plan entire from beginning to end in my mind; but I fear I could not carry on with equal success the execution of the idea, an extremely subtle and difficult one."[84]

If, however, Coleridge's early associates, like Wordsworth and Lamb, were hesitant to accept his later affirmations, two of his new friends, Allsop and Gillman, claimed special knowledge as to what had been in the poet's mind.[85] Allsop's reminiscence, dating from about 1821, is the more modest, but superficially the more inexplicable. According to him, Coleridge informed him that Crashaw's verses on St. Teresa, beginning,

> Since 'tis not to be had at home,
> She'l travel to a martyrdom,

"were ever present to my mind whilst writing the second part of Christabel; if, indeed, by some subtle process of the mind they did not suggest the first thought of the whole poem."[86] Though this might be interpreted as a tacit admission that the perfect design had not been in the author's mind from the first, it adds a further element of mystery to the circumstances. The only person, as a matter of fact, to whom there is no mystery in "Christabel", either in what Coleridge wrote or in what he intended to write, is James Gillman. For, maintained Gillman, during the period when Coleridge had come to him to be treated for his drug habit and was actually living in his home, entirely separated from his own family, the poet divulged to him and their circle a detailed outline of the remaining three books of the story. "It has been said," Gillman asserted, "that 'Coleridge never explained the story of Christabel.' To his friends he did

---

[84] *Table Talk*, p. 241.

[85] Although Walter Graham, "Contemporary Critics of Coleridge the Poet," *PMLA*, XXXVIII (June, 1923), 284, says that John Sterling, in attending the Highgate "Thursdays" during the winter of 1827–28, "had caught from the lips of the 'sage' further explications of the meaning of the much-misunderstood poem, *Christabel*," I can find no such claim in his *Athenaeum* essay of 1828, which is merely a thorough appreciation and interpretation of the poem as it affected the young writer. Nor does the essay printed by Coleridge's other young "disciple", his nephew Henry Nelson Coleridge, in *The Etonian* (No. 4) for 1821, contain more than a passing reference to the poem. See *Etonian* (London, 1823), I, 406–20; and Graham, p. 284 n.

[86] Allsop, I, 195–96.

explain it; and in the Biographia Literaria, he has given an account of its origin."[87] The synopsis which he then proceeds to offer, but which to my mind is totally at variance with the first two cantos and all that they imply, is so important a part of Coleridgeana that it must be treated in a separate chapter, along with the other attempts that have been made to explain or complete the poem.

[87] Gillman, p. 283.

II

REVIEWS AND SPECULATIONS

EXCLUDING Gillman's, which is by far the most complete and dogmatic, and is a composite of the others, some three main types of suggestion for explaining or finishing "Christabel" have been offered the curious world, all of them with one or another sort of authority behind them—and none of them satisfying the demands of the judicious in poetry or of the connoisseur in the realms of the Gothic.

There is, for instance, the lurid, or scandalous, approach, according to which "Christabel" was once pronounced "the most obscene poem in the English language" and was linked with Byron's "Parisina" as "poems which sin as heinously against purity and decency as it is possible to imagine".[1] Astonishing and incredible as this verdict may seem, the activating force behind it appears even more surprising. Coleridge himself is responsible for leveling the minatory forefinger at his old friend William Hazlitt, whose promise and merits he had recognized and encouraged as far back as 1798, as Hazlitt himself was soon to confess with his usual delightful and picturesque candor in "My First Acquaintance with Poets".

Coleridge at one time or another suspected Hazlitt of writing two of the most bitter of all the attacks on his poem.[2] His first

---

[1] So says the anonymous author of *Hypocrisy Unveiled and Calumny Detected: In a Review in Blackwood's Magazine* (4th ed.; London, 1818), p. 50. This was a pamphlet attacking John Wilson (i.e., "Christopher North") and J. G. Lockhart for traducing Coleridge and others in *Blackwood's*. See Griggs, II, 247; Mary Gordon, '*Christopher North*' *A Memoir of John Wilson* . . . . (Edinburgh, 1879), pp. 203–7; and Alan Lang Strout, "Samuel Taylor Coleridge and John Wilson of *Blackwood's Magazine*," *PMLA*, XLVIII (March, 1933), 113 and n. Strout gives reasons for believing that the author was probably James Grahame rather than Macvey Napier.

[2] A general perspective of the early reviews may be obtained by supplementing E.H.C.'s excerpts (pp. 99–102) with the brief article by Walter Graham, "Contemporary Critics of Coleridge the Poet," *PMLA*, XXXVIII (June, 1923), 278–89.

mistrust was fixed on Francis Jeffrey's *Edinburgh Review*, for he had long felt that Jeffrey had harbored an animosity against him and his friends. Not long before, in an effort to obtain a favorable hearing for a book by one of these friends, he had gone so far as to invite Jeffrey to Keswick and had entertained him briefly there. Imagine, then, the shock to a man who believes himself to have made a favorable impression on an editor to discover a leading article on himself in that editor's magazine, ending, "Upon the whole, we look upon this publication as one of the most notable pieces of impertinence of which the press has lately been guilty. . . . ."[3] Coleridge's dazed attempt to understand and explain this dastardly treatment appears first in the postscript to a letter which he wrote his publisher Murray soon afterward: "I have not seen either the 'Edinburgh' or the 'Quarterly' last Reviews. The article against me in the former was, I am assured, written by Hazlitt. Now what can I think of Mr. Jeffrey, who knows nothing personally of me but my hospitable attentions to him, and from whom I heard nothing but very high seasoned compliments, and who yet can avail himself of *such* an instrument of his most unprovoked malignity towards me, an inoffensive man in distress and sickness?"[4] The attribution of this criticism to Hazlitt, however, was very likely an error in which Coleridge confused the article at first with another, for Hazlitt's name was never closely associated with *The Edinburgh Review*.[5] Yet Coleridge repeated his charges when in a postscript to the *Biographia Literaria* in the same year he continued the battle with Jeffrey, accusing him again of unjustified animosity and charging publicly that the other had commissioned an unnamed person to review the book prejudicially.[6] Jeffrey promptly replied with a counterblast written with his customary cutting good humor and appended, as a long foot-

[3] *Edinburgh Review*, XXVII (September, 1816), 66.

[4] Letter of February 27, 1817, *Letters*, II, 669–70.

[5] A. R. Waller and Arnold Glover, however, in their edition of *The Collected Works of William Hazlitt* (London, 1902–6), X, 411, are "disposed to think that the review is substantially the work of Hazlitt, though . . . . it may be conjectured that Jeffrey used his editorial pen freely."

[6] *Biographia Literaria*, II, 299–304.

note of his own, to the review which his periodical published of the *Biographia* in 1817. In this he not only denied all his antagonist's allegations but added that, so far as his memory sustained him, the entertainment he had received at Keswick in 1810 consisted of a cup of coffee at Southey's home and one meal which Coleridge had taken with him at the inn.[7]

This was the series of episodes which Gillman later described with considerable heat as follows: "The Fragment had not long been published before he was informed, that an individual had been selected (who was in truth a great admirer of his writings; and whose very life had been saved through the exertions of Coleridge and Mr. Southey,)[8] to 'cut up' Christabel in the Edinburgh Review. The subject being afterwards mentioned in conversation, the reviewer confessed that he was the writer of the article, but observed, that as he wrote for the Edinburgh Review, he was compelled to write in accordance with the character and tone of that periodical. This confession took place after he had been extolling the Christabel as the finest poem of its kind in the language, and ridiculing the public for their want of taste and discrimination in not admiring it."[9] Gillman here is certainly alluding to Hazlitt, and yet there is absolutely no

---

[7] *Edinburgh Review*, XXVIII (August, 1817), 508–9 n. Jeffrey (p. 511 n.) denies explicitly that he himself wrote the review, but does not name his hireling. Another peculiar side light on the affair appears in Jeffrey's letter to John Wilson on October 17, 1817, in which he says of the latter's desire to write a favorable review of Coleridge: "I had intended to review him fairly, and, if possible, favourably, myself, at all events mercifully; but, on looking into the volume, I can discern so little new, and so much less good than I had expected, that I hesitate about noticing him at all. I cannot help fearing, too, that the discrepancy of our opinions as to that style of poetry may be too glaring to render it prudent to venture upon it, at least under existing conditions; and, besides, if I must unmask all my weakness to you, I am a little desirous of having the credit, though it should be only an inward one, of doing a handsome or even a kind thing to a man who has spoken ill of me, and am unwilling that a favourable review of this author should appear in the *Review* from a hand other than my own" (see Gordon, pp. 171–72). Strout (pp. 100 ff.) discusses the whole mystery thoroughly and shows how Coleridge quickly forgave his former intimate friend, Wilson, for his treacherous attack on the *Biographia* in *Blackwood's* for October, 1817, and how "*Maga*" later made up for its ill-treatment of him by many flattering references and by making him a contributor. Wilson's treachery seems to have been due partly to his extraordinarily changeable nature and partly to his temporary annoyance because of Coleridge's abuse of Jeffrey, with whom Wilson was just then getting on excellent terms.

[8] See Percival P. Howe, *The Life of William Hazlitt* (London, [1922]), p. 80.

[9] Gillman, pp. 276–77. However, this is a much stronger statement than Coleridge's own in the *Biographia*, for which see n. 12, below.

evidence beyond Coleridge's suspicion and Hazlitt's so-called, but highly unlikely, confession to connect him with the *Edinburgh* review.[10] The anonymous author, whose identity Jeffrey jealously guarded, as was his policy, may very possibly have been Henry Brougham, later Baron Brougham, who had been associated with the magazine since its founding, and whose style and political views would accord with those revealed in the article.[11]

But if Hazlitt may probably be exculpated from the sally in *The Edinburgh*, he was with little doubt deeply implicated in an even more serious and far-reaching assault in *The Examiner*, which his friend Leigh Hunt was then editing. Strangely enough, Hazlitt's candidacy for the authorship of *two* reviews of the same poem seems to have escaped nearly all of the commentators—or at least did not trouble or mystify them. Yet what is more likely than that the rumors about the composer of the earlier review, which was *The Examiner*'s, should have been mistakenly attached by Coleridge to the later, *The Edinburgh*'s? For Hazlitt was openly engaged in writing for Hunt, and modern scholars have pretty generally agreed to assign the article on "Christabel" to him.[12] The review, which appeared in the issue

[10] Wilson wrote a little later in *Blackwood's* (III, 77) that Jeffrey "committed the task to a savage and truculent jacobin, the very twitching of whose countenance is enough to frighten the boldest man into hysterics" (see Strout, *op. cit.*, p. 107 n.). This description, of course, might apply to many men, although it was evidently intended to refer to Hazlitt. Lockhart, writing as "Z." in *Blackwood's*, invented the phrase "pimpled Hazlitt", which had great currency, although Hazlitt indignantly maintained that he was not pimpled at all, "but remarkably pale and sallow." See Strout, "Pimpled Hazlitt," *ELH*, IV (June, 1937), 156–59.

[11] So thinks P. L. Carver, in "The Authorship of a Review of *Christabel* Attributed to Hazlitt," *Journal of English and Germanic Philology*, XXIX (October, 1930), 562–78. Carver's evidence is mostly internal; it is plausible, but not conclusive.

[12] Arnold and Glover do not absolutely commit themselves, but reprint the article in a note (Hazlitt, *Works*, XI, 580–82). Edmund Blunden, however, in *Leigh Hunt's Examiner Examined* (London, 1928), p. 58, assigns it to Hazlitt unqualifiedly. James Dykes Campbell, *Samuel Taylor Coleridge A Narrative of the Events of His Life* (London, 1894), p. 222, refers to Coleridge's belief that the author was Hazlitt, but calls attention to the final chapter of the *Biographia Literaria*, in which Coleridge describes the reception of "Christabel" in the *Edinburgh* (etc.): "and this review was generally attributed (whether rightly or no I know not) to a man, who both in my presence and in my absence has repeatedly pronounced it the finest poem of its kind in the language." This passage, however, was made much less personal and individual in later editions of the *Biographia*.

for June 2, 1816, not only was a masterpiece of misinterpretation by innuendo but admitted openly that its author had had access to the original manuscript, upon which his main charges revolved. After predicting that many of the squeamish readers of the poem would be offended by such a brazen phrase as "mastiff bitch", but commending Coleridge for his "manliness" in retaining it, the critic continued: "We the rather wonder at this bold proceeding in the author, as his courage has cooled in the course of the publication, and he has omitted, from mere delicacy, a line which is absolutely necessary to the understanding of the whole story. The *Lady Christabel*, wandering in the forest by moonlight, meets a lady in apparently great distress, to whom she offers her assistance and protection, and takes her home with her to her own chamber. This woman,

> '————beautiful to see,
> Like a lady of a far countree,'

is a witch. Who else she is, what her business is with *Christabel*, upon what motives, to what end her sorceries are to work, does not appear at present; but this much we know that she is a witch, and that Christabel's dread of her arises from her discovering this circumstance, which is told in a single line, which line, from an exquisite refinement in efficiency, is here omitted. When the unknown lady gets to *Christabel's* chamber, and is going to undress, it is said—

> 'Then drawing in her breath aloud
> Like one that shuddered, she unbound
> The cincture from beneath her breast:
> Her silken robe, and inner vest,
> Dropt to her feet, and full in view,
> *Behold! her bosom and half her side*—
> A sight to dream of, not to tell!
> And she is to sleep by Christabel!'

The manuscript runs thus, or nearly thus:—

> 'Behold her bosom and half her side—
> *Hideous, deformed, and pale of hue.*'

This line is necessary to make common sense of the first and second part. 'It is the keystone that makes up the arch.' For that reason Mr. Coleridge left it out."

Any critic who assigns such a motive to Coleridge has obviously confessed his own lack of taste and intelligence; but nevertheless Hazlitt—if it be he—has pitched upon one of the pivotal lines in the poem, though not for the reason he thought. This problem, however, must be postponed until later. In the meantime the review, after commending certain parts of the poem, continued: "The poet, like the witch in *Spenser*, is evidently

'Busied about some wicked gin.'—

But we do not foresee what he will make of it. There is something disgusting at the bottom of his subject, which is but ill glossed over by a veil of Della Cruscan sentiment and fine writing—like moon-beams playing on a charnel-house, or flowers strewed on a dead body."

If this article was intended to pique a curiosity about forbidden things without allaying it, it was eminently successful. What could there be that was so disgusting about the relationship between Geraldine and Christabel—so disgusting that it could not be named on a printed page, but that the critic, with a "We could, and if we would" air, hinted that he was able to divulge? Only one person who had been really intimate with Coleridge ever went about whispering such a secret—and that was William Hazlitt. According to Coleridge himself, it was Hazlitt who was responsible for originating and promulgating the before-mentioned charge of obscenity against his poem: "Some genius in a pamphlet entitled Hypocrisy Unveiled written against Mr. Wilson has pronounced poor Christabel 'the most obscene Poem in the English Language'—It seems that Hazlitt from pure malignity had spread about the Report that Geraldine was a man in disguise. I saw an old book at Coleorton in which the Paradise Lost was described as an 'obscene Poem,' so I am in good company. . . . ."[13]

This sexual interpretation of the poem, which would have

[13] Letter to Southey, [February, 1819,] in Griggs, II, 247.

turned it into nothing more than a novel and supernatural kind of seduction, or rape (incidentally, the *Edinburgh*'s review had also hinted at seduction),[14] so fascinated and shocked the moralists, with their memory of the dreadful night Christabel had spent in Geraldine's embrace, that they spread their horrid accusations throughout the nation. Rossetti knew of the scandal in the latter part of the century as a bit of choice and racy gossip which was still filtering through literary circles, his particular channel of information having been P. G. Patmore, father of Coventry Patmore.[15] Gillman was of course familiar with it and felt called upon to deny it with suitable horror and loathing.[16] Outrageous as the idea was, however, there was after all some slight basis for the charge, as revealed in Gillman's own continuation—not to mention the fact that in Coleridge's poem "Love", composed between the first and second parts of "Christabel", there is a somewhat similar impersonation, with the sexes reversed, when the anonymous knight is deceived by a fiend which has usurped the shape of his beauteous lady.[17]

Acting on these discreditable suggestions from journals which should have had more integrity than they did, the parodists gleefully jumped into the mud-throwing exhibition. The vulgarest of these performances was sponsored by J. Duncombe, a purveyor of middle-class erotica, who in the year 1816 brought out a work with the following title-page: *Christabess. By S. T. Colebritche, Esq. A Right Woeful Poem, Translated from the Doggerel, by Sir Vinegar Sponge.* Fortunately for his reputation, the identity of Sir Vinegar was kept a secret, as the content of his "Poem" shall also be, since only the most reckless and impervious scholar is likely to dare its clumsy and vulgar humors.

As a final black monument to this scandalous interpretation, the coarse and brutal continuation in *Blackwood's Edinburgh*

[14] *Edinburgh Review*, XXVII, 62–63.

[15] T. Hall Caine, *Recollections of Dante Gabriel Rossetti* (London, 1882), pp. 155–56. The elder Patmore's associations with, and contributions to, *Blackwood's* at the time of the Hazlitt controversy are discussed by Strout, "Pimpled Hazlitt," *ELH*, IV, 154–56.

[16] Gillman, pp. 293–94.

[17] *Poems*, pp. 330–35; published first in *The Morning Post*, December 21, 1799, as an "Introduction to the Tale of the Dark Ladie".

Magazine for June, 1819, still stands.[18] This parody has been persistently assigned to the great William Maginn. This Irish journalist, who received an LL.D. from Trinity College in 1819, began his contributions to *Blackwood's* in the same year; and the verses published frequently under the pen name of "Morgan Odoherty" (or O'Doherty) have generally been regarded as his. One of the earliest of these appearances was a parody of "Christabel", which set the vulgar, and even the insensitive among the intelligentsia, to guffawing all over the nation. Ridiculing in a clumsy, bludgeon-like fashion certain of the superficial characteristics of Coleridge's style, the satirist related how, after nine "moons" had waxed and waned, and Christabel was faced with the imminent birth of her child, she at first contemplated suicide in the brook, but finally, funking the deed, temporarily escaped her troubles by drinking herself boozy on her mother's wild-flower wine.

Coleridge was a long-suffering man. It is hard to understand how he could have been as tolerant of this amateurish balderdash as he was. Yet he remarked mildly not long afterward to his friend Allsop: "I laughed heartily at the continuation in Blackwood, which I have been told is by Maginn: it is in appearance, and in appearance *only*, a good imitation; I do not doubt but that it gave more pleasure, and to a greater number, than a continuation by myself in the *spirit* of the two first cantos."[19]

Not content with this half-hearted private reproach, however, Coleridge wrote a letter of encouragement and gratitude to Blackwood himself, assuring him of his own enjoyment of "the droll Christabelliad" by a man of such "undoubted genius" as that of O'Doherty, and concluding, "Let only no poison of personal moral calumny be inserted, and a good laugh is a good thing; and I should be sorry, by making a wry face, to transfer it from my Lady Christabel to myself."[20] This kissing of the rod

---

[18] *Blackwood's*, V (April–September, 1819), 286–91.

[19] Allsop, I, 94–95.

[20] Mrs. Margaret Oliphant, *Annals of a Publishing House. William Blackwood and His Sons, Their Magazine and Friends* (New York and Edinburgh, 1897), I, 412–13.

so pleased "Odoherty" that in the July number he inserted a little note to the editor, asking him to thank Coleridge for the "kind and good-tempered way" in which he had received the parody, and calling this mildness the sign "of a true genius and a true poet."[21]

One wonders, nevertheless, whether Coleridge would have laughed quite so loudly or thanked *Blackwood's* quite so humbly if he had known that "Odoherty" was after all not the celebrated Irish wit Maginn but much smaller fry, David Macbeth Moir, known as "Delta". For, many years later, after Allsop's reminiscences had come out, Moir wrote modestly in reference to Allsop's anecdote and his own contributions to *"Maga"*: "In one of his conversations, I see, Mr. Coleridge imputes some imitations of his more remarkable compositions (to which I plead guilty) to Dr. Maginn, a much abler man. They were dashed off, twenty years ago, in no unkind spirit; but it is pleasing to know, that the author of *Kubla Khan* and the *Ancient Mariner* felt this."[22]

How can one explain a reading public which will gag on a "mastiff bitch" and yet applaud such dull obscenities as Moir's? Gillman, too, wondered, when he spoke of Coleridge's sufferings and misunderstandings, and quoted from the famous passage on friends in "Christabel": "Surely he could not be compared to the generality of his fellows—to men who, though possessing great worldly reputation, never gave him their support; but, on the contrary, were sometimes even ready to whisper down his fair name!

> 'For whispering tongues can poison truth;
> 'And constancy lies in realms above.' "[23]

---

[21] *Blackwood's*, V (July, 1819), 433.

[22] D. M. Moir, "Life of Dr. Macnish," *Tales, Essays, and Sketches by the Late Robert Macnish* (London, 1844), I, 392 n. See also Thomas Aird's "Memoir" prefixed to *The Poetical Works of David Macbeth Moir*, Δ (London and Edinburgh, 1860), I, 28, and W. Lindsay Alexander, "Delta and His Writings," *Hogg's Instructor*, third series of *Titan: A Monthly Magazine* (January–June, 1855), IV, 176. The whole matter is discussed compactly by Strout, *PMLA*, XLVIII, 110–11.

[23] Gillman, p. 173.

The second approach is the purely supernatural, or marvelous. In 1815, it will be remembered, an unidentified poetaster
who was a frequent contributor of verse narratives to *The European Magazine* under the austere signature "V.", beguiled that
periodical into publishing his "Christobell. A Gothic Tale."[24]
This desecration he went on to describe as "Written as a sequel
to a beautiful legend of a fair lady and her father, deceived by a
witch in the guise of a noble knight's daughter." "V.'s" well-
intentioned but appalling production, which rises to its climax
amid a flurry of tolling bells, fairy rosebuds, and purple fire, is
forced to enlist in "Christobell's" cause no less a magician than
Merlin, into whom Bracy is transformed, and who recognizes
Geraldine as his long-since-vanquished enemy, the "Witch of
the Lake", whom he now successfully commands to "descend
forever!" All is ready, therefore, for the marriage of Christabel
to Sir Roland's son, who is apparently her "true lover". Inept
and downright risible as this continuation is, however, it was
obviously written by someone near enough to Coleridge's own
group to have read, or at least to have heard of, the original.
The spelling "Christobell" is one that Coleridge himself had
used in early versions of his poem, and that Southey was also
familiar with.[25] On the other hand, the imitator disagreed with
his original on the pronunciation of "Geraldine" and "Leoline",
Coleridge riming them with "divine", and "V." with "mien".
Nevertheless, in spite of these discrepancies in genius and pronunciation, the opinion was advanced in good faith by an anonymous memoirist in *Fraser's Magazine* in 1834 that "Christobell" had been sired by S. T. C. himself in an effort to sound out
public reaction to this ending, which was the best he could do
with his original situation at the moment, although "A better
solution was in the mind of the poet, and therefore, though he
took care that this should be preserved in case the better one
was not produced, he was desirous of its being so published that
it might be easily suppressed, whenever the *new dénouement*

[24] *European Magazine, and London Review*, LXVII (April, 1815), 345–46.

[25] E.H.C., pp. 39, 45. Coleridge used *both* spellings in the *Biographia Literaria*, even
after his poem had been published!

should come forth to supply its place." To prove his authority as an authentic "insider", the writer added that a friend of his had once heard Coleridge about to elucidate his curious production; but unfortunately, according to his usual habit, the poet had carelessly digressed to another topic and had never got back to his main theme. First, however, he had informed his hearers of his intention to add a detailed description of the local scenery to be passed in the journey of "Bracey [*sic*] the Bard".[26]

Several other continuators or parodists believed, like "V.", that the solution of the mystery lay simply and easily within the boundaries of magic and diablerie. In the mind of W. F. Deacon, the reaction was one of pure burlesque; and in "The Dream, a Psychological Curiosity," published in *Warreniana*, a collection of travesties of contemporary poets, he was content to tell a rickety tale of bogles, broomsticks, devils, and the most talented manufacturer of shoeblacking of the day.[27] Similarly, in another piece of anonymous doggerel, published in *The Déjeuné; or, Companion for the Breakfast Table* in 1820, the author of "A Parody of Christabelle. The Baron Rich" saw nothing in Coleridge's poem but the most obvious and conventional supernaturalism, coupled with a few stylistic peculiarities.[28] Two or three hundred lines on how the mastiff bitch turned into Satan himself and carried the Baron off to hell on another broomstick are far too many.

A degree above both of these is the work of James Hogg, who had at least persuaded many of his contemporaries that he should be considered as a real poet. Before any of his fellow-parodists, he had entered the field with a whole volume of satirical mimicries, which he called *The Poetic Mirror; or, The Living Bards of Great Britain*. Among these imitations, which were pretty wretched stuff even for the "Ettrick shepherd", he in-

---

[26] "Reminiscences of Coleridge, Biographical, Philosophical, Poetical, and Critical," *Fraser's Magazine for Town and Country*, X (October, 1834), 393–94.

[27] [W. F. Deacon,] *Warreniana; with Notes, Critical and Explanatory, by the Editor of a Quarterly Review* (London, 1824), pp. 93–108.

[28] *Déjeuné*, November 6, 1820.

cluded one entitled "Isabelle, by S. T. Coleridge".[29] Here, in an atmosphere of rainy moonlight, croaking rails, and the harsh murmuring of a river, sits and shivers the Lady Isabelle, with only a quaking "cut-tail'd whelp" (a metamorphosis, of course, of the famous "mastiff bitch") to bear her company. And so the pair sit and wait, apparently for the coming of three spirits of the dead; but what happened after that Hogg never told.

Martin Farquhar Tupper, on the other hand, was a sincere and appreciative admirer of "Christabel". Though the thousand lines or so which, under the title "Geraldine", he composed in 1831 to complete Coleridge's three unfinished cantos are as dull as anything he ever wrote, and can scarcely be regarded as much more than a miserable sacrilege, he at least realized his own temerity and apologized for it.[30] In one or two points, indeed, he seems almost to have caught a glimmer of certain of Coleridge's intentions, though his handling of the story is bald and inept. The changes and additions in his dramatis personae —Geraldine, a "dragon-maid"; "Ryxa the Hag," a horrible dwarf; Amador, Sir Roland's "long-lost child" and Christabel's former lover, now returned from the Holy Land—indicate sufficient of his conception of the comparative ease of his task in finishing the plot.

Most interesting of these supernatural continuations, in spite of its poetic inadequacies and grammatical solecisms, was the attempt of Eliza Stewart to go on with Coleridge's story in the relatively unknown *Smallwood's Magazine* for June, 1841.[31] Here, in her "Canto III", she at least did not sin by telling too much, as her competitors had done. In fact, much of the success of her effort probably resides in her breaking off her narra-

[29] [James Hogg,] *The Poetic Mirror* . . . . (Philadelphia, 1817), pp. 147–53. The first edition appeared in 1816.

[30] *The Poetical Works of Martin Farquhar Tupper* (New York, 1849), pp. 113–47. John Wilson, in reviewing it for *Blackwood's* in December, 1838 (XLIV, 836–38), wrote: "So far from soaring through the sky like a Daedalus, he labors along the sod after the fashion of a Dodo."

[31] "Christabel. Continued from Coleridge by Eliza Stewart," *Smallwood's Magazine*, June, 1841, pp. 432–38.

tive at a new climax at the end of her third part and leaving her readers in almost as great a suspense and mystery as when they had begun to read. Miss Stewart's originality did not lie in her attempt to enrich Coleridge's setting with croaking ravens and prophetic announcements, or in her unearthly fordoing of the mastiff bitch, or even in her allowing Christabel's returned lover, Sir Gamelyne, to be ridden off with by the gloating Geraldine. Rather, her shiver was contained in the last line of the speech of Roland de Vaux to Sir Leoline after Bracy had returned from his mission—a speech which revealed that Geraldine de Vaux had been placed in her grave a month before, in spite of Christabel's horrified insistence that the lady walked "the green earth still." Nevertheless, as the two knights and the bard ride back to examine the grave of the dead Geraldine, Miss Stewart's inspiration expires, leaving the mystery of the girl's death and resuscitation (for such it appears to be) unsolved. It is an admirable essay, far more intelligent than any other, as will be seen.[32]

The third approach is the moral, or didactic. In the *Biographia Literaria,* in the famous passage discussing the relationship which he and Wordsworth had determined to maintain between the supernatural and the humanly sympathetic, Coleridge said: "In this idea originated the plan of the 'Lyrical Ballads;' in which it was agreed, that my endeavours should be directed to persons and characters supernatural, or at least romantic; yet so as to transfer from our inward nature a human interest and a semblance of truth sufficient to procure for these shadows of imagination that willing suspension of disbelief for the moment, which constitutes poetic faith. . . . . With this view I wrote 'The Ancient Mariner,' and was preparing among other poems, the 'Dark Ladie,' and the 'Christobel,' [*sic*] in which I should have more nearly realized my ideal, than I had done in my first attempt."[33]

[32] The persistency of this simplest of supernatural explanations, which sees nothing further in the poem than an illustration of the theme of witchcraft, is shown by Lawrence Hanson's unquestioning acceptance of it in *The Life of S. T. Coleridge The Early Years* (London, 1938), pp. 256–57.

[33] *Biographia Literaria,* II, 2–3.

Derwent Coleridge, the poet's second surviving son, whose profession as a cleric may of course have biased him in favor of the instructive interpretation, unites with James Gillman in this view, which, when one considers the S. P. C. A. ending of "The Ancient Mariner", seems not totally inharmonious with its author's philosophy. According to Derwent's surprising elucidation of his father's mystery, "The sufferings of Christabel were to have been represented as vicarious, endured for her 'lover far away'; and Geraldine, no witch or goblin, or malignant being of any kind, but a spirit, executing her appointed task with the best good will, as she herself says:—

> All they who live in the upper sky,
> Do love you, holy Christabel, &c. (ll. 227–32).

In form this is, of course, accommodated to 'a fond superstition', in keeping with the general tenour of the piece; but that the holy and the innocent do often suffer for the faults of those they love, and are thus made the instruments to bring them back to the ways of peace, is a matter of fact, and in Coleridge's hands might have been worked up into a tale of deep and delicate pathos."[34] This provocative suggestion buttresses the earlier but more meager one of Gillman on this same point, but contradicts it flatly on another: "The story of Christabel is founded on the notion, that the virtuous of this world save the wicked. The pious and good Christabel suffers and prays for

> 'The weal of her lover that is far away,'

exposed to various temptations in a foreign land; and she thus defeats the power of evil represented in the person of Geraldine. This is one main object of the tale."[35]

[34] Derwent Coleridge, *The Poems of Samuel Taylor Coleridge* (E. Moxon, Son & Co., [1870?]), p. xlii; quoted by E.H.C., p. 52 n. I am forced to rely on E. H. C.'s quotation because I have been unable to locate this edition in the British Museum, the Huntington Library, or the Union Catalogue. If it were not for the fact that E. H. C. again refers to this same volume in his bibliography at the end of his Oxford, 1912, edition of Coleridge's *Complete Poetical Works*, II, 1173, saying that it contains an introduction (an "Essay in a Brief Model") which has never been reprinted, I should be almost tempted to think that he had invented the passage for just such an investigation as my present one.

[35] Gillman, p. 283.

The two men therefore agree on their interpretation of the moral purpose behind the character of Christabel, but are completely at variance in their attitude toward the function of Geraldine.[36] On this point, if there is anything in the belief in a spiritual kinship between members of the same family, the decision must go to Derwent Coleridge. Moreover, in the next generation Ernest Hartley Coleridge was to side with his father, when, in quoting the other's statement, he commented: "The writer speaks with authority, and it is possible that this suggestion of 'vicarious' suffering on the part of Christabel was made by Coleridge himself. It must be received with respect, but it does not add much to the interpretation of the poem as a whole."[37] The truth of the last observation will be discussed later, but E. H. C. was not always so alert and sensitive as he might have been. Perhaps his grandfather's own cryptic reference to Crashaw's St. Teresa and her desire for a martyrdom might have aided him to a wiser conclusion if he had considered it more carefully.

Gillman, however, in his endeavor to prove how intimate in the counsels of Coleridge he had been, was not content to restrict his contribution to generalities, but pressed recklessly on to follow the adventures of Bracy, Sir Leoline, and the two ladies in full detail. In so doing, he not only lent support to the sensational and supernatural, as well as the moral, schools, but he precipitated a new war of the critics, at least one of whom, Professor B. R. McElderry, has recently accepted *in toto* the following synopsis by Gillman, as being in complete harmony with the two original cantos and the known characteristics of the author:[38]

[36] John Sterling, writing in 1828, would have agreed with Gillman in seeing only the malicious and menacing side of Geraldine's character, though once he implies a slight doubt, when he writes of "the fiendish damsel, if such she were . . . ." (*Essays and Tales*, I, 105–6).

[37] E.H.C., p. 52 n.

[38] B. R. McElderry, "Coleridge's Plan for Completing *Christabel*," *Studies in Philology*, XXXIII (July, 1936), 437–55. McElderry takes this stand even after conducting a survey of the attitude of previous critics toward this ending, and finding the results as

"Over the mountains, the Bard, as directed by Sir Leoline, 'hastes' with his disciple; but in consequence of one of those inundations supposed to be common to this country, the spot only where the castle once stood is discovered,—the edifice itself being washed away. He determines to return. Geraldine being acquainted with all that is passing, like the Weird Sisters in Macbeth, vanishes. Re-appearing, however, she waits the return of the Bard, exciting in the mean time, by her wily arts, all the anger she could rouse in the Baron's breast, as well as that jealousy of which he is described to have been susceptible. The old Bard and the youth at length arrive, and therefore she can no longer personate the character of Geraldine, the daughter of Lord Roland de Vaux, but changes her appearance to that of the accepted though absent lover of Christabel. Next ensues a courtship nost distressing to Christabel, who feels—she knows not why—great disgust for her once favoured knight. This coldness is very painful to the Baron, who has no more conception than herself of the supernatural transformation. She at last yields to her father's entreaties, and consents to approach the altar with this hated suitor. The real lover returning, enters at this moment, and produces the ring which she had once given him in sign of her betrothment. Thus defeated, the supernatural being Geraldine disappears. As predicted, the castle bell tolls, the mother's voice is heard, and to the exceeding great joy of the parties, the rightful marriage takes place, after which follows a reconciliation and explanation between the father and daughter."[39]

---

follows: *for*—D. G. Rossetti, in Caine's *Rossetti*, p. 154: ". . . . the conclusion as given by Gillman from Coleridge's account to him is correct enough, only not picturesquely worded"; *against*—James Dykes Campbell, *The Poetical Works of Samuel Taylor Coleridge* (London, 1893), p. 604: "One suspects and hopes, this was mere quizzing on the part of Coleridge, indulged in to relieve the pressure of prosaic curiosity . . . ."; the rest do not consider Gillman's conclusion significant enough even to refer to it: E.H.C., p. 34; A. T. Quiller-Couch, *Coleridge's Poems* (Oxford, 1907); H. W. Garrod, *Coleridge's Poetry and Prose* (Oxford, 1925); and E. L. Griggs, *The Best of Coleridge* (New York, 1934), p. 688. Lately, however, Donald R. Tuttle, in his article on "*Christabel* Sources," *PMLA*, LIII, 446 n., has acquiescently referred to McElderry: "That the Gillman ending or one similar to it was planned by Coleridge seems highly probable."

[39] Gillman, pp. 301–2.

BOOK II

THE CENTRAL MYSTERY

I

THE FIGURE IN THE CARPET

WAIVING the likelihood that a bald synopsis of this
type might make even "The Ancient Mariner" sound
stale and unprofitable, is there anything in Gillman's
extension to justify Coleridge's assurance that his idea was "an
extremely subtle and difficult one"? The physician was certainly sincere in presenting his account of his patient's intentions;
but he was not a person of much imagination, and he did not
become acquainted with the poet until many years after the
other's once heated brain had cooled to a mist of tepid vapors.
Few would feel that there is in Gillman's plot much more than
the most pedestrian and uninspired of ghost stories, pranked
out in the romantic trappings of the "lovers-reunited" school of
fiction. Admitting, as we must, however, that Gillman was
probably reflecting, in a stained and twisted mirror, something
of Coleridge's own treacherous recollections as he grew farther
and farther away from the untamed transports of his youth, can
we find here any satisfaction of the curiosity which the fragment has aroused on a dozen or two points? In other words,
does the continuation explain the most mysterious and the most
vital passages in the original—the ones which have given it its
place as perhaps the most fascinating and enigmatic of literary
conundrums? What does it tell of the very center of the secret
—the Lady Geraldine, her origin, her behavior, and her motivation? Nothing at all. The two parts might almost as well be
separate stories.

This conclusion becomes the more incredible when the blind-
ness and obtuseness of practically all the other exegetes and
speculators are added to Dr. Gillman's. For has Coleridge left
no clues as to the solution of his mystery—no traces of his initial
conception of the Lady Geraldine—no hints as to the accumula-

of his material, as he did in "The Ancient Mariner" and Kubla Khan"? What would happen if "Christabel" were really analyzed as it stands, with due and adequate attention to every precious detail, to every preserved revision, to every figure of speech and every association of ideas? Listen again to the well-known story, with the truly significant details pricked out in the pattern, as in a picture puzzle which contains hidden figures of birds, beasts, and famous persons from myth and history disposed among foliage, clouds, brooks, and buildings, so that they can be discovered only when the page has been turned to a certain angle and the eye has attained the one necessary focus.

It is twelve o'clock on a chilly night in April. The full moon shines through the thin gray clouds. The old watchdog of the castle, which has a strange habit of echoing the clock every midnight, no matter what the weather, utters sixteen short howls, one for each quarter and twelve for the full hour; some people, indeed, say that the dog on these occasions sees the shroud of the lady of the castle, who has died in childbirth years ago.

Now the gentle Christabel, cause of her mother's death, steals along the path to the wood, intending to pray for her distant lover, for

> She had dreams all yesternight
> Of her own betrothèd knight

—dreams that, as Coleridge added in a couplet to the 1816 edition, but later removed,

> made her moan and leap,
> As on her bed she lay in sleep.[1]

Scarcely has she prayed, however, when she hears a low moaning on the other side of the great oak tree near which she is kneeling. Terrified, she nevertheless moves around it and discovers a lovely damsel dressed in white silk, with jewels entangled in her hair. With a breathless prayer to the Virgin, Christabel inquires the lady's identity; and the lady answers in

[1] E.H.C., p. 63 n.

a voice which, Coleridge twice insists, is "faint and sweet".
"Stretch forth thy hand, and have no fear!" beseeches the
stranger; "I scarce can speak for weariness." But when Christabel presses her further, she gives her name as Geraldine, of
noble lineage, and tells a story of how, the day before, she had
been seized by five unknown warriors (in some versions they are
described as "ruffians", with their number varying from three
to five),[2] who had tied her on a white palfrey and, themselves on
white horses, had driven her before them until "Once we crossed
the shade of night" (again, some versions read "twice").[3] Finally the wild ride had stopped, the tallest of the men had unbound her from her horse, had placed her under the oak, and
had ridden away with his companions, promising soon to return.
Exactly how long ago this happened she does not know, "For
I have lain entranced I wis," or, as the earlier versions had it,
"For I have lain in fits, I wis."[4] Ending her story she again
begs Christabel to stretch forth her hand.

The innocent Christabel complies, and guarantees the other
the protection of her father, Sir Leoline, and a safe convoy back
to Geraldine's home. The two girls then slowly start back to
the castle, where Christabel offers to share her bed with the
stranger. At the postern gate, however, Geraldine sinks to the
ground, "belike through pain," and Christabel is forced to lift
her over the threshold, whereupon

> the lady rose again,
> And moved, as she were not in pain.

As they cross the courtyard, Christabel suggests that they praise
the Virgin for her aid; but "Alas, alas!" sighs Geraldine; "I cannot speak for weariness." The old watchdog moans angrily in
her sleep as the pair, moving stealthily so as not to disturb the
infirm Sir Leoline, pass her kennel; and even the dying fire in
the hall spurts up as they go softly by, so that

> Christabel saw the lady's eye,
> And nothing else saw she thereby,

except the boss of her father's shield on the wall.

---

[2] *Ibid.*, p. 67 n.   [3] *Ibid.*   [4] *Ibid.*, p. 68 n.

So they come to the bedchamber, lighted by a lamp fastened with a silver chain to an angel's feet. But, as its owner trims it and leaves it swinging, her guest sinks wretchedly down on the floor underneath. When the latter is offered a cordial made of wild flowers by Christabel's mother, she learns that the dying woman had predicted that she would hear the castle bell strike twelve on her daughter's wedding day. "That thou wert here!" exclaims Christabel piously, thinking of the mother she has never known. The response is totally unexpected to both Christabel and the reader. "I would she were!" replies Geraldine—but then her voice alters, and she cries,

> Off, wandering mother! Peak and pine!
> I have power to bid thee flee.

With "unsettled eye" she stares as if she could see "the bodiless dead", and continues hollowly,

> Off, woman, off! this hour is mine—
> Though thou her guardian spirit be,
> Off, woman, off! 'tis given to me.

Christabel, bewildered, attributes the fit to her guest's "ghastly ride" and administers the cordial, whereupon Geraldine's "fair large eyes 'gan glitter bright" and she rises refreshed to her full stature. Again she speaks soothingly and reassuringly, almost as if with divine authority:

> All they, who live in the upper sky,
> Do love you, holy Christabel!

—and for their sakes and her own she vows that, in her degree, she will try to reward her new friend.

She then requests Christabel to disrobe and retire to bed, while she herself prays. But Christabel cannot sleep; she opens her eyes and watches Geraldine, who slowly prepares to undress. Shudderingly the strange lady draws in her breath, loosens her girdle, and lets her robe fall to her feet. What does the observer see? "A sight to dream of, not to tell!" avers Coleridge. "Behold! her bosom and half her side—" reads the poem, and breaks off direly, leaving the preceding rime dangling. But in three early manuscripts the sentence goes on to specify the horror: Geraldine's bosom and half her side "Are lean and old and foul of hue". Moreover, instead of the following relatively innocent line, "O shield her! shield sweet Christabel!" the earlier versions all allude to the fact that Geraldine is to sleep with Christabel.[5]

We never learn the direct effect of the sight on the watcher; it is the sinister Geraldine upon whom Coleridge dwells. She seems stricken when she realizes that she has been observed; weakly she appears to be trying to lift some heavy weight from deep inside herself; then, proudly and scornfully, she lies down by Christabel and takes the luckless maid in her arms, murmuring with low voice and doleful look that in the touch of her bosom is a spell of silence. The other, she says, knows and will continue to remember "This mark of my shame, this seal of my sorrow"; but the knowledge will be useless, for all that Christabel can declare will be the story of how she found "a bright lady" in the forest and brought her to shelter.

And so Christabel sleeps, "With open eyes (ah woe is me!). . . . ." She is

> Fearfully dreaming, yet, I wis,
> Dreaming that alone which is—[6]

This time Coleridge does not go on, even in the early manuscripts. "O sorrow and shame!" is his only commentary. But Geraldine, "the worker of these harms"—Geraldine, who holds Christabel in her embrace—ah, Geraldine is slumbering as gently and quietly as if she were a mother enfolding her child. So for one hour, as she had claimed, she holds command, she has her will. "A star hath set, a star hath risen," says Coleridge, since her arms imprisoned her captive. During that hour all the night-birds have been silent, but now they burst jubilantly again into song. Christabel gathers herself from her trance; her limbs relax and her face grows soft and sad; she sheds tears, and yet

---

[5] *Ibid.*, pp. 75–76 n.

[6] Of the powers and effects of dreams, Coleridge had set down in his memorandum book: "Dreams sometimes useful by giving to the well-grounded fears and hopes of the understanding the feelings of vivid sense. . . . . In a distempered dream things and forms in themselves common and harmless inflict a terror of anguish" (*Archiv*, pp. 256–57).

she often smiles in her sleep. Perhaps she knows that the guardian spirit of her mother is near.

> And, if she move unquietly,
> Perchance, 'tis but the blood so free
> Comes back and tingles in her feet.

And here the poetic frenzy departed. Here, in 1797 or 1798, Coleridge broke off his first canto. Not until two or three years later, perhaps by the double stimulus of his new home among the Cumberland hills and his travels through the stirring scenery of the Harz Mountains, with all the associations of the Brocken, did he display to his friends the completed second part, with its scene now specifically set in the Lake District.

The canto opens on a note of doom. "Each matin bell," affirmed Sir Leoline when he rose one morning and found his lady dead, "knells us back to a world of death." And so he will continue to say until his own dying day. Thus, every dawn, the sacristan must toll the bell heavily, telling forty-five beads before each new stroke. As the echoes, distorted by the ghosts of three sinful sextons who continue to rend the atmosphere of the near-by mountains with their "ropes of rock and bells of air", come pealing back merrily from the hills, Geraldine, shaking off her dread, rises lightly, dresses with care, and confidently awakens her companion. Christabel is astounded at what she sees. Surely this is not the same woman who had lain down beside her—not even the one whom she had rescued from the forest:

> Nay, fairer yet! and yet more fair!
> For she, belike, hath drunken deep
> Of all the blessedness of sleep!
> And while she spake, her looks, her air
> Such gentle thankfulness declare,
> That (so it seemed) her girded vests
> Grew tight beneath her heaving breasts.

Contrite, and puzzled by her dreams, Christabel leads the lady to her father. Now for the first time Geraldine announces that she is the daughter of Lord Roland de Vaux of Tryermaine. The name arouses in Sir Leoline sad memories of his youth, for he and Lord Roland had once been close friends; but "whispering tongues can poison truth", and the two had parted with insults and hatred. The beauty of the lovely and distressed Geraldine, however, is too much for his chivalrous spirit; and he swears that he will avenge her, that he will appoint a tourney where, if they dare, her attackers may come, and where he may properly

> dislodge their reptile souls
> From the bodies and forms of men!

In the ecstasy of his remorse he clasps Geraldine in his arms, and she not only meets his embrace but prolongs it "with joyous look". And at the sight the hideous vision of the night before descends upon Christabel:

> The vision of fear, the touch and pain!
> She shrunk and shuddered, and saw again—
> (Ah, woe is me! Was it for thee,
> Thou gentle maid! such sights to see?)
> Again she saw that bosom old,
> Again she felt that bosom cold. . . . .

The first line of this passage was the result of meticulous revision, for in some manuscripts Coleridge had written, "The vision foul of fear and Pain" and "The vision of fear, the touch of pain".[7] There is no doubt, then, that he wanted all three elements in his picture: the fear, the touch, and the pain. But what happens further to Christabel when the memory of her delirium returns to her? She "drew in her breath with a hissing sound", which so startles her father that he wheels wildly about —to see nothing but his daughter with her eyes raised heavenward as if in prayer, for now

> The touch, the sight, had passed away,
> And in its stead that vision blest,
> Which comforted her after-rest,
> While in the lady's arms she lay,
> Had put a rapture in her breast. . . . .

(Again, in the first line, earlier readings had substituted "pang" for "touch".)[8] The spell, then, is proving so potent that Christabel has no power to tell the truth.

[7] E.H.C., p. 87 n.   [8] *Ibid.*, p. 88 n.

So deep is Sir Leoline's contrition for his youthful behavior that he refuses Geraldine's request that she be sent to Tryermaine without delay. Rather, he plans to dispatch his bard, Bracy, with a boy harp-bearer, to inform Lord Roland of his daughter's safety and to arrange a mutual excursion in which parties from both castles will meet each other halfway, so that the lady may be returned with appropriate ceremony. Yet Bracy hesitates. He has had a dream so ominous that he has vowed to cleanse the wood with his music from some "thing unblest". He has seen a favorite dove of Sir Leoline's, called by the very name of Christabel, struggling with a bright-green snake which has thrown its coils around the bird's wings and neck.

> Green as the herbs on which it couched,
> Close by the dove's its head it crouched;
> And with the dove it heaves and stirs,
> Swelling its neck as she swelled hers!

The knight, however, is in the toils; he turns to Geraldine with wonder and love in his eyes, addresses her as "Lord Roland's beauteous dove", and promises that he and her father will crush any threatening snake with force more powerful than music. Thereupon, blushing, Geraldine turns so that only Christabel can see her face; then she

> couched her head upon her breast,
> And looked askance at Christabel—
> Jesu, Maria, shield her well!
>
> A snake's small eye blinks dull and shy,
> And the lady's eyes they shrunk in her head,
> Each shrunk up to a serpent's eye,
> And with somewhat of malice, and more of dread,
> At Christabel she looked askance!

Although the sight lasts only an instant, it is too much for the victim. Christabel, in a "dizzy trance", stumbles and shudders aloud, once more "with a hissing sound". Geraldine, "like a thing, that sought relief," turns back to Sir Leoline; but Christabel, so deeply has she drunk in the look of those sunken serpent eyes, unconsciously imitates in her own features "That look of dull and treacherous hate". When at length she recovers from her trance, she prays her father, by her mother's soul, to send Geraldine away. But the old knight, instead of being struck with pity and understanding, is driven to a mad anger that he has been thus dishonored in his generosity and hospitality by "more than woman's jealousy". Sternly and sharply he commands Bracy to depart. Then, averting his face from Christabel, he leads forth the Lady Geraldine.

"The Conclusion to Part II", written in 1801, is little more than an expression of Coleridge's paternal sentiment toward his young son Hartley, and adds nothing to help solve the mystery which he here left dangling to baffle posterity.

Nevertheless, there are obviously plenty of materials here to work with. Is it not possible, by revolving the drawing in different directions, to get some inkling of the hidden design—to find Jack concealed crosswise among the leaves of the beanstalk; to unearth the ogre somewhere in the vegetation, even though he may be standing on his head; perhaps even to discover the needle in the haystack? The venture is at least worth attempting.

Certain of the supernatural paraphernalia of the poem may first be temporarily discarded as merely incidental to the heart of the situation—such matters as the psychic time-telling powers of the old "mastiff bitch" who guards the castle, or the ghosts of the three sinful sextons who continue to ring their phantom bells in Dungeon-ghyll. It is Geraldine, and Geraldine alone, who can afford the key to the riddle. What clues does Coleridge offer concerning this strange and "subtle" being whom he has conceived and begun to create?

The first part is rather vague and conventional in its folklore and superstitions. The lady is manifested suddenly out of nowhere and tells a patently fabricated story about being kidnaped by marauders. She cannot pass the entrance to the house alone, but has to be lifted over the threshold. A dog groans in its sleep when she passes, and a dying fire leaps up. The name of the Virgin distresses her, and the shadows from the angel on the lamp sap her strength so that she almost faints. She casts a spell of silence over a person who might betray a dangerous secret. So far, though unrolled by a master, the basic plot is quite commonplace.

But another element is introduced very early: the eagerness of the weak and weary Geraldine to establish physical contact with Christabel. "Stretch forth thy hand, and have no fear!" she begs in her first speech; and again, at the end of her brief narrative, she reiterates her plea, "Stretch forth thy hand. . . . ." When Christabel finally complies, she is able to walk slowly to the castle. When she sinks at the gate as if in pain and Christabel lifts her through it, she immediately rises refreshed on the other side. When she sleeps with Christabel in her arms, Christabel's dreams are fearful and unspeakable; but Geraldine slumbers happily, like a mother with her child. When the hour of her dominion expires, it is Christabel who sleeps happily, but even then the younger girl moves restlessly; perhaps, says Coleridge, it is the blood coming back and tingling in her feet.

The hints so far seem explicit, but perhaps they might be overlooked. In the second part, however, they are so developed and underlined that they almost shout. Geraldine, when she awakes, is so full of new life and vigor that her breasts swell tight against her undervest. Christabel, however, remembers the shrunken bosom of the night before—"lean and old and foul of hue"; she recalls the cold and clammy touch; she cannot forget the pangs and the pain she felt. Nor is she the only prey. On Sir Leoline, too, Geraldine practices her wiles; and when he takes her fondly in his arms, she prolongs the embrace joyously. This is the sight which swiftly calls up the nausea of the previous night in Christabel's memory and makes her cry out so wildly.

What else could such a creature be but a vampire? Of course, in the hands of a poet like Coleridge, it would not be the common graveyard variety of vampire, or ghoul, with a gaunt body bloated to repletion, with eyes (preferably blue in color) inflamed and glowing, with flesh cold as ice, with sharp white

canine teeth, and with full, sensual lips beslobbered with gore—
such vampires as the Reverend Montague Summers has described for the warning of his readers, in the devout belief that
the world still suffers from their depredations. Nor does this
vampire stalk only at night, being doomed at cockcrow to crawl
again into its tomb, where it lies quietly, distended and bloody,
until conditions are favorable again for its prowling—a moonlight night being especially salutary for its resuscitation.[9] Father
Summers knows, and explains at magnificent length in *The
Vampire, His Kith and Kin*, that there are many subspecies in
the race. There are even "spiritual vampires" or "psychic
sponges", who sap the strength of anyone who is merely in the
same room with them.[10] As he explains this type, "Sensitive
people will often complain of weariness and loss of spirits when
they have been for long in the company of certain others. . . . .
In an article on Vampires, *Borderland*, vol. III, No. 3, July,
1896, pp. 353–358, Dr. Franz Hartmann mentions the 'psychic
sponge' or mental vampire. He says: 'They unconsciously vam-
pirize every sensitive person with whom they come in contact,
and they instinctively seek out such persons and invite them to
stay at their houses. I know of an old lady, a vampire, who thus
ruined the health of a lot of robust servant girls, whom she took
into her service and made them sleep in her room. They were
all in good health when they entered, but soon they began to
sicken, they became emaciated and consumptive and had to
leave the service.' "

Obviously, Geraldine's appearance is not so easily detectable
as that of Summers' first type, nor are her methods quite so incorporeal as those of his second; but she gets identical results.
The subtlety of Coleridge's conception is manifest: by a series
of the most delicate—perhaps, in view of their general failure to
be recognized, overdelicate—suggestions he implies the characteristics and personality of his gruesome but fascinating visitant.
Yet I realize that in such a statement I may be making assump-

[9] Summers, pp. 77, 179, 171, 181, 287. Also, "Those whose hair is red, of a certain
peculiar shade, are unmistakably vampires" (p. 182).

[10] *Ibid.*, pp. 134–35.

tions which the reader may not be willing so far to admit. *Is Geraldine a strange and highly original form of vampire?* What did Coleridge know of vampires anyhow? Can it be proved that he was familiar with their peculiarities and operations? I believe that it can, with considerable certainty; but I believe, too, that even if the succeeding argument be rejected the internal evidence in the poem itself is so clear, and so impossible to explain by any other hypotheses (at least, by any other hypotheses which have occurred to me or any of my predecessors), that this conclusion is virtually inevitable.

What is the likelihood that Coleridge had come across the lore of the vampire not once, but many times, in his reading both before and during the time that he was writing "Christabel"?

II

VAMPIRES AND MEDICAL DEMONOLOGY

AS JOHN LIVINGSTON LOWES discovered, one of the works in which Coleridge was much interested, and of which he made considerable use in "The Ancient Mariner", was the *Memoirs of the Literary and Philosophical Society of Manchester.*[1] This was the official publication of a group of provincial intellectuals—chiefly scientists, clergymen, and literati—whose organization was, to a large extent, modeled on that of the Royal Society of London; and in these *Memoirs* they were accustomed to print, sporadically, the best of the papers which had been presented to their membership. With the early volumes of this publication, the first of which appeared in 1785, Coleridge was extremely intimate. Perhaps he originally became acquainted with them soon after their appearance, but, if so, he certainly renewed his knowledge at the time when he was one of the most assiduous patrons of the Bristol Library. On April 20, 1798, for example, he carried Volume II home with him for study, and kept it for over a month.[2] What his object was in drawing it, or what use he made of what he found, is not clear; but the incident at least manifests his interest.

It was, however, Volume III, printed in 1790, which was stuffed with ore for his mining. Although it does not appear on his list of withdrawals, he had studied several of its articles carefully, as his notes and allusions make abundantly clear. Perhaps he became so engrossed in what he found that he could not wait to read it at home, but carried it immediately to a table in the library itself. For in this volume is John Haygarth's article, "Description of a Glory" (with a full-page illustration),

---

[1] Lowes, pp. 29, 30, 205, 470, 501, 546, 553, 557, 565. This work is referred to hereafter as *"Manchester Memoirs"*.

[2] Kaufman, p. 320.

an account of an optical phenomenon of a halo, which impressed Coleridge so much that he set down a special reminder of it in his memorandum book, extracted several phrases from it,[3] and remembered it so vividly that in his poem "Constancy to an Ideal Object", written over twenty-five years later, he described a similar experience of his own and appended a footnote referring to "one of the earlier volumes of the *Manchester Philosophical Transactions. . . . .*"[4]

Striking as was Haygarth's essay, however, there was still more enticing material in the third volume. Probably the most conspicuous and versatile member of the Manchester society since its inception had been John Ferriar, physician of wide and esoteric learning, philosophical bent, and literary taste. *The British Critic*, in reviewing his *Medical Histories and Reflections*, had once described him as "Physician to the Manchester Infirmary, Dispensary, Lunatic Hospital, and Asylum."[5] Again and again Ferriar had turned up in the earlier volumes of the *Memoirs* with challenging and remarkable papers on the most diverse and unexpected subjects.[6]

In the third volume in particular was a contribution by him which could not but have made a tremendous impression on a man of Coleridge's temperament. Conspicuous not only by its position and length but also by its recondite scholarship, Ferriar's discourse "Of Popular Illusions, and Particularly of Medical Demonology", first delivered on May 12, 1786, draws the

[3] *Archiv*, p. 367; *Manchester Memoirs*, III, 463–67. Earlier in the volume there is a similar article by the Rev. James Wood, "On Halos" (pp. 336–43). Wood's article, which Lowes does not mention, though he makes some use of Haygarth's (Lowes, pp. 29, 138, 205), concerns halos around the sun and moon; Haygarth's deals rather with the colored halo cast by the sun around a shadow on a cloud.

[4] *Poems*, p. 456 n. In this passage he also quotes from his own *Aids to Reflection* (1825), his personal copy of which, now in the Harvard College Library, he annotated with a reference to the same phenomenon and a slightly inaccurate allusion to "the 1st or 2nd vol. of yᵉ Manchester Phil¹. Transactⁿˢ "(see Lowes, p. 471).

[5] *British Critic*, XII (August, 1798), 120.

[6] E.g., on October 25, 1786, he had read an "Essay on the Dramatic Writings of Massinger", which was later printed in the third volume, pp. 123–58; and he had soon afterward proved his abiding interest in this author by editing his works. Was it pure coincidence that on August 18, 1797, and again on June 8, 1798, Coleridge drew Vols. I–IV of Massinger's works from the Bristol Library? (Kaufman, pp. 319–20.)

reader's eye like a lodestone even today.[7] As Lowes (who has noticed the article in a casual footnote) has put it, "That is something which Coleridge would never have passed by"; and again, "It is learned and interesting and skeptical, and I suspect that it was to read it that Coleridge got hold of the volume."[8] And here it is that the explorer of Xanadu himself teeters on the brink of the valley, but, unlike his poet, after a brief glance recovers his balance and passes on. Clearly perceiving the nature of much of Ferriar's material, he diffidently hazards an application of a piece of it to a minor aspect of "The Ancient Mariner", and abandons it, obviously with sadness, for it has cast the same spell over him as it seems to have done with Coleridge.

It was before December 31, 1796, as can be demonstrated with considerable conclusiveness, that Coleridge had been reading Ferriar's work in this volume. For on this date the poet wrote a long and significant letter to his friend, the political reformer John Thelwall, carrying on the discussion in which the two were engaged concerning the various theories of life offered by the scientists and philosophers. Here, in the midst of his allusions to Dr. William Hunter, Plato, and Thelwall's own recent essay on "Animal Vitality", he remarked: "Ferriar believes in a soul, like an orthodox churchman."[9] This remark would not be important except for the fact that the third volume of the *Memoirs* also contained another article by the Manchester virtuoso— "Observations concerning the Vital Principle".[10] If Coleridge read these "Observations", it is very unlikely that he would

[7] *Manchester Memoirs*, III, 25–116. Thomas Cooper, in a long article, "Observations respecting the History of Physiognomy," in the same volume, also treated many of the same subjects as Ferriar (pp. 458, etc.). He is the same Cooper that Coleridge referred to in his notebook in April, 1796, as the author of a work on materialism (*Archiv*, p. 344); in Cooper's *Tracts, Ethical, Theological and Political* (Warrington, 1789) is a section entitled, "Of the Impossibility of the Existence of an Immaterial Indiscerptible, Immortal Soul" (see Lowes, p. 604*s*). Coleridge's probable personal acquaintance with Cooper is shown by Lowes (pp. 453, 554–55).

[8] Lowes, pp. 565, 546.

[9] *Letters*, I, 211–12.

[10] *Manchester Memoirs*, III, 216–41. Ferriar does not state directly that he believes in a soul, but this idea is implied in his rejection of a vital principle separate from the mind or brain (*ibid.*, pp. 237–41). He also (pp. 222, 227 ff.) thoroughly discusses Hunter's doctrine in the latter's *Medical Commentaries*.

have overlooked the companion essay on "Medical Demonology" which preceded it.

For this lengthy treatise is a veritable condensed encyclopedia on superstitions and the lore of the supernatural. There seems to be nothing that the credulous—clergy, laity, or scientists—have believed and practiced that Ferriar has overlooked or failed to expose in his sharp, ironical fashion. Witchcraft, ocular fascination, secret marks, spells and "ligatures", demoniacs, ghosts, reanimation—all these and many other similar topics pass in review before his skeptical and amused eye. Nor in the bibliography of popular illusions has he much to learn. From Johannus Wierus, *De praestigiis daemonum* to Cicero's *De divinitate;* from the *Malleus maleficarum* of the medieval inquisitors to the *Occult Philosophy* of Cornelius Agrippa; from Apuleius to Paracelsus; from Joseph Glanville to Sir Kenelm Digby; from Moses to Boyle and van Helmont and Mesmer— no leap is too herculean and no tome too ponderous in weight or Latinity for Dr. Ferriar to conquer with ease and satisfaction. As a compendium and guide by an adept for a neophyte, "Of Popular Illusions, and Particularly of Medical Demonology" can scarcely be excelled, for it refers to close to a hundred and fifty sources and authorities on the subject.

It is unlikely that a savant and connoisseur in the domain of such curiosa would miss one of the weirdest and most appalling of all the creations of man's imagination—the vampire. Nor does Ferriar. In fact, he devotes seven pages toward the end of his treatise to this grisly creature.[11] In discussing the subject of reanimation and the return of the dead, he begins: "Paracelsus found a ready theory in his philosophy, for this species of reanimation; the devil, according to him, can do what he will in his own kingdom, and he can preserve a dead body for any length of time, by his knowledge of the true balsam. . . . ." Commenting on the eccentric contradictions among the Christian sects in the belief of some that preservation of a corpse intact indicates sainthood or beatitude, and of others that it proves diabolic possession, he then passes to the most morbid of all the applica-

---

[11] *Manchester Memoirs*, III, 84–91.

tions of the notion—the tradition of the vampire. "This strange delusion prevailed very generally among the modern Greeks, and they knew the remedy for the disturbance, which consisted in publicly burning the carcase of the *vroucolacas*, as they termed the *redivivus*. But the triumph of this absurdity was reserved for an advanced period of the eighteenth century." He then relates the well-known story of the so-called outbreak of vampires in a certain district of Hungary in the year 1730, as narrated in the *Jewish Letters* of the Marquis d'Argens. These unnatural beings, according to the tale, "sucked the blood of some of the family, during their sleep. The sufferers were sensible of this terrible operation, and commonly recognized the features of the apparition. . . . . In consequence of these practices, the persons sucked became weak and emaciated, the corpse of the Vampire, on the contrary, was found, even after long interment, fresh, florid, and full of blood. . . . ." These gory, but basic, details he then substantiates by reference to further authorities: ". . . . the learned Dom Calmet, well known by his critical dissertations on the Bible, published a history of Vampires, rich in absurdity, of which the following passage is a specimen, but it is necessary to add, quoted from Voltaire." The illustration from Calmet, through Voltaire, concerns two Hungarian officers of Charles VI who investigated a vampire and found that the reports had not been at all exaggerated. Finally, as a clenching proof of the preposterousness of the whole delusion, he cites the record of a fellow-physician, a skeptic like himself: Joseph Pitton de Tournefort, who in his *Relation d'un voyage du Levant, fait par ordre du roi* ... ,[12] described with somewhat nauseating frankness his visit to the Greek island of Mycone in 1701, where he found the town in an utter panic over a supposed vampire, which was eventually dug up under the supervision of the clergy and, though obviously already badly decomposed, was thoroughly exorcized and burned.

Ferriar's review and anecdotes thus open up the whole field of vampire legendry. For, as Lowes has many times pointed out, Coleridge had the pedantic habit of regularly verifying his

[12] See pp. 52–55 of the Amsterdam, 1718, edition.

source references. In fact, concerning this particular passage Lowes appends this note: "The reference to Calmet is precisely the sort of thing which Coleridge, as we have seen, was extremely apt to verify—the more, since he had probably read the article on vampires in Voltaire. . . . . Did he do so in this case?"[13] Answering his own question with an "I suspect he did", he goes on to suggest an echo of this bit of research in the famous re-animation of certain corpses of the crew of a becalmed ship by a troop of angelic spirits. So, closer and closer, did Professor Lowes come. He could smell the tracks of vampires in "The Ancient Mariner", but his sense was numbed when he neared the most fascinating of the whole tribe in "Christabel".

If it was Ferriar's dissertation which reminded Coleridge of vampires about 1796, there is still no reason why notions of the genus should not have been incubating in his imagination for many years. Ferriar's reference to Voltaire might have sent him scurrying back to the *Dictionnaire philosophique* to verify his recollections, but he had actually been familiar with the work of the French skeptic and priest-tormentor for many years— since his school days, in fact. Even while he had been a charity boy at Christ's Hospital, according to the notes which he himself furnished Gillman for his biography, he had turned from a consuming interest in medicine "to a rage for metaphysics, occasioned by the essays on Liberty and Necessity in Cato's Letters, and more by theology. After I had read Voltaire's Philosophical Dictionary, I sported infidel! but my infidel vanity never touched my heart. . . . ."[14] Whatever the permanency of the effect of Voltaire's free thought on Coleridge's own religious convictions, there is little doubt that the article on "Vampires" would have made a profound impression upon him, for in it Vol-

---

[13] Lowes, p. 565; see also p. 282.

[14] Gillman, p. 23. Coleridge's statement here about his early interest in medicine might suggest another reason why he would be attracted to an article about "Medical Demonology": "I became wild to be apprenticed to a surgeon. English, Latin, yea, Greek books of medicine read I incessantly. Blanchard's Latin Medical Dictionary I had nearly by heart." Steven Blankaert's *Lexicon novum medicum Graeco-Latinum*, translated into English as *The Physical Dictionary* of Stephen Blankard (2d ed.; London, 1693), contains nothing bearing on vampires, however.

taire's anticlericalism reached one of its highest levels of bitter irony. Vampires, in fact, were merely stalking horses for the real object of the article, the theme of which, as stated at the climax, was that "the true vampires are the monks, who eat at the expense of both kings and people." In other words, after examining the vampire literature most accessible in his day, Voltaire turned his whole exposure into a diatribe against superstition and the church, especially the Jesuits.[15]

In the article, which was the first and therefore the most prominent under the letter "V", Voltaire first spat out his contempt in general and then embarked on his own description and history of the vampirical superstitions: "These vampires were corpses, who went out of their graves at night to suck the blood of the living, either at their throats or stomachs, after which they returned to their cemeteries. The persons so sucked waned, grew pale, and fell into consumption; while the sucking corpses grew fat, got rosy, and enjoyed an excellent appetite." This sort of primitive blood transfusion of course went on only in the outlying and little-known districts of such countries as Poland, Hungary, Silesia, Moravia, Austria, and Lorraine; the wise vampire carefully avoided metropolises like London and Paris. Nevertheless, hard as it may be to believe, he pointed out, the conception of the vampire derived from Greece—"Not from the Greece of Alexander, Aristotle, Plato, Epicurus, and Demosthenes; but from a Christian Greece, unfortunately schismatic. . . . . The Greeks are persuaded that these dead are sorcerers; they call them '*broucolacas*,' or '*vroucolacas*'. . . . . The Greek corpses go into the houses to suck the blood of little children, to eat the supper of the fathers and mothers, drink their wine, and break all the furniture. They can only be put to rights by burning them when they are caught. But the precaution must be taken of not putting them into the fire until after their hearts are torn out, which must be burned separately." He then concludes this part of his account by epitomizing the most sensa-

---

[15] *The Works of Voltaire* (Akron, 1904), XIV, 148–49. The form in which Coleridge first knew the *Dictionnaire philosophique* is uncertain, but it was probably not in French, since he apparently did not begin to learn that language until some years later, and even then read it with difficulty.

tional and best-attested tales from Tournefort, Calmet, D'Argens, and the rest.[16]

Again, as in Ferriar, the same characteristics of vampire behavior have been singled out for mention: the faintness and emaciation of the victim, the well-being and renewed vitality of the assailant, and the latter's additional parasitism on other members of the victim's family. All these details are obviously exemplified in the three main characters in Coleridge's poem—Christabel, the victim; Geraldine, the assailant; and Sir Leoline, the father. The poet has thrown a beautiful and many-colored veil about his horrors; their crude bloodiness and ghastliness have disappeared, but the essential outlines are easily discernible beneath the veil.

In the accounts of both Ferriar and Voltaire the name of the Benedictine priest, Dom Augustin Calmet, was mentioned so conspicuously and temptingly that certainly Coleridge would have desired to consult his work if he could discover it within his reach. No irrefragable proof that he ever held it in his hands has occurred, but there are plenty of ways in which he might have done so. His omnivorousness as a reader developed early,[17] and he never lost this bookish voracity. On November 19, 1796, in a highly significant letter to his friend Thelwall, he wrote: "I am, and ever have been, a great reader, and have read almost everything—a library cormorant. I am deep in all out of the way books, whether of the monkish times, or of the puritanical era. I have read and digested most of the historical writers; but I do not *like* history. Metaphysics and poetry and 'facts of mind,' that is, accounts of all the strange phantasms that ever possessed 'your philosophy:' dreamers, from Thoth the Egyptian to Taylor the English pagan, are my darling studies. . . . ." Then, after remarking, apropos of some French reading that he contemplated, that "I cannot *speak* French at all and I read it slowly", he commissioned Thelwall to buy him certain out-of-the-way books from a secondhand catalogue.[18] With such facilities and such a temperament, despite the weakness of his

---

[16] *The Works of Voltaire*, XIV, 143–46.   [17] Gillman, pp. 17, 20.

[18] *Letters*, I, 180–81. The secondhand books will return to the story later.

French, there is no inherent improbability in Coleridge's having got access to Calmet somehow during this time.

Dom Augustin Calmet, described by Voltaire more scathingly than he deserved, was best known to the educated world through his learned commentaries on the Bible and his *Histoire ecclésiastique et civile de la Lorraine,* all published during the first three decades of the eighteenth century. In 1746, however, incited by the popular agitation over supernatural manifestations and vampirism, he published from Paris his *Dissertation sur les apparitions des anges, des demons, et des esprits. Et sur les revenans et les vampires.* Five years later he issued a new edition with the word *"Traité"* substituted for the earlier *"Dissertation".*[19] All of this surprising work might well have attracted Coleridge and given him hints, as Lowes suggests, but it is obviously only the latter part which might have a direct bearing on "Christabel". Calmet's study of *"revenans"* was thorough, and his attitude toward vampires much less credulous than that toward apparitions in general. In fact, after regaling his readers with all the tales of these bloodsuckers that he could collect, and examining them in the light of reason and science, he came to this decision concerning their believers: ". . . . all these things are mere illusions, and the consequences of a heated and prejudiced imagination. They cannot cite any witness who is sensible, grave and unprejudiced. . . . ."[20] This good sense, however, Voltaire and Ferriar failed to give him proper credit for, perhaps because of his belief in other mystic phenomena and perhaps because of the way his argument was built up. Until the very end of the investigation, that is, one is uncertain of the author's own opinions; in other words, Calmet marshaled his material, both documentary and argumentative, in a scholarly and impartial fashion, weighing his evidence, until the last sentence.

Much of what he has to say is by this time familiar to the

[19] My citations of Calmet will be from the translation (with an introduction and notes) made by the Rev. Henry Christmas (London, 1850). His edition, in two volumes, is entitled *The Phantom World; or, The Philosophy of Spirits, Apparitions, &c.;* the second volume, however, has a separate heading: *Dissertation on Those Persons Who Return to Earth Bodily, the Excommunicated, the Oupires or Vampires, Vroucolacas, etc.*

[20] *Ibid.,* II, 241.

reader, through Ferriar and Voltaire, both of whom were considerably indebted to him. All the accepted stories of returns from the dead, of the so-called vampires of Hungary, Moravia, etc., based on D'Argens, Tournefort, and the rest, are retailed at length. He derives the name "vampire", or "oupire", from the "Sclavonic, a leech." He announces at the outset that only God can resurrect a person really dead.[21] But his most interesting story is that dealing with the celebrated case of Arnold (or Arnald) Paul, of Madreiga. This weird tale so fascinated the writers of the eighteenth and early nineteenth centuries that they told it over and over again, or alluded to it so casually that they clearly counted on every reader's familiarity with it.

Arnold Paul was a Hungarian, a well-known and important person in his district. It was his misfortune, however, to have been sucked by a Turkish vampire during his life. This fact was not divulged until, after his death and burial, an extensive and vicious outbreak of vampirism occurred in his village, whereupon one of his comrades recalled that Paul had once confided to him the history of his mishap in Turkey. This revelation was all the clue that was necessary, for a person who has been sucked by a vampire, no matter how innocent he may be, will invariably become a vampire himself after his death, if he does not do so in life. Living human beings, that is, inoculated by the oupire's fangs and embrace, must become passive vampires; after they have died, there is no escape for them—their passive traits become active at once, and they must join the depredations of their horrible tribe: "those who have been sucked, suck also in their turn. . . . ." Thus one vampire, unless quickly discovered and exterminated, may create dozens more, in an endless chain of multiplication. The epidemic in Arnold Paul's village was cured only by a wholesale exhuming, impaling, and burning of corpses of those suspected to have been preyed upon by Paul or some other of his victims.

Of these victims at second or third hand, one of the saddest cases was that of the daughter of one of the village leaders, the Heyducq Jotiützo. This young girl, named Stanoska, had ap-

[21] *Ibid.*, pp. 6–7.

parently been bitten when no one, not even she herself, knew it.
Only afterward did her family recollect that at night, in the days
before her death, she had formed the habit of moaning, trembling, and shrieking in her sleep; for this behavior, according to
the authorities, was indubitable evidence of her fate.[22]

Is it necessary to recall the troubled slumbers of Christabel,
her "dreaming fearfully", her moving "unquietly", the tears
which afterward trickle from under her sleeping eyelids?[23] And
here, too, in the story of Paul is a *female* vampire, though
through no fault of her own. Female vampires are relative rari-
ties in early vampire literature, though they do occur; it is the
male who makes the most dreaded of the assaults. Only in our
own day has the term "vampire" taken on a primarily female
connotation. Yet not only is Geraldine a woman, with vampire
characteristics; in the second canto Christabel also shows unmistakable signs of turning into the same sort of creature. In
her manner, in her appearance, in the sounds she utters, she
imitates all that is most sinister in her previous night's bedfel-
low. Whatever Geraldine may be, Christabel is clearly being
transformed into a similar being—likewise through no fault or
willingness of her own. Those who have been infected by a vampire become vampires themselves.

This is a point which Coleridge would not have learned from
Voltaire and Ferriar, but would have seized on quickly from
Calmet. On another matter, however, he would have found a
confirmation of their remarks—the preying of the vampire on
an entire family, not on an individual member only. For Calmet quotes a considerable extract from the *Mercure Galent* of
1693–94, containing the following dogmatic assertion: "This
reviving being, or *oupire*, comes out of his grave, or a demon in

---

[22] *Ibid.*, pp. 37–40, 47–48.

[23] Tuttle (pp. 462–65) compares such behavior with Emily's in *The Mysteries of Udolpho* and Ellena's in *The Italian*, both by Ann Radcliffe, and again (p. 473) with Sabina's in Mary Robinson's *Hubert de Sevrac*. But, of course, no vampires are involved. Note also, incidentally, that just the night before, in dreaming of her lover, Christabel had had

> "Dreams that made her moan and leap,
> As on her bed she lay in sleep. . . . ."

his likeness, goes by night to embrace or hug violently his near relations or his friends, and sucks their blood so much as to weaken and attenuate them, and at last cause their death. This persecution does not stop at one single person; it extends to the last person of the family, if the course be not interrupted....."[24] Thus, if this theory means anything in the light of the completed portion of "Christabel", Sir Leoline, as the only other surviving member of his family, was clearly marked out as the next quarry of Geraldine. She had, in fact, already begun her operations upon him and had enfolded him tentatively in her silken embrace.[25]

Through one, or all, of these channels, then, Coleridge might well have become acquainted with the essentials of vampire lore. These works, however, belong in the domain of scholarship—medical science, psychopathology, religion, travel, and pseudo-history. They can scarcely be classified as literature. The vampire, in fact, was surprisingly slow to forge its way into

[24] Calmet, II, 52.

[25] Certain further characteristics of the vampire, or of certain types of vampire, are also given by Summers (see especially pp. 77, 84, 100–101, 133, 171, 195, 205), although they do not seem to have colored Coleridge's conception—if, indeed, he was familiar with them at all. With these beautifully specific details it may be interesting to compare the general views of Cornelius Agrippa on the behavior of the souls of the wicked after death, in *Three Books of Occult Philosophy, Written by Henry Cornelius Agrippa, of Nettesheim, Counsellor to Charles the Fifth, Emperor of Germany, and Iudge of the Prerogative Court* (London, 1651), pp. 476–83: "But if it [the soul] hath done ill, the spirit judgeth it, and leaves it to the pleasure of the devil, and the sad soul wanders about Hell without a spirit, like an image..... This image therefore of the soul enters into the ghost as an *Aerial* body, with which being covered doth sometimes advise freinds, sometimes stir up enemies..... So the Spirit of *Naboth* .... because at the end of its life it went forth with a desire of revenge, was made, to execute revenge..... For the impure soul of a man, who in this life contracted too great a habit to its body, doth by a certain inward affection of the elemental body frame another body to it self of the vapours of the elements, refreshing as it were from an easie matter as it were with a suck, that body which is continually vanishing..... Sometimes also (which yet is very rare) souls are driven with such a madness that they do enter the bodies not only of the living, but also by a certain hellish power wander into dead Carkasses, and being as it were revived commit horrid wickednesses." After giving various such anecdotes, he concludes this passage with "And we have heard that oftentimes the bodies of the dead were by the devils taken from the graves, without doubt for no other use than to be imprisoned, and tortured in their hands." It will be remembered that Agrippa's *Occult Philosophy* was one of Ferriar's authorities (*Manchester Memoirs*, III, 36, 42–43) and that, in view of Coleridge's hermetic interests and reading, it is not at all unlikely that he had also looked up Agrippa.

literature; by the end of the eighteenth century it had hardly got even a precarious foothold there. Nevertheless, that foothold had been established, and was to be rapidly consolidated.

Can it be only a coincidence that the first introduction of a vampire into English literature to be recognized up to the present occurs within the narrow precincts of Coleridge's own circle—in other words, in a poem on which his friend Southey was to begin actual work at least by July, 1799, and which he was to finish just a year later, at Cintra?[26] This long verse narrative, *Thalaba the Destroyer*, was the object of Coleridge's special interest, as indicated by his letters extending from 1799 to 1817. Sometimes bits of advice about the poem, such as he apparently was accustomed to give in private conversation, also crept into these letters, as it did on September 30, 1799;[27] yet, in spite of his admiration for the work, he was obviously uncertain of the other's ability to handle such a story with sufficient finesse, as his advice on November 10 of the same year suggests: "I would to Heaven that you could afford to write nothing, or at least to publish nothing, till the completion and publication of the 'Madoc'. . . . . Whereas 'Thalaba' would gain you (for a time at least) more ridiculers than admirers, and the 'Madoc' might in consequence be welcomed with an *ecce iterum*. Do, do, my dear Southey! publish the 'Madoc' *quam citissime*, not hastily, yet speedily. I will instantly publish an Essay on Epic Poetry in reference to it. . . . ."[28] Yet Southey published *Thalaba* in 1801. As late as December 13, 1817, an echo of the basis for Coleridge's doubt appears in his letter to J. H. Green, in which he refers to a sentence of his in "a fragment of an Essay on the Supernatural many years ago, viz. that the *presence* of a ghost is the terror, not what he *does*, a principle which Southey, too, overlooks in his 'Thalaba' and 'Kehama.' "[29]

---

[26] Summers, pp. 278–80; Lowes, p. 557.

[27] *Letters*, I, 126.

[28] *Ibid.*, p. 314; see also p. 319. In a letter of December 14, 1807, Coleridge again promised to refer at large to *Thalaba* and *Madoc* in a series of lectures he was contemplating on English poetry.

[29] *Letters*, II, 683–84, and n., which refers also to *Table Talk*, January 3 and May 1, 1823, and *The Friend*, Essay iii of the First Landing Place, etc.

For not only are there ghosts in *Thalaba:* the whole poem moves in an atmosphere of supernatural apparitions and demons. And one of this gruesome gallery is a vampire—a woman-vampire! Her passage through the story is brief, it is true, but it is emphasized by a whole battery of footnotes, which in scope and length overshadow the episode itself. In stanzas 8–10 of Book VIII, the supposedly shivering reader is given the explanation of the mystery surrounding the rumored revival and nocturnal appearances of the dead girl Oneiza.[30] The hero, Thalaba, and his father-in-law, Moath, resolve to explore and to end the horrors which have been occurring, and go to her tomb. There they see a being resembling Oneiza; but her cheeks are livid, her lips are blue, and her eyes gleam with a

> Brightness more terrible
> Than all the loathsomeness of death.

Momentarily shocked and stunned, they nevertheless recover control of themselves, and Moath thrusts his trusty lance "through the vampire corpse". The fiend which has been reanimating the body flees, and Oneiza's true spirit appears. Apparently, though Southey does not make the point too clear, the demon is Kharola, fiercest of the woman-fiends in Domdaniel, the home of the sorcerers under the ocean. Bulwarking the entire passage and solidly filling the lower halves of several pages is Southey's detailed and extensive explanatory footnote, citing his authorities and recounting the most famous of the vampire stories with which he was familiar. Here again appear the *Lettres juives* of D'Argens, the account by Tournefort, the history of Arnold Paul, the story of the vampires at Gradisch, and many similar collectanea.

Is it likely that Southey would be acquainted with all this material while his intimate friend and adviser was not? For many months the two men had used the same library at Bristol, often signing one another's names for books they had borrowed.[31] They read together, talked together, and wrote to-

---

[30] *The Poetical Works of Robert Southey* (London, 1850), pp. 275–79 and n.

[31] Kaufman, pp. 318–20.

gether. Why should not Oneiza in *Thalaba* and Geraldine in
"Christabel" have been born of the same seed? It would be
typical of Southey's talent to label his character a vampire;
it would be just as typical of Coleridge's genius not to label his
at all. Moreover, Coleridge knew and watched *Thalaba* as it
grew. Did Southey similarly know "Christabel"? Obviously he
did—and to the extent that several reminiscences of it also appear in his poem. Much as Christabel tells Geraldine that her
dead mother had promised that she would hear the castle bell
ring on her daughter's wedding day, so at the beginning of the
fourth book of *Thalaba* the spirit of Thalaba's dead mother appears and promises that she will appear to him again "in the
hour of death"; this promise she later redeems, and guides him
to Paradise.[32] When Thalaba encounters Oneiza, the "Arabian
maid" (soon to be a vampire), at the end of the sixth book and
the opening of the seventh, she has just escaped from some
enemies, who have seized her and carried her off; it is the same
sort of story that Geraldine tells of her capture and wild ride.[33]
Most interesting of all, however, is the speech of Okba, father
of the beauteous Laila, in the presence of Thalaba:

> "Servant of Allah, thou hast disobeyed;
> God hath abandoned thee;
> This hour is mine!" cried Okba,
> And shook his daughter off. . . . .[34]

Who can forget here how Geraldine cries out in anguish to the
invisible spirit of Christabel's mother, "Off, woman, off! this
hour is mine—"?[35]

Another threading of the shuttle and one of the main patterns
of Coleridge's plan will be complete. In 1794, in Germany,
Friedrich Schiller conceived the plan of starting a new periodical, *Die Horen;* and among those whom he invited to collaborate
and contribute was Goethe. The magazine ran until 1797; but
since it did not prove so popular as he had hoped, he started

---

[32] Southey, *Poetical Works*, pp. 243, 312.

[33] *Ibid.*, pp. 268–69.   [34] *Ibid.*, p. 300.

[35] E.H.C., p. 74. As a source for Coleridge's line, Tuttle (pp. 470–71) suggests a
speech in Mary Robinson's *Hubert de Sevrac*, in which an unknown horseman warns:
"This is not thy hour, de Sevrac. . . . ." The similarity does not seem very close.

his *Musen-Almanach* in 1796. The two publications—one a monthly magazine and the other a sort of annual poetical anthology—during this time provided both men with a medium for some of their most deservedly popular lyrics and ballads. *Die Horen* quickly became known in England and was regularly noticed in the literary journals. For instance, in January, 1797, *The British Critic* called attention briefly to "Die Horen. *Eine Monatschrift herausgegeben von* Schiller. *Des Jahrgangs 1795. I–X Stück.*" At this time, as well as later, Coleridge was an assiduous reader of *The British Critic* and had picked up several useful hints from it.[36] However, his general interest in, and knowledge of, German literature and its two greatest glories, Schiller and Goethe (a passion which was to betray him into his arduous translation of *Wallenstein* in 1798), could easily account for a knowledge of *Die Horen* and the *Musen-Almanach*, without his needing to rely on any notice in a critical review. And in the latter of these German publications, the *Musen-Almanach für das Jahr 1798*, just at a time when Coleridge's imagination seems to have been storing itself with curious fancies and facts about vampires, appeared Goethe's justly famous little verse narrative, "Die Braut von Corinth", or "The Bride of Corinth".[37] The romantic stimulus of the new folk poetry and the ballad had apparently reminded Goethe of his own youthful studies in the occult, even in alchemy and astrology; and now, in "Die Braut von Corinth", which he labeled "Romanze", he produced a delicately finished piece of Gothic horror which could not fail to appeal to a reader of Coleridge's temperament. Moreover, although the volume containing the poem is dated 1798, it was actually published late in 1797, as was the custom with such annuals, planned especially to take advantage of the holiday sales centering around the Christmas fairs and general gift-giving. "Christabel", it will be remembered, was begun, according to the best evidence, in the spring of 1798.

In Goethe's poem, the scene of which is laid many centuries ago, a handsome youth arrives one day in Corinth from Athens.

[36] Lowes, p. 181.   [37] *Op. cit.*, pp. 88–99.

He has come to claim as his bride a Corinthian girl to whom he had been contracted in his childhood, but whom he has never seen, since the parents of the two families have managed the whole affair. He is a pagan, but in the meantime her family have become Christians. When he reaches her home, she does not appear. No one mentions her absence, but there is a curious sense of restraint about the family, although they entertain him courteously. Soon after he has gone to bed, however, the figure of a beautiful young woman appears in his room. She learns who he is and attempts to leave. But he is entranced by her beauty and pleads with her to remain. At last she tells him her identity and laments the passing of the old gods. Her mother had vowed her to Christ against her will and belief, and now plans to marry the young man to the girl's sister instead. Completely infatuated, he swears that he will not listen to the plan, and they thereupon plight their troth. She asks for a ringlet of his hair, which he gladly grants her; and she gives him a golden chain in exchange. The youth now grows importunate, claiming her as already his bride; but she begs him not to force her to yield to him, warning him earnestly but sorrowfully that the touch of her limbs will chill and freeze him to the heart. Believing that these are merely maidenly scruples, however, he renews his pleas, and she finally consents to him. In the midst of their passionate embrace the mother enters and discovers them. Then the girl reveals, to the horror of both her hearers, that she has been forced to come from her grave every night (for her mother and her mother's religion have killed her in her youth) to seek her beloved and "draw the lifeblood from his heart". Now, against her will, she has fulfilled her mission and must at once depart to seek another prey. As the youth feels a sudden iciness stealing through his blood, she begs her mother to open her tomb and, as soon as possible, to burn both her and her lover's bodies, so that they may flee together to the old gods.

Could such a story as this have been the crystallizing agency in Coleridge's imagination? It may well have been. It is wrought with a fineness and subtlety which he would have ad-

mired intensely. The mystery and suspense are brilliantly sustained, and the real character of the lovely but lethal *"revenant"*
is cunningly concealed to the end; in fact, the reader is never
informed of her exact status in the kingdom of demonology.
She is a ghost of some sort, certainly; but, although Goethe intended her to be a vampire, he never said so publicly. Nevertheless, the clues are obviously there: the nightly return from
the grave, the chill of the touch, the drawing of the lifeblood,
the compulsion of the unearthly visitor to act against her will,
the proposed burning of the corpses. The sinister central figure,
moreover, is a beautiful woman. No other classification fits
her so well as that of she-vampire.

And so Goethe himself recognized her to be.[38] According to
his diary, he began this "Vampyrische Gedicht" on June 4,
1797, finished it the following day, and gave Schiller a copy for
the next *Musen-Almanach* on June 6. All of Goethe's entries in
his diary at this time (one on each day) refer to the poem under
this name; none uses its later title, although in a letter to his
wife he called it "eine grosse Gespensterromanze".[39] Early in
August, Schiller had sent it to Herder for the press.[40] If Goethe
intended his heroine to be a vampire and privately recognized
her as such, there is little reason for doubting that Coleridge
might have regarded his villainess-heroine in the same way.

Where did Goethe get his suggestion for the poem? Although,
like Coleridge, he may have carried the seeds in his mind for a
long time, his immediate source seems to have been one of the
books he had been excerpting for his Walpurgisnacht scene in
Faust: the chapter on dead people, "Von gestorbenen Leuten,"
in *Eine neue Weltbeschreibung, von allerley wunderbaren Men-
schen,* written by Johannes Praetorius (also known as Anthro-
podemus Plutonicus), and printed at Magdeburg in 1668. The
story which Goethe appropriated and remade is that of Ma-
chates and Philinion, the dead daughter of Demostrates and

---

[38] Erich Schmidt, "Quellen Goethescher Balladen," *Goethe-Jahrbuch,* IX (1888),
229–34, discusses the history and sources of the poem.

[39] Hans Gerhard Gräf, *Goethe ueber seine Dichtungen* . . . . (Frankfort, 1912), III,
Part I, 274–75.

[40] Schmidt, p. 229.

Charito, who returned from the dead to her unsuspecting lover's arms. Praetorius, however, freely admitted that he was indebted for his marvelous tale to Pierre le Loyer's *IIII livres des spectres*, also known as *Discours et histoire des spectres;* and Le Loyer cited Phlegon Trallianus' *De mirabilibus et longaevis* as his authority. The same story was also available in *Daemonolatria oder Beschreibung von Zauberen und Zauberinnen*, published by Nicolaus Remigius at Hamburg in 1693; nor had it been overlooked by Martinus del Rio in his *Disquisitionum magicarum libri sex* in 1599–1600. In all of these, the setting of these weird events was Syria. Goethe's scene, Corinth, however, was in all likelihood suggested by the even more famous story of Philostratus concerning the student Menippus and his philosopher-teacher Apollonius, who rudely shattered the lad's love-idyll with a strange and lovely creature from another world. I mention these works and authors thus at length—all literally names to conjure with in the realm of the occult—because practically every one of them, from Del Rio to Remigius and Le Loyer, from Phlegon Trallianus to Apollonius and Philostratus, is prominently alluded to in Ferriar's article on medical demonology.[41] In other words, even without "Die Braut von Corinth", Coleridge could easily have got back to the sources of Goethe's "vampirical poem" for himself and then worked forward in his own direction. I believe it more likely, indeed, that he knew the German "Romanze"; but in any case, here, in one form or another, he might well have found the necessary element to precipitate his own fantasies. In the alembic of his imagination such a transmutation could easily have taken place, whether consciously or unconsciously, as in "The Ancient Mariner" and "Kubla Khan".

In this chapter I have attempted to show something of the materials and processes of assimilation, selection, and modification through which Coleridge may have reached his conception of certain aspects of the focal figure in "Christabel", the Lady Geraldine. I repeat, "*may* have reached", and not "reached".

[41] *Manchester Memoirs*, III, 38, 46, 50, 55, 75, 84, 98.

I have no assurance that the manner was exactly, or even nearly, as I have presented it here. But I am confident that some
such assumption, based on some such material, is inescapable
if one is to explain the clues which the author himself has left
behind in his poem. Moreover, if I am right, then to Coleridge
must go the additional distinction of being the first to introduce
the vampire into English literature.

Before, the claimants for this somewhat dubious honor have
been two, perhaps three, in number. It will be recalled that, as
the aftermath of Byron's reading "Christabel" aloud to Shelley
and several other friends, two tangible Gothic tales eventuated:
Mrs. Shelley's *Frankenstein* and Dr. John William Polidori's
The Vampyre. But Byron himself had also been at work on a
story about a vampire, and at first Polidori's story was mistaken
for Byron's and actually printed as his,[42] though Byron later
repudiated it. Obviously, Coleridge's poem had somehow fixed
the unconscious thought of vampires in its hearers' minds.
Among the critics and historians, then, Byron and Polidori have
been the rival candidates for having brought the vampire into
English story-telling. Eino Railo, in his amusing study, *The
Haunted Castle*, after remarking on the appearance of the creature in Slavonic myth, has said: "The first English author to
take up the idea was Byron: when Mary Shelley began *Frankenstein*, Byron simultaneously began a story called *The Vampire*, which was never finished." Also mentioning *Lara* and *The
Giaour*, he adds that the original story was completed by
Polidori, who published it in 1819.[43] Similarly, Father Summers, easily forgetting the claims of Southey, which he is just
preparing to discuss, remarks: ". . . . until we come to Polidori's novel . . . . , nowhere, so far as I am aware, do we meet
with the Vampire in the realms of Gothic fancy. So vast, however, is this fascinating library and so difficult to procure are
these novels of a century and a quarter ago that I hesitate

---

[42] The editor of *The New Monthly Magazine*, XI, 195, stated that the story had been
sent him as Byron's, but added that he had also in his possession a sketch for another
similar tale by Polidori, which he might print later. But he never did.

[43] Eino Railo, *The Haunted Castle. A Study in the Elements of English Romanticism*
(London and New York), pp. 310, 381.

sweepingly to assert that this theme was entirely unexploited. .... I am at least prepared to say that the Vampire was not generally known to Gothic lore, and had his presence made itself felt in the sombre chapters of one votary of this school I think he would have re-appeared on many occasions, for the writers were as accustomed to convey from one to another with an easy assurance, as they were wont deftly to plunder the foreign mines."[44] Perhaps if Summers had not confined his attention so largely to prose fiction, he would have taken his *terminus a quo* back at least to 1798. But he, like all the rest of Coleridge's readers, was looking for something gross as a mountain, open, palpable—something as glibly detectable as Falstaff's lies.[45]

[44] Summers, p. 278.

[45] Others, too, have apparently had subconscious inklings of what was in Coleridge's mind. For instance, Hogg, in his imitation "Isabelle", brings in three hair-raising but unexplained *"revenants"*. This is even more definitely the interpretation which Eliza Stewart intended to give to her continuation. Also in Byron's *The Siege of Corinth* (1816) there is a scene which has reminded some scholars of "Christabel". Actually, though, there is little similarity, except that the effect of the touch of the ghost of Alp's just-deceased sweetheart is somewhat like that of Geraldine. Eugen Kölbing, in *The Siege of Corinth by Lord Byron—In kritischem Texte* . . . . (Weimar, 1896), pp. xxv, 104 ff., claims more than can be proved in this respect. He also maintains that *Thalaba*, Book V, stanzas 20 ff., should be regarded as the real source of passages in "Christabel", *The Siege of Corinth*, and *The Lay of the Last Minstrel!* In spite of Byron's own *mea culpa*, this is Teutonic source-hunting with a vengeance. Albert Eichler is hero-worshiping enough to follow him (see his *Samuel Taylor Coleridge The Ancient Mariner and Christabel* . . . . , in *Wiener Beiträge zur englischen Philologie* for 1907, XXVI, 44).

III

LAMIA THE QUEEN AND LAMIA THE
SERPENT-DEMON

THE figure in the carpet as outlined in the preceding
chapters seems a relatively simple and uncomplicated
one. Yet, if Coleridge had done no more in "Christabel"
than create a fascinating she-vampire, the first in English literature, he would scarcely have left a poem which has both attracted and baffled as this one has. The main design in a Persian
rug may clarify itself easily to the eye, or it may continue to
tease and tantalize it, as did Cronshaw's gift to Philip Carey.
It may at first seem to have no meaning, or it may take on a
meaning from what the observer brings to it. In life, perfect
simplicity almost never exists unentangled with the involu-
tions and complexities of human existence. So Coleridge, in
weaving the design for "Christabel", found that his imagination
had stored itself with many intricate smaller devices and would
not let them go.

The ordinary Gothic romancer would have been satisfied with
an ordinary witch or malignant otherworldly spirit.[1] As the
didactic interpreters of "Christabel" have been almost alone in
realizing, however, here is a case

> Of forests, and enchantments drear,
> Where more is meant than meets the ear.

There is more than the obvious external conflict in the story;
and the one which most intrigues is the one which is most often

---

[1] Especially, perhaps, such blood-curdling, dangerous, and night-walking female
demons as are listed and classified by Ludwig Lavater under the names of Empusa,
Mormo, Gilo, Striges, Volticae, Gorgon, Acco, Alphito, Ephialtae, Hyphialtae—"that
is *Incubi* and *Succubi*, (which we call Maares) . . . . ." See pp. 2–6 of the first book of
Lavater's *De spectris, lemuribus, et magnis atque insolitis fragoribus* as it was translated
into English in 1572 under the title *Of Ghostes and Spirites Walking by Nyght, and of
Strange Noyses, Crackes, and Sundry Forewarnynges, Which Commonly Happen before
the Death of Menne, Great Slaughters, & Alterations of Kyngdomes*, and as edited with
an introduction and appendix by J. Dover Wilson and May Yardley (Oxford, 1929).
Lavater was well known to Ferriar.

missed—the conflict within Geraldine herself. It is not merely
her great beauty which enlists the sympathy of the yielding
reader against his will. As Derwent Coleridge insisted, and
Ernest Hartley Coleridge agreed, Geraldine seems often to be
acting under compulsion; her heart is by no means in her acts;
she is struggling against some power stronger than herself,
which is governing her for some unexplained object of its own—
an evil object, thought Gillman; a beneficent one, asserted the
poet's own son. According to E. H. C., "There are indications
that the Geraldine of the First Part of the poem was at the
mercy of some malign influence not herself, and that her melt-
ing mood was partly genuine. She is 'stricken' with horror at
her unwelcome task, because she cannot at first overcome the
temptation to do right. She was in a strait between the contending powers of good and evil."[2] When Christabel first meets
her, she is moaning, in "sore distress". When Christabel mentions her mother, Geraldine, who has sunk to the floor in her
weakness, inquires innocently,

> And will your mother pity me,
> Who am a maiden most forlorn?

And when the girl exclaims sorrowfully,

> O mother dear! that thou wert here!

the other echoes with apparent sincerity,

> I would, said Geraldine, she were!

Then comes the sudden change, in which, "with hollow voice",
she informs the mother's spirit of her power and commands her
to leave. Then she assures her hostess:

> All they, who live in the upper sky,
> Do love you, holy Christabel!
> And you love them, and for their sake
> And for the good which me befell,
> Even I in my degree will try,
> Fair maiden, to requite you well.

Is this merely diabolical hypocrisy? How does Geraldine behave when she is forced to bare her bosom to Christabel's gaze?

[2] E.H.C., p. 76 n.

Not, certainly, like a demon or hardened evildoer. First she draws

> in her breath aloud
> Like one that shuddered. . . . .

Then, after dropping her silken robe, she

> nor speaks nor stirs;
> Ah! what a stricken look was hers!
> Deep from within she seems half-way
> To lift some weight with sick assay,
> And eyes the maid and seeks delay;
> Then suddenly, as one defied,
> Collects herself in scorn and pride,
> And lay down by the Maiden's side!—

And as she sets her spell of silence on the girl, she does so "with low voice and doleful look", calling her disfigurement "This mark of my shame, this seal of my sorrow." As she sleeps, she

> Seems to slumber still and mild,
> As a mother with her child.

Nor in the second canto is this element entirely missing, though it is not quite so strong. When Geraldine awakes and hears the matin bells ringing, she "shakes off her dread". Later, when she speaks with Sir Leoline, she looks like a divine being, "Such sorrow with such grace she blended. . . . ." Some minutes afterward, when Bracy has related his ominous dream, she first fixes her baleful gaze on Christabel "with somewhat of malice, and more of dread," and then, as Christabel almost faints, she turns away,

> And like a thing, that sought relief,
> Full of wonder and full of grief,
> She rolled her large bright eyes divine
> Wildly on Sir Leoline.

There is, of course, no possible doubt as to Coleridge's main purpose in these scenes. Geraldine is at this time an evil and threatening element. But it is evil not untempered with compunction and understanding. The reader both hates her and at the same time grieves for her.

In the opening of the famous fourteenth chapter of the *Biographia Literaria* Coleridge later described how, in the period of the *Lyrical Ballads*, his conversations with Wordsworth had turned on "the two cardinal points of poetry": "first, the power of exciting the sympathy of the reader by a faithful adherence to the truth of nature," and second, "the power of giving the interest of novelty by the modifying powers of imagination." For the second type, the supernatural, "the excellence aimed at was to consist in the interesting of the affections by the dramatic truth of such emotions as would naturally accompany such situations, supposing them real." Further, the two friends agreed that Coleridge's efforts "should be directed to persons and characters supernatural, or at least romantic; yet so as to transfer from our inward nature a human interest and a semblance of truth sufficient to procure for these shadows of imagination that willing suspension of disbelief for the moment, which constitutes poetic faith."[3] The essential and recurring ideas here are: sympathy, truth of emotions, nature, human interest. Could these feelings be aroused in the reader if the leading figure in a poem were utterly malignant and unnatural, an inhuman creature of an entirely unfeeling and unsympathetic order of beings? For Coleridge to have attempted to do so would have been a perfect contradiction of his basic principles.

The tracker of his footsteps should therefore be on the lookout for some conception which will permit this two-phased interpretation and which at the same time will explain the several other characteristics of Geraldine which have not yet been dealt with. The vampire-lady is the keystone to the whole structure, and in her, too, this element of sympathy is to be found; but the analyst cannot stop here. Fortunately, another possibility is also easily at hand.

One of the most extravagant of the fabulous inventions of the Greek imagination, classical and modern, was the lamia. Many myths about this grotesque creature have been circulated from ancient days down to our own; and, as is the frequent peculiarity of such myths, some of them disagree with, or actually contradict, one another concerning the origin, the history, the powers, and the activities of this fearsome female demon. In

[3] *Biographia Literaria*, II, 2–3.

general, though, her story is supposed to run more or less as follows:[4]

There was once a queen of Libya, named Lamia. She was the beautiful daughter of Belos and Libya—so beautiful, in fact, that she soon became the object of one of the amours of celestial Zeus. The jealous and alert Hera, however, in her usual annoying way, suspected her errant husband and watched him. As a result she eventually discovered his trespasses, which by this time had begun to bear fruit in several lovely children. The king of the gods attempted to escape his wife's vengeance by transferring his human mistress to Italy (whence came the name of the town Lamia), but he could not deceive the keen-eyed Hera, who maliciously watched for each new child and as methodically destroyed it. The misery of this persecution, combined with the continuation of Zeus's attentions, seems to have driven Lamia almost to madness. At any rate, she finally retired to live among the barren rocks and caves along the sea-coast; and thence, out of her despair and her envy of the happy mothers of living children, she issued to prey upon these children, afflicting them with wasting diseases or seizing them outright from their mothers and killing them by sucking their innocent blood. She was therefore a prototype of the more modern vampire—nor should it be forgotten that Greece, along with Hungary, was one of the two chief centers of eighteenth-century vampire lore.

According to one of the more grotesque embroideries upon this basic story, Hera was not content with her simple cruel revenge, but she also condemned her rival to sleeplessness, so that Lamia should never cease to be tormented by the memory of her dead offspring. Zeus, thereupon, in a very unscientific and irrational attempt to compensate at least partially for his wife's curse, gave his now ugly former mistress the power to

[4] This account of the lamia is based particularly on the following works: W. H. Roscher, *Ausführliches Lexikon der griechischen und römischen Mythologie* (Leipzig, 1894–97), II, Part II, 1819–21; *The Encyclopaedia Britannica* (New York, 1910), XVI, 130; Walter Woodburn Hyde, *Greek Religion and Its Survivals* (Boston, 1923), pp. 136–89, *passim;* and M. Oldfield Howey, *The Encircled Serpent A Study of Serpent Symbolism in All Countries and Ages* (London, n.d.), pp. 328–34.

remove her eyes at will, so that she might sleep. Thus, when Lamia, exhausted with weeping, placed her eyes in the basket which she always carried with her, she was not to be feared, but rather pitied; but when she replaced them in their sockets, then the memory of her losses drove her once more on her hideous depredations. To increase her terrors, according to some commentators, Zeus also granted her the power to turn herself into all kinds of forms, Proteus-fashion.

In a later stage of the legend, Lamia became a beautiful woman once more, haunting lonely roads, forests, or seacoasts and luring handsome young men into her toils by lasciviously showing them her breasts or promising them her love. Sometimes, however, she, or her descendants (for the name soon became generic and was applied to a whole class of similar beings), extended her attacks to old men and women; but always her purpose was the same: to suck their lifeblood from their hearts. This vampirism, being but one aspect of cannibalism, naturally came to associate her with Lamus, the cannibalistic king of the Laestrygones, with whom Odysseus had one of his more unpleasant adventures: Lamia, that is, has been regarded by some folklorists as merely the feminine form of the name Lamus, and thus, as a Lesbian young woman, was mentioned by Sappho. Both Lamus and Lamia have been called the children of Poseidon, and it has been suggested that originally they were a pair of minor deities, whose worship finally died out and who then degenerated into mere demons.[5]

Can it be assumed, or even proved, that Coleridge was familiar with the essentials of the old story of Lamia? It would, as a matter of fact, be more unbelievable if he were not acquainted with it. Of course, Lavater and the other demonological commentators had not overlooked the lamia, but they had not usually attempted to recount the whole story of Lamia the queen and her transformation into lamia the demon.[6] Coleridge, however, as a student at Christ's Hospital and at

---

[5] Roscher, p. 1819; Howey, pp. 333-34. Howey also sees a connection between these names and that of the Lama, or chief priest, of Tibet.

[6] E.g., Lavater, pp. 5-6.

Jesus College, had been well founded in Latin and Greek—not always in the most scholarly and best-regulated way, perhaps, but in a degree sufficient to permit him to indulge sometimes in a little harmless vanity about the matter.[7]

In its earlier outlines the story of Lamia, which clearly contains the two necessary elements of pity and terror, is to be found alluded to or treated, more or less fragmentarily, by such Greek and Latin writers as Diodorus Siculus, Horace, Plutarch, Suidas, Duris, and various other scholiasts on Aristophanes, Euripides, and other authors.[8] The simple Greek of the historians would have been child's play to Coleridge, whether he read them as part of the assigned exercises of the curriculum or as a voluntary entertainment. Moreover, in 1795, Wessling and Wachler's new edition of Diodorus had been published, a review of which (though not very favorable) had appeared in Coleridge's admired *British Critic* in 1797.[9] Here, however, this line of proof must stop, with mere likelihood. Yet, if Coleridge's friend Carlyon, during their trip to Germany in 1799, borrowed Diodorus, among other books, from the library of the University of Göttingen, as he did,[10] there is little reason for hesitating to believe that Coleridge had also read it, and that perhaps Carlyon's interest had been aroused by his friend's reference to it in one of the brilliant discursive lectures with which he was spontaneously accustomed to enliven the trip.

Luckily, however, the net can be drawn much closer about Queen Lamia, the pitiable but horrible. Professor Lowes has again obligingly pointed the road, without following it. As he reminds the reader,[11] Coleridge said in his *Aids to Reflection* that

[7] See, e.g., his letter of May 1, 1794, in *Letters*, I, 70–71.

[8] Perhaps the two best specimens of the handling of the myth are those by the Greek historian of the first century before Christ, Diodorus Siculus, and his fourth-century predecessor, Duris of Samos, from whom Diodorus gleaned much. See Διοδώρου του Σικελιώτου . . . . . *Diodori Siculi bibliothecae historicae quae supersunt* . . . . (Paris, 1855), II, 375; J.G. Hullman, *Duridis Samii quae supersunt* (Trajecti ad Rhenum, 1841), pp. 123–24; and F. Jacoby, *Die Fragmente der griechischen Historiker* (Berlin, 1926), Zweiter Teil, Kommentar zu nr. 64–165, p. 120.

[9] *British Critic*, IX (April, 1797), 459.

[10] Alice D. Snyder, "Books Borrowed by Coleridge from the Library of the University of Göttingen, 1799," *Modern Philology*, XXV (February, 1928), 377.

[11] Lowes, p. 538.

he wrote "The Wanderings of Cain", "The Ancient Mariner", and "Christabel" in the same year. The Gutch memorandum book shows that he was preparing for the task of composing "Cain" by studying *The Jewish Antiquities* of Flavius Josephus, for two Greek excerpts from it containing "certain uncanonical information about Cain"[12] are set therein. But the prime source book of unorthodox information about the patriarchs was Pierre Bayle's great *Dictionnaire historique et critique*, which had been several times translated into English under such titles as *An Historical and Critical Dictionary* (in 1710) and *A General Dictionary, Historical and Critical* (in 1734 ff.). Now just after one of the Greek quotations from Josephus in the notebook Coleridge had jotted down, with what Lowes describes as "a faintly discernible touch of zest, the following brief but suggestive memorandum: '*Ham*—lustful rogue—Vide Bayle under the Article *Ham*.' "[13] Lowes's general conclusion from this evidence —that Coleridge had been "consulting the lively and reprehensible articles in Bayle on the patriarchs"—is correct enough, although, if he had followed Coleridge's own example and verified his sources, he would have discovered no article on Ham in Bayle. At least, the editions and translations that I have been able to consult contain none. Nor is there any on Ham's father Noah. Only in Bayle's learned predecessor, the universal lexicographer Louis Moreri, to whom Bayle is continually referring (usually with blistering scholarly scorn), does one find a separate treatment of Noah, which refers to Ham's uncovering his father's nakedness while the latter was drunk.[14] This must be the story which was in Coleridge's mind when he made his note. Consequently, his entry in the notebook must be interpreted as a memorandum to look Ham up in Bayle rather than as an assertion that he had done so.

All this may seem to be a far cry from Lamia and lamias, but

---

[12] *Ibid.*, p. 237.

[13] *Ibid.*, p. 255. Lowes corrects Brandl's reading of "rogues" (*Archiv*, p. 370) to "rogue".

[14] See the translation, with additions, into English: Lewis Morery, *The Great Historical, Geographical, Genealogical and Poetical Dictionary* (London, 1701), II, n.p. (under "Noah"). The 1820 Paris edition, which contains all the notes and additions from succeeding commentators, also contains no article on Ham.

let the reader be reassured. The more devious the path to the goal, the more alluring that goal may sometimes seem. For it was the poet's study of Bayle which makes his acquaintance with the story of Lamia indubitable. The student of the Old Testament will recall that, according to the commentators, Cain, the murderer, was himself killed by Lamech, whose name means "the destroyer". But there were two Old Testament Lamechs, the other being the father of Noah and the son of Methuselah. To both of these Lamechs, then, Bayle devotes an article, each fortified with long and learned footnotes. If Coleridge had been following out his self-admonition to investigate Ham, he would probably have eventually come to Lamech. If, as is even more likely, he had been hot in pursuit of Cain, he would again have come out at Lamech, inasmuch as Bayle referred to him as the avenger in his article on Cain. By one route or the other Coleridge must have turned to the pages in his edition of Bayle describing the two Lamechs.

Yet the Lamechs are of no importance in themselves. The vital matter is that Coleridge opened his Bayle to these pages. For, in alphabetical terms, the name Lamech just precedes the name Lamia in such a dictionary. And Bayle had printed a complete account of Lamia and lamias, giving most of the stories about the unfortunate queen, stressing her cannibal characteristics, but also making much of her "terrible grief" at the death of her children. Moreover, for the benefit of those who might wish to read further, he stated his sources: Diodorus Siculus, Suidas, Pausanias, Philostratus, Duris, Hesychius, etc.[15] The whole philological journey was therefore mapped out for anyone who might wish to follow it.

However, there were several Lamias, just as there were two Lamechs; and Bayle, like a thoroughgoing encyclopedist, set down his accounts of the chief three (with another paragraph for the city): Lamia the African queen, bogey of children; Lamia the courtesan; and Lucius Aelius Lamia, the Roman leader. Of this last Lamia, Bayle wrote, according to his Eng-

---

[15] Bayle, *General Dictionary* (London, 1734 ff.), VI, 610–11; or *Historical and Critical Dictionary* (London, 1710), III, 1876.

lish translator: " 'Tis thought it was he, who being accounted (E) a dead Man, so that Fire was put to his Funeral Pile, recovered his senses by the Activity of the Fire. Consult *Streinnius's* Roman Families, and *Glandorp's Observations.*"[16] The portentous "(E)" leads to a footnote quoting the Latin of *Valerii Maximi dictorum factorumque memorabilium* to this effect: "It was agreed also that a voice similarly came to L. Lamia, the praetorian, upon the funeral pile." The authority of that other historian of the marvelous, Pliny, is then also called upon. But the footnote just preceding this (also quoted from Valerius Maximus) is still more paradoxically chilling: "The funeral pile of Acilius Aviola also brought something of wonder to our state, who, believed dead by both the doctors and by his household, when he had lain for awhile on the ground, rising, after the fire had attacked his body, proclaimed himself alive, and called for aid upon his teacher (for he alone remained there). But now, surrounded by flames, he could not be dragged from his fate."

These prodigies, with their burning pyres and their corpses returning from the dead, are striking enough in themselves, especially when associated with the word Lamia, but they become of decisive import when read in conjunction with one of the most cryptic passages in the Gutch memorandum book: "The Wicked aiming from Death to Life in order to be annihilated compared to the apoplective Man who was awoken by the funeral Pile, just to shriek and be utterly consumed—"[17] This brief glimpse at the reviving corpse amid the flames is followed by a long paragraph (the source of which I have been unable to identify) describing a sort of vision of a future state of life which a sick woman experienced while in a trance. These views of heaven, Coleridge reminds himself, are not to be taken as pure illusions.

From three different directions, then, the evidence has converged upon the article concerning Lamia in Bayle's *Dictionary*. But how explain the phrase "The Wicked aiming from Death to

---

[16] Bayle, *Historical and Critical Dictionary*, III, 1876.   [17] *Archiv*, p. 355.

Life"? How does it fit into the pattern? But what other purpose does a vampire have in its vampirism than an effort to
cling to the world of the living after it should long before have
surrendered to death, by all the laws of nature? Again, the
vampire and the lamia have taken visible form together.

It would, indeed, have been almost as hard for Coleridge to
avoid the lore of the lamia if he had followed up the authorities
of Ferriar as it would have been to avoid the lore of the vampire. Lowes, again, imperfectly realized this fact when, in the
course of tracking down Josephus and Cain, he remarked: "In
the curious treatise, for example, of Balthazar Bekker, Doctor
of Divinity, entitled *The World Bewitched*, he [Josephus] is
drawn on for pertinent evidence, and that eminent authority on
all matters daemonological, Johannes Wierus, takes issue with
him on a knotty point, when, in his edifying work on the Illusions of Daemons (*De Praestigiis Daemonum*), he discusses the
treatment of those who are so hapless as to fall victims to the
sorceries of lamias."[18] One may add that Wier's section on
lamias was one of the most famous of all his works and was even
published independently.[19] But it almost seems as if Lowes had
determined not to let himself be numbered among the "victims
to the sorceries of lamias", for on the very next page he cites
"a remarkable passage" on "Daemons and the Dead" ("Dae-
mones et mortui") in Jerome Cardan's sixteenth-century *On the
Variety of Things (De rerum varietate)*. This was in Book XVI;
but in Book XV Cardan had had another remarkable chapter,
entitled "Striges seu lamiae et fascinationes", that is, "Witches
or Lamias and Spells".[20] Wier is the first authority whom Ferriar
calls upon; his name is probably the most recurrent of the whole

---

[18] Lowes, pp. 236-37. As a matter of fact, it was Bekker who took issue with Wier,
and not Wier with Bekker, since Wier brought out his trail-breaking book in 1563,
whereas the *Betooverde Wereld* of Bekker, another zealous skeptic, was not published
until 1691.

[19] As, e.g., in *De Lamiis. Das ist: Von teuffelsgespenst Zauberern vnd Gifftbereytern.
Kurzer doch gründlicher Bericht was für vnterscheidt . . . .* (Franckfort am Mayn,
1586). In his *Omnia opera . . . .* (Amsterdami, 1659), "De lamiis liber" appears on
pp. 669-747.

[20] *Hieronymi Cardani Mediolanensis Medici de rerum varietate libri XVII* (Basiliae,
1557), II, 983-1000.

group of witch doctors and witch-exposers; and it is told how he served and studied under the great Cornelius Agrippa. Ferriar describes Cardan as "one of the most celebrated medical astrologers". He knows the French translation of Bekker, *Le Monde enchanté*.[21] He knows Calmet also,[22] and Calmet widens the field still further. "Some learned men," wrote the French Benedictine, "have thought they discovered some vestiges of vampirism in the remotest antiquity; but all that they say of it does not come near what is related of vampires. The lamiae, the striges, the sorcerers whom they accused of sucking the blood of living persons, and of thus causing their death, the magicians who were said to cause the death of new-born children by charms and malignant spells, are nothing less than what we understand by the name of vampires; even were it to be owned that these lamias and strigae really existed, which we do not believe can ever be well proved."[23] Calmet was bold enough to take this stand in spite of the opposite implication of Holy Scripture itself—which was a highly courageous act for a man of his position and time. All these commentators, from Calmet to Wier, are familiar to Ferriar; it would be a miracle if at least some of them were not known to Coleridge too.[24]

[21] *Manchester Memoirs*, III, 25, 29, 31, 38, 42, 43, 55, 61, etc.

[22] *Ibid.*, p. 85.   [23] Calmet, II, 64.

[24] Certain other conceptions are allied with that of the lamia and perhaps might have influenced Coleridge. The first is that of the "lilith", a name often used interchangeably with "lamia" and applied to a blood-sucking woman who preyed on children. The rabbinical history of Eve's unmentionable predecessor is related by Coleridge's favorite, Samuel Purchas, in *Purchas His Pilgrimage. Or Relations of the World and the Religions Observed in All Ages and Places* . . . . (London, 1626), p. 179. The story may also be followed in Calmet, II, 64–65; A. K. Donald, *Melusine* ("Early English Text Society," Extra Series, No. 68; London, 1895), p. 382, quoting E. B. Tylor and referring to Lenormant's *La Magie chez les Chaldéens*; Martinus del Rio, *Disquisitionum magicarum libri sex* . . . . (Coloniae Agrippinae, 1679), pp. 368–69; and Father Sebastien Michaëlis, *The Admirable Historie of the Possession and Conversion of a Penitent Woman.* . . . . *Whereunto Is Annexed a Pnevmology, or Discourse of Spirits* . . . . (London, 1613), pp. 79–81 (see also p. 138). Putting all these versions and others together, we see how the Hebrew and the Greek have commingled and how the Kabbala, the Old Testament, and pagan mythology and history have coalesced.

The second is the undine. Railo (p. 263) has glanced briefly at the possibility of finding Geraldine standing in the damp shadow of this water nymph, seeing in her a "being symbolizing forces injurious to natural man", but overlooking the fact that she also enlists the sympathy of the observer for her fate. Of course, Coleridge could not have

So far Geraldine has been established as some sort of beautiful vampire being—a creature human, yet not human; suddenly materializing out of the night and attaching herself to the girlish and innocent Christabel; dominated to a considerable extent by some compulsion outside herself; and capable, like the genus of lamias, of enlisting the reader's unwilling sympathy in spite of her obviously dark intentions. There are, however, other features which distinguish her from her fellows and place her in quite a separate, and relatively rare, category. These evidences are grouped almost entirely in the second canto and may indicate an expansion of Coleridge's original plan as he continued to ponder his material.

The first striking detail makes its impact just after Christabel sees the demon (for such it now indubitably is) embrace her father. The shock makes her shudder; but what else? She *hisses*. Yet this development is not totally unprepared for. Serpents, their venom and their behavior, have been much in Coleridge's mind in the preceding lines. Perhaps his initial description of Geraldine in the first canto, in which he draws her with gems glittering in her hair, may have been a reflection of the conventionalized drawings of serpents with designs of brilliant jewels in their heads. However this may be, just before the hissing scene he has symbolically alluded to the poisoning of truth by gossiping tongues in Sir Leoline's recollection of his quarrel with Lord Roland. But, most palpably, just before the hissing occurs, Coleridge has confessed how serpents are dominating his imagination when, by a simple association of ideas, he lets Sir Leoline threaten Geraldine's attackers (or con-

---

known Friedrich de la Motte Fouqué's sentimental little romance, *Undine*, since it was not published until 1811; but he could have found descriptions of this sort of being in F. M. Guazzo's *Compendium maleficarum* (tr. Montague Summers, London, 1929), p. 73, or in Paracelsus' treatise on elemental spirits, Paracelsus being another of Ferriar's favorites (see *Manchester Memoirs*, III, 38, 47, 70, 80, etc.). Sabine Baring-Gould, *Curious Myths of the Middle Ages* (Boston, 1882), p. 357, discusses and classifies the Undine legend. Curiously, in what Coleridge had completed of "Christabel" there is no suggestion of such a watery background for Geraldine, but in "V." 's completion and in Gillman's continuation there definitely is, since in "V." Geraldine turns out to be none other than the "Witch of the Lake", and in Gillman, when Bracy tries to deliver his message to Lord Roland, he finds that the castle of that nobleman has been completely washed away by "one of those inundations supposed to be common in this country", and that while he has been away, Geraldine has also vanished.

federates—if, indeed, they existed at all) by announcing the
tournament at which he will

> dislodge their reptile souls
> From the bodies and forms of men!

Clearly, then, Coleridge knew that serpent demons sometimes
hid themselves in human shapes. But this is only the beginning.
Bard Bracy's nightmare is not merely allegorical. The snake
coiled around the dove named Christabel stirs and swells just
as the dove stirs and swells. The pulse of the dove seems to become the pulse of the snake. So, too, has Geraldine wound herself about Christabel and arisen replenished and vigorous. More
and more explicit becomes the serpent imagery. Sir Leoline
ignorantly or wilfully misunderstands Bracy's narrative and
promises to kill any snake which may menace his beautiful visitor. Then, like Bracy's snake, Geraldine "couches" her head
upon her breast and gazes at Christabel. Her eyes shrink up
into small, dull, serpent's eyes; they strike such terror into the
girl that she turns faint, shudders, and again *hisses*. She is
acquiring the characteristics of a snake herself. Her whole expression duplicates that which she has seen in Geraldine, and
she "passively" imitates that colubrine "look of dull and
treacherous hate". No wonder that she prays her father to
send Geraldine away forthwith!

Evidently the lovely demon belongs to that large class of
supernatural beings which combine in themselves the characteristics of both human and serpent kind. Classical antiquity
and medieval fairy lore are rife with these creatures, which may
adopt the land, sea, or air impartially as their habitat. They
may be part woman and part snake; they may have the power
of turning completely from one into the other; or they may
merely have certain viperine faculties without taking on the
actual form. The Gorgons, the Graiae, and the Empusae all
belonged to this family, having the faces, necks, and breasts of
women, but being provided also with snaky ringlets of hair, or
with scales instead of skin on their lower bodies, or even with
serpents' tails instead of legs.[25]

[25] Howey, pp. 157–58.

There was, however, another principal member of this ophidian lineage, whose name has just appeared conspicuously in
this study in an entirely different connection. For the index
of evidence would not point half so clearly at Coleridge's knowledge of Lamia the queen of Africa if that strange figure did not
also emerge in mythology in still another metamorphosis—
Lamia the serpent-demon. Somewhere in the tortuous history
of this apparition—no one seems to know exactly where or
why—Lamia acquired the reputation of being a snake endowed
with the power of assuming human form. Perhaps the legend
arose from the commonly accepted tale that Zeus had granted
her, like Empusa, the ability to take any shape that she desired
—ox, tree, fly, viper, or beautiful woman. She is, as the Germans have put it, a "Proteus-Elfin".[26] A further suggestion may
also be made: According to Diodorus Siculus, the country
about Libya was savage and desolate, inhabited by wild
beasts and all kinds of serpents, so that when Ophellas led his
army through it he and his men were much impressed by its
dangers. Since this section of Diodorus's history immediately
follows that in which he relates the fables about Lamia the
queen, it would have been easy to establish an association between the cruel ruler and the snakes among which she dwelt.[27]
M. Oldfield Howey, in his book *The Encircled Serpent*, has also
suggested that the assumption of a serpent form by the lamias,
which were jinn first recognized in Egyptian mythology, "was
probably an intermediate stage which marked their passage
from the visible to the invisible."[28] It is the visible Geraldine
of Coleridge that we are dealing with, however—not the Geraldine of Gillman, who has the power to vanish and return in a
different shape.

Whatever the influence of Diodorus Siculus or of the protean transformation theory, the chief basis for the conception
of Lamia as a serpent-demon is to be found in what is probably

[26] Eichler, p. 24. [27] Diodorus Siculus, II, 375.

[28] Howey, p. 329. He then refers to the better-known stories about lamias and sum-
marizes several modern tales, from Marie Trevelyan, *Folk-Lore and Folk-Stories of
Wales* (London, 1909); J. Lockwood Kipling, *Beast and Man in India* .... (London,
1891); and Baring-Gould.

the most celebrated passage in Φιλοστρατου τα Ες τον Τυανα
Απολλωνιων, that is, *The Life of Apollonius of Tyana*, by Philostratus the Elder. It is the same passage that prompted Goethe
to locate the scene of "Die Braut von Corinth" in Corinth; for
in this Greek city the sage Apollonius, whose life and philosophy
were once even set up as a pagan rival to combat the growing
ascendancy of Christianity, discovered, exposed, and put to
flight a lamia whose evil designs upon one of his young disciples
had almost succeeded.[29] The famous story is recounted in considerable detail by Philostratus, who completed his work in
A.D. 217, though he gives full credit to the notes of Damis,
Apollonius's Boswellian biographer, who had kept them as a
sort of journal while he accompanied his master on his travels
during the first century after Christ. It occurs in the twenty-
fifth chapter of the fourth book, although Philostratus mentions
it again with some pride in the fifth chapter of Book VIII.[30]

Menippus the Lycian, a handsome and athletic young man
of twenty-five, with a great intellectual endowment, had been
the promising pupil of the Cynic philosopher Demetrius in
Corinth. Demetrius, however, regarded Apollonius so highly
that he turned over to him the best of his own disciples, among
whom was Menippus. The gossip was spreading abroad, nevertheless, that the young man was the lover of a certain beautiful
woman, from a foreign country, who was young and dainty, and
apparently very wealthy. She had met him one day while he
was walking alone on the road to Cenchreae, had clasped his
hand, declared that she had long been in love with him, announced that she was a native of Phoenicia, now living in a particular Corinthian suburb, and invited him to call upon her there
that evening. She promised him singing and such wine as he
had never drunk, and added that, if he would come to dwell with
her, he should never have any rival to disturb him and their

[29] There are two good modern translations of Philostratus, the first also containing
the Greek text: *The Life of Apollonius of Tyana the Epistles of Apollonius and the
Treatise of Eusebius with an English Translation by F. C. Conybeare* .... (2 vols.; London and New York, 1912); and *Life and Times of Apollonius of Tyana*, by Charles P.
Eells (Stanford University, 1923).

[30] Conybeare, I, 402–9; Eells, pp. 105–7, 226.

love-making. Menippus, though a philosopher, could not resist, and allowed himself to be seduced, for she was lovely and wealthy, and he could scarcely be expected to realize that she was only a "φάσμα", or apparition.

But Apollonius was more suspicious. He at once looked over Menippus as a sculptor might do, divined his character, and said: "You are handsome, and are courted by a beautiful woman, as you believe, but as a matter of fact you are cherishing a serpent, and a serpent is cherishing you." While Menippus wondered, the other continued by asking whether the youth thought that the woman, who was his mistress but not his wife, really loved him, and whether he was willing to marry her. Menippus replied that he would probably marry her the next day.

Apollonius said no more; but, when the wedding feast arrived, he presented himself just as the guests appeared, asking them: "Where is the delicate bride you have come to see?" Blushing, Menippus introduced her. Apollonius inquired to whom the gold and silver and other decorations of the hall belonged. "They are hers," answered the youth, "for this is all that I own," and he pointed to his philosopher's cloak. Turning to the guests, Apollonius asked: "Did you ever see the gardens of Tantalus, which exist and do not exist?" They answered that of course they had never seen them, but that they had read of them in Homer.

Then said the old philosopher: "Believe them to be like this establishment, for none of these things is real either, but only illusion. For this fair nymph is actually one of the empusae, the lamias, and the mormolykes whom the people tell of. These creatures love and are devoted to the delights of Aphrodite, but still more to human flesh, and they seduce with such sensual pleasures those whom they mean to devour." The bride shrieked and protested, railed at all philosophers and their inventions, and commanded him to be gone. But suddenly, under the exorcism of Apollonius, the golden goblets and silver plate vanished into nothingness; and the cooks, cupbearers, and other servants followed them into thin air. Then the phantom pretended to weep and begged him not to torture her or force her to confess her identity; but he persisted, until she acknowledged that she was a lamia and was fattening Menippus with dainties so that she might devour him, for it was her custom to feed on young and beautiful bodies, because their blood was pure and life-giving.

Here Philostratus ended his account of this, "the most celebrated exploit of Apollonius", without specifying the fate of the perfidious lamia or of the ensorceled Menippus; but it may be assumed that the vampire-demon evaporated like her retinue and that the sad and disillusioned youth returned to his philosophic meditations.

This original version of the story of a lamia and her intended human victim is told, it will be noted, entirely from the viewpoint of the real hero of the episode, Apollonius. There is no sympathy for the lamia herself, for her purpose is purely cannibalistic; nor is there much more for young Menippus. But, when the fable was transported into English literature, its atmosphere became quite different. To the Greeks the thought of such a love was merely horrible; to the English there was something fascinating about its romantic morbidity. Consequently, when Robert Burton retold the tale in the first subsection of the first member of the second section of the third partition (!) of *The Anatomy of Melancholy*, he carefully suppressed all the distressing details of vampirism and lust and summarized it as follows:

"*Philostratus*, in his Fourth Book *de Vita Apollonii*, hath a memorable instance in this kind, which I may not omit, of one *Menippus Lycius* a young man 25 years of age, that going betwixt *Cenchreae* and *Corinth*, met such a phantasm in the habit of a fair gentlewoman, which, taking him by the hand, carried him home to her house in the suburbs of *Corinth*, and told him she was a *Phoenician* by birth, and if he would tarry with her, *he should hear her sing and play, and drink such wine as never any drank, and no man should molest him; but she being fair and lovely, would live and die with him, that was fair and lovely to behold*. The young man, a Philosopher, otherwise staid and discreet, able to moderate his passions, though not this of love, tarried with her a while to his great content, and at last married her, to whose wedding, amongst other guests, came *Apollonius;* who by some probable conjectures found her out to be a Serpent, a *Lamia,* and that all her furniture was like *Tantalus'* gold described by *Homer,* no substance, but mere illusions. When she saw herself descried, she wept, and desired *Apollonius* to be silent, but he would not be moved, and thereupon she, plate, house, and all that was in it, vanished in an instant: *many thousands took notice of this fact, for it was done* in the midst of Greece."[31]

Here, in this brief idyll of thwarted love, the element of human sympathy has returned and been accentuated. The cold-hearted, austere philosopher-magician has become the villain; and Menippus and his lamia are the hero and heroine. Gone are all references to the lamia's real purpose; in fact, her real nature is never explained, for she is simply "a serpent, a lamia." If such creatures can be so beautiful and attractive, Burton implies, why should the fact that they are from a different world deter them from loving human beings? It was, of course, in this form that Keats came across the story. Luckily he did not know Greek, or his gorgeously decadent "Lamia", with all its pathos and tenderness and anti-rationalism, would never have been written.

Coleridge, however, knew both Greek and Latin, and he was undoubtedly acquainted with Burton. If it was necessary for Ferriar to have called his attention to them, however, Ferriar would have done so, for Apollonius, Philostratus, and Burton's *Anatomy* are all on his reading list.[32] And it is in these three, chiefly, that the serpent enters into the lamia and becomes one substance with her. Most oddly, however, if one reads Philostratus with any care, one begins to doubt whether he really meant that the lamia was literally a serpent.[33] It is true that

[31] Burton, *The Anatomy of Melancholy* (London, 1904), III, 50–51. Burton also has a chapter on the nature of devils, in which he mentions Lilith (I, 207), Lamiae (I, 214), and most of the demonological writers.

[32] *Manchester Memoirs*, III, 47, 50, 55, 98.

[33] Roscher, e.g. (II, 1819–21), in his discussion of Lamia says nothing about her serpent characteristics, although he refers to Philostratus.

Apollonius twice uses the word "ὄφις" to describe her, but is it not possible that he was using it in a figurative sense? He tells, it is true, how Menippus is cherishing and being cherished by a serpent, but cannot this remark be interpreted proverbially to mean that the young man is nourishing in his bosom a viper which will soon turn and sting him? The fact that the earliest accounts of lamias do not contain this element would suggest that the ophidian characteristics of the latter were the result of a late agglomeration, deriving perhaps from a misinterpretation of Philostratus. For all practical purposes, however, this fusing was made by the beginning of the Christian Era and was well established by the eighteenth century.[34]

The affinity between serpent-kind and a being like Geraldine is, however, both realistic and mystical.[35] The snake has been

[34] So several of Ferrier's authorities make clear. One to be noted in particular is, as he calls it (see *Manchester Memoirs*, III, 38), that "very extraordinary book" by the Abbé Laurent Bordelon, translated into English as *A History of the Ridiculous Extravagancies of Monsieur Oufle; Occasion'd by His Reading Books Treating of Magick, the Black-Art, Daemoniacks, Conjurers, Witches, Hobgoblins, Incubus's, Succubus's . . . .* [etc.]. *With Notes Containing a Multitude of Quotations Out of Those Books, Which Have Either Caused Such Extravagant Imaginations, or May Serve To Cure Them* (London, 1711). The pertinent passage is in the footnote to p. 177.

[35] As in the case of the serpent-demon, there were various tales of dragon-ladies which had been in popular circulation for centuries, which were available to Coleridge, and which may therefore have been vaguely in the background of his mind. I shall content myself with mentioning them briefly. One of them, become part of the Arthurian cycle, had been summarized by Bishop Percy as "Libius Disconius" in 1765, when he published his *Reliques of Ancient English Poetry* (see the London, 1877, edition, III, 362). This story was unquestionably known to Coleridge, like all the rest of the materials in the *Reliques*. The book was a central one in his library, and when he went away he had to have it sent after him. On August 6, 1800, Lamb wrote him at Keswick: "I have taken to-day, and delivered to Longman and Co., *Imprimis:* your books, viz., three ponderous German dictionaries, one volume (I can find no more) of German and French ditto, sundry other German books unbound, as you left them, Percy's Ancient Poetry, and one volume of Anderson's Poets" (see Lamb, *Letters*, I, 197). This condensed synopsis of "Libius Disconius" was the only form in which the story was easily obtainable until Joseph Ritson published it as "Lybeaus Disconus" in his *Ancient Engleish Metrical Romanceës* (London, 1802); Ritson, however (II, 84–85; III, 253–54), informed his readers not only that the tale had been printed before 1600 but that it had several parallels: Herodotus; *The Voiage and Travaile of Sir John Maundeville, Kt. . . . .* (pp. 23–26 of the London, 1866, edition); and "a pretendedly ancient Northumberland ballad, intitled 'The laidly worm of Spindleton-heugh,' written, in reality, by Robert Lambe, vicar of Norham, author of *The history of chess*, &c. who had, however, hear'd some old stanzas, of which he avail'd himself, sung by a maid-servant."

These all suggest the most renowned of all the dragon myths of this particular genus, that of the fairy, or woman-serpent, Melusina. It was in 1387 that Jean d'Arras first recounted her fabulous history in his *Chronique de la princesse*, and the story was soon

regarded symbolically by man for ages. Contradictorily, it
has been worshiped by cultists as a god; it has been accepted
and used as a proof of, and a means of achieving, rejuvenation
and eternal youth; and it has, most commonly, been taken as a
symbol of the principle of evil, based on the almost universally
accepted error that Genesis had presented Satan and the Serpent as synonymous. Coleridge had apparently not reconciled
his own views completely, but his dominant position was the
last. Once more, his reading in his favorite recondite authors
during this period of incubation may have confirmed his conception.

No more significant an autobiographical letter was ever
written by Coleridge than that which he sent to John Thelwall
on November 19, 1796, banking on the complete friendship and
sympathetic assistance of a man whom he had not yet seen.
Lowes has realized the importance of this letter, in its manifold
clues as to the poet's favorite authors, his manner of reading
and research, his haunting of first- and secondhand bookshops,
and his poring over the catalogs of secondhand books. With
such a man, indeed, it would be a risky and unsafe matter to
maintain that any book which was accessible in London or any
of the places he had visited could not have passed under his avid

---

afterward versified by Couldrette. So popular did it become that it was translated
into Spanish, German, Flemish, and English and was printed and reprinted during the
fifteenth and sixteenth centuries. Ever since its first appearance, indeed, it has fascinated romantic readers by its fantasticality and pathos. Since the tale is not only well
known but also extremely long and complicated, the curious reader is referred to any
of its complete editions, as, for example, that by A. K. Donald (already referred to)
from an English prose translation, *ca.* 1500, or the verse translation edited by W. W.
Skeat, also in the "Early English Text Society," Original Series, No. 22 (London,
1866). Later, in the unbridled imagination of Paracelsus the Great, both Melusina
and her sister Melior, like Lamia before them, spawned a whole race of aerial sprites
and essences longing to have conjunction with the terrestrials. For these "melosiniae",
see *The Hermetic and Alchemical Writings of Aureolus Philippus Theophrastus Bombast,
of Hohenheim, Called Paracelsus the Great* (tr. Arthur E. Waite, London, 1894), II, 254;
W. Johnson, *Lexicon Chymicum* (London, 1652), quoted by Donald, pp. 374–75; and
Cornelius Agrippa, p. 404. (For Ferriar's references to Agrippa, see *Manchester Memoirs*, III, 36, 42.) In all these the main theory of Paracelsus was dominant: Melusina
and her kind represented some spiritual principle without a soul or a real body in the
human sense; but it was an essence which could achieve final humanity by living in close
physical relationship with some human being until the time came for its death under
normal human conditions. Consequently, this might have been one of the motives for
Geraldine among which Coleridge was vacillating.

gaze. The most important passages in this letter, already
quoted in part, follow:

". . . . I am, and ever have been, a great reader, and have read
almost everything—a library cormorant. I am *deep* in all out
of the way books, whether of the monkish times, or of the
puritanical era. I have read and digested most of the historical
writers; but I do not *like* history. Metaphysics and poetry and
'facts of mind,' that is, accounts of all the strange phantasms
that ever possessed 'your philosophy;' dreamers, from Thoth
the Egyptian to Taylor the English pagan, are my darling
studies. In short, I seldom read except to amuse myself, and
I am almost always reading. Of useful knowledge, I am a so-so
chemist, and I love chemistry. All else is *blank*; but I *will* be
(please God) an horticulturalist and a farmer. . . . . Such am I.
I am just going to read Dupuis' twelve octavos, which I have
got from London. I shall read only one octavo a week, for I cannot *speak* French at all and I read it slowly.

"P.S. I have enclosed a five-guinea note. The five shillings over
please to lay out for me thus. In White's (of Fleet Street or the
Strand, I forget which—O! the Strand I believe, but I don't
know which), well, in White's catalogue are the following
books:—

"4674. Iamblichus, Proclus, Porphyrius, etc., one shilling
and sixpence, one little volume.

"4686. Juliani Opera, three shillings: which two books you
will be so kind as to purchase for me, and send them down with
the twenty-five pamphlets. But if they should unfortunately
be sold, in the same catalogue are:—

"2109. Juliani Opera, 12s. 6d.

"676. Iamblichus de Mysteriis, 10s. 6d.

"2681. Sidonius Apollinaris, 6s.

"And in the catalogue of Robson, the bookseller in New Bond
Street, Plotini Opera, a Ficino, £1.1.0, making altogether
£2.10.0.

"If you can get the two former little books, costing only four
and sixpence, I will rest content with them; if they are gone,

be so kind as to purchase for me the others I mentioned to you, amounting to two pounds, ten shillings. . . . ."[36]

Thelwall obtained both of the cheaper volumes, which remain in the Coleridge family today, having passed through the hands of the poet's son Derwent on to those of the Reverend Gerard H. B. Coleridge, in whose possession Lowes saw them.[37] But most of the books cited in the postscript of the letter must wait until they are needed in a later chapter. Besides, Lowes has discussed these Neo-Platonists and their revival during the Renaissance and again during the seventeenth and eighteenth centuries so eloquently that anything added of a general nature would be supererogatory.[38] It is, rather, the testimony of that sensationally popular anti-Christian Frenchman, C. F. Dupuis, whose twelve octavos promised to give the ambitious young linguist so much trouble, that is first pertinent in this matter of serpent lore and ophiolatry.

Dupuis published his prolixly erudite work in 1794, with the title *Origine de tous les cultes, ou La religion universelle*. Naturally it met with the wild approval of the Revolutionists because it attempted to discredit Christianity by tracing all religion to nature-worship, especially worship of the sun. Lowes remarks: "I doubt whether Coleridge got anything from it beyond those unconsidered trifles which genius has the trick of filching as it goes, for conversion into jewels rich and strange."[39] And he may be right, so far as thefts of a tangible and criminally demonstrable form are concerned. The fact remains, nevertheless, that, wound through all of Dupuis's argument revealing the basic sun-worship of the early civilizations, runs a twisting

[36] *Letters*, I, 180–82. Coleridge's consuming curiosity for authors of this ilk had begun some time before, as Lamb's somewhat aggrieved remonstrance with him on July 1 of the same year proves: "Coleridge, what do you mean by saying you wrote to me about Plutarch and Porphyry—I received no such letter, nor remember a syllable of the matter, yet am not apt to forget any part of your epistles, least of all an injunction like that. I will cast about for 'em, tho' I am a sad hand to know what books are worth, and both those worthy gentlemen are alike out of my line" (Lamb, *Letters*, I, 33).

[37] E.H.C., in Coleridge, *Letters*, I, 182 n.; also his edition of *Christabel*, p. 9; and Lowes, p. 533. Lowes also cites some evidence to suggest that Thelwall may likewise have picked up the Sidonius Apollinaris.

[38] Lowes, pp. 230–33.   [39] *Ibid.*, p. 233.

strand showing that everywhere the principle of evil had simultaneously been symbolized as a serpent.[40] The Hebrews, the Persians, the Egyptians, the Greeks, and the Romans all taught that the world was created from the two contending forces of good and evil. Symbolizing the latter, Greek art gave feet made from serpents to the Giants, or Titans, in their battle against Jupiter, the principle of goodness and light. In modern times, Dupuis pointed out, the natives of Madagascar similarly acknowledge the two principles and give to the evil one the same serpent attributes. So, in the sacred books and heroic literature of many nations, the same identification is to be found. The Christian Bible, in both Genesis and the Apocalypse, discloses the belief. The story of Christ himself (whom Dupuis derives from the Sun) agrees with the others. Among the twelve labors of Hercules, who is another culture hero identified with the sun, appear several encounters with the evil principle in the form of serpents and dragons. The story of Jason lends itself very obviously to such an interpretation, and even in the heroic poem of Nonnus on Bacchus a similar personification occurs. Finally, in the Boundesh (the Persians' Genesis), the Zoroastrian spirit of evil, Ahriman, penetrated into heaven itself in a serpent's form, accompanied by his Dews, or bad genii, whose only business was to destroy; Ahriman it was, indeed, who had introduced evil into the happiness of the world and had created all savage beasts, poisonous reptiles, and noxious plants. Often in such religions this serpent, typifying the spirit of evil, emerges as an emblem for the harshness and cruelty of winter. Almost universally, in fact, wherever a dualistic system has existed, evil has been represented in its cosmogony as a subtle, insidious snake.

Thus, as Coleridge plowed his way perseveringly, week by week, through the twelve octavo volumes of Dupuis, he would have encountered reference after reference, figure after figure, fable after fable, all bearing on the allegory of iniquity incarnated in serpent form. And it was late in 1796 and early in

[40] See, especially, in C. F. Dupuis, *The Origin of All Religious Worship* (New Orleans, 1872), pp. 72–75, 79, 94 ff., 131 ff., 210, 218, 223.

1797 that this unorthodox conception of the religious development of mankind was impressing itself on him. He would,
moreover, have found a very similar view expressed by the
demonologists. Lavater, in fact, would have embodied the
eternal conflict between the opposing principles still more
definitely, graphically enumerating the different transformations under which each might be manifested: "Moreover
popishe writers teach vs to discerne good spirits from euill by
four meanes. . . . . For if they appeare vnder the forme of a
Lyon, beare, dog, tode, serpent, catte, or black ghoste, it may
easly be gathered that it is an euill spirit. And that on the
other side good spirits do appeare vnder the shape of a doue, a
man, a lambe, or in the brightnesse, and clere light of the
sunne."[41] Does the vision of Bard Bracy spring to the mind
here—the vision of a cruel green snake throttling the innocent
dove among the grasses beneath the ancient tree in the midst
of the forest? If so, remember it, for it will make more of itself
later.

But the Neo-Platonists of Coleridge's postscript to Thelwall
must not be overlooked either. The second name on his list was
Proclus, among whose scholia on the *Cratylus* of Plato, concerning the class of "terrestrial heroes" (that is, all the great
men of the world) who have been generated by the good demons
on mankind, occurs the statement: "Not only a daemoniacal
genus of this kind sympathizes with men, but other kinds
sympathize with other natures, as nymphs with trees, others
with fountains, and others with stags or serpents."[42] Note here,
however, that Proclus is not referring to evil demons, but to
generally benevolent ones. Once more the antinomy asserts itself. Beings from another order of creation may identify themselves with serpents, but the nature of these beings is by no

[41] Lavater, p. 108.

[42] Thomas Taylor, in Apuleius, *The Metamorphosis, or Golden Ass, and Philosophical
Works* (London, 1822), p. 320 n. I use Taylor's version, even though it came out after
the period of "Christabel", because Taylor, a credulous but indomitable enthusiast
who at this very time was engaged in translating into English the works of the whole
Neo-Platonic school as rapidly as his Greek and his financial resources would permit,
was one of the "darling studies" mentioned by Coleridge in his letter to Thelwall.

means fixed. According to one school of thought, they were dangerous and depraved spirits; according to another, they were harmless and even well-wishing. Coleridge knew both schools; he was reading both at the same time.

Though this particular commentary on the *Cratylus* did not happen to be in the "one little volume" Thelwall had bought him at White's bookstore, Coleridge had had other ways of studying his author, as his pointed remark to Lady Beaumont later, concerning Thomas Taylor's translation of the *Platonic Theology* of Proclus, makes amply clear. This work, he said, has been in part "translated by Taylor, but so translated that difficult Greek is transmuted into incomprehensible English."[43] The obvious conclusion is that Coleridge owned or had access to his own copies of the works in fifth-century Greek and that he was comparing them with Taylor's modern renderings as these were published. He was a scholar as well as a poet. The hand of the former is at work beneath the surface in "Christabel"; the world, however, has seen only the hand of the latter, imperfectly but still triumphantly shaping the exterior.

Some such backgrounds of allegorical serpentry as these, then, were probably behind the picture which Coleridge was painting, as the lovely Geraldine melted imperceptibly into the snake and the gentle Christabel found herself involuntarily imitating her.

[43] *Memorials of Coleorton, Being Letters from Coleridge, Wordsworth and His Sister, Southey, and Sir Walter Scott to Sir George and Lady Beaumont of Coleorton, Leicestershire, 1803 to 1834*, ed. William Knight (Boston and New York, 1887), II, 107.

IV

OPHIOLOGY, OCULAR FASCINATION, AND THE
MARK OF THE BEAST

THE perception of the peculiar serpent characteristics of Geraldine as detailed in the preceding chapter has been common because certain of their aspects are so obvious, even without any realization of the complex background which lies behind them.[1] As E. H. C. has put the matter in comparing the Geraldine of the first canto with the Geraldine of the second: "But the Geraldine who paced into the Baron's presence-room is not the Geraldine who held the slumbering maiden in her arms, and sealed her with the seal of her own bewitchment. As Coleridge himself might have put it, the Geraldine of the First Part is a supernatural, of the Second Part a trans-natural being. The half-mythical, half-pathological conception of the *witch* Geraldine as a human snake denotes a 'transition to another kind', a development of the idea. What suggested or determined this departure from the original?"[2] He then proceeds to cite the most astute and suggestive of all the analyses and discussions of Geraldine up to the time of his own introduction—in Oliver Wendell Holmes's strange "Romance of Destiny", as its author calls it, *Elsie Venner*. This citation poses still another question concerning the antecedents and relationships of the bewilderingly many-sided creature, the villainess of "Christabel".

Says E. H. C.: "Oliver Wendell Holmes in his psychological novel, *Elsie Venner* (ed. 1861, cap. xvi, p. 202), compares *Christabel* with Keats's *Lamia*. 'Geraldine,' writes one of the char-

---

[1] They have, in fact, formed the whole basis of Martin Farquhar Tupper's "Geraldine", in which that ambiguous lady is referred to interchangeably as a "serpent-monster" and a "dragon-maid", and the implications of those terms are made all too concrete through Tupper's substantial, unmistakable descriptions of fact. So much of Coleridge's intention, at least, has communicated itself to some of his readers.

[2] E.H.C., p. 29.

acters, 'seems to be simply a malignant witch-woman with the *evil* eye, but no absolute ophidian relationship. Lamia is a serpent transformed by magic into a woman.[3] The idea of both is mythological, and not in any sense physiological.' The idea of the Geraldine of the Second Part is, in my judgement, physiological as well as mythological."[4]

I agree with him in his main point—and it is an important one: the second Geraldine is "physiological as well as mythological". And, if he had read more carefully, he would have found Holmes's opinion to be the same.[5] It is, then, Coleridge's par-

---

[3] Both Holmes and E. H. C. fail to recognize that although Keats's Lamia "is a serpent transformed by magic into a woman", she has also been a woman before she was transformed into a snake, as Keats has his heroine make very clear in her pathetic and passionate plea to Hermes to return her to her woman's shape. Her original nature, as E. H. C. seems not to recognize, is female and human.

[4] E.H.C., p. 29.

[5] E. H. C. can scarcely have read *Elsie Venner* with any care when he accepts the statement of "one of the characters" that Geraldine has "no absolute ophidian relationship". The passage he quotes, although in a letter written by the "Professor" (admittedly Holmes himself), represents the viewpoint of an outsider who has not been on the ground to witness the nerve-wracking events of the story and who is obviously only trying to reassure the young hero, Bernard Langdon, in his anxieties and fears. The scientific arguments of the "Professor" are perfectly contradicted and destroyed by the story itself. For Elsie Venner's case is thoroughly physiological— the mythological does not enter into it at all; and obviously it has been suggested to Holmes by "Christabel" and "Lamia". As a matter of fact, the "Professor" is attempting to answer a point-blank question from Langdon, as follows: "Have you read, critically, Coleridge's poem of 'Christabel,' and Keats's 'Lamia'? If so, can you understand them, or find any physiological foundation for the story of either?"

Certain phases of Holmes's romance are extremely interesting because of their implications of what he saw in his two forerunners. For of course he wanted his readers to believe that he intended the influence of the rattlesnake, *Crotalus durissus*, on Elsie to be both physical and spiritual. She is several times described as having diamond eyes (though black) and a low, slanting forehead. When she looks at people intently, she fascinates them and weakens them by her gaze. She wears dresses of curious barred and checkered patterns, she has sharp white teeth which leave small stinging scars where they have bitten, and she possesses a queer enunciation, which has been a sort of lisp in her childhood. Sometimes people have visions of serpents (the Laocoön, for instance) after they have been with her. She always wears a broad necklace, jealously guarded, to conceal a faint but hideous birthmark. She loves to frequent the snake ledge and other dangerous places outside the town, and she has a mysterious power over snakes which compels them to obey her will. What more physiological evidence of her sinister strain could be adduced?

The presence of "Christabel" in Holmes's mind is shown in other ways also. Not only do his characters refer to the poem, but in the first part of the novel the relationship between Elsie and Helen Darley is too much like that between Geraldine and Christabel to be mere coincidence. Toward the end, too, there is a dove episode involving Elsie which is reminiscent of Bracy's dream. Finally, just before her death, Elsie's

tially physiological conception of Geraldine, like Holmes's of Elsie (a similarity which Holmes perceived), with which I am next concerned. Outside of Coleridge's probable knowledge of the mythology of serpents and dragons as it appeared in many famous ancient and medieval legends, and his incidental encounters with snakes and other reptiles on his rambles about the English countryside, what information about ophiology was he likely to have gleaned from his reading during this period? And of this information about the natural history and behavior of snakes, and about the effects of their presence and their bites on human beings, what portions may possibly be reflected in those passages of "Christabel" wherein Geraldine assumes her ophidian character?

It will now be appropriate to recall the specific details of Geraldine's reptilian appearance, conduct, and influence. She has eyes which at one time are bright and beautiful, but at another have the power of shrinking up and blinking dully like a "snake's small eye". She couches her head upon her breast—and the picture the reader gets is that of a snake drawing back its head to strike. Twice, Christabel, who has been embraced by her, hisses so much like a snake that those near her draw away in alarm. In the allegory of the bird which has fallen into the toils of the serpent ("bright green" in color), the necks of both victim and attacker swell and heave together. It is as if, as in the popular conception, the snake is actually feeding on its victim and sucking its blood; it has become a sort of vampire substitute. Moreover, Geraldine's body is cold and unhuman to the touch, and upon her bosom the skin is shriveled and foully colored. These are not simply the generalized and conventionalized details as-

---

serpent characteristics disappear, and she is left a pathetic and sympathetic woman—just as, I suspect, Geraldine would have become if Coleridge had found himself able to guide her plausibly to such a conclusion.

These elements—"Lamia" and "Christabel", coupled with Holmes's medical studies, his observations of the New England rattlesnake, and his ingrained moralistic tendencies—were the main ingredients of *Elsie Venner* (even the name "Venner" contains an echo of "venom"). In his 1883 preface he disclaimed any knowledge of the legend of Melusina until a French critic referred to Elsie as "cette pauvre Melusine"; nor did Hawthorne's *The Marble Faun* appear until after his book was "well advanced". "So that my poor heroine found her origin, not in fable or romance, but in a physiological conception, fertilized by a theological dogma."

sociated with the serpent-demon or dragon of mythology. They belong to the flesh and cold blood of realistic snakedom.

Since E. H. C. has already attempted to point out parallels to one or two of these items in Coleridge's reading, a few other similar details may well be added. For instance, the poet's abandoned intention to become an American farmer as part of the pantisocracy scheme had led him to read all the books he could lay hands on concerning American geography, American colonization, American customs and habits of mind, and American farming methods and rural conditions.[6] As a result, on February 26, 1796, he appeared at the Bristol Library and signed for the volume of *The Annual Register* for 1782; this volume he kept until March 10[7]—ample time for perusing with some care those articles in which he might have any interest. Of these articles, only one stands out as likely to have had any personal appeal— and it was probably because his eye had been caught by part of its title that he drew out this periodical volume, which was now fourteen years old. The article, or rather excerpt, was headed: "From the Letters of J. Hector St. John, an American Farmer."[8] The quotation itself, after Coleridge once got into it, can scarcely have been of much agrarian aid; but it contained at least one vividly memorable passage, and it could easily have sent the reader to the original book in which this passage appeared. The excerpt was headed: "Some Account of the Snakes of North America, and of the Humming Bird." The editor had selected, as a specimen likely to interest his readers, an account of the behavior and fate of a man bitten by a copperhead. Soon after his misfortune, the poor fellow's body had begun to swell and puff; different-colored spots had appeared and disappeared on parts of his skin; "his eyes were filled with madness and rage, he cast them on all present with the most vindictive looks: he thrust out his tongue as the snakes do; he hissed through his

[6] His list of borrowings from the Bristol Library in 1795 includes such titles as "Clarkson, Essay on the Slave Trade", "Wedstrom, on Colonization", and "Edwards' West Indies" (Kaufman, p. 319).

[7] Kaufman, p. 319.

[8] *Annual Register, 1782*, p. 99.

teeth with inconceivable strength, and became an object of
terror to all bye-standers." And finally he died. The venom of
the snake had obviously induced in him all the possible physical
characteristics of reptilian behavior, and he acted exactly as if
he himself were turning into a snake.[9]

Another very striking instance (though belonging to an entirely different order) of a complete assimilation of man and
serpent is to be found in canto 25 of Dante's "Inferno". Here
the poet recounts how, while in the circle of thieves, he saw three
of his countrymen so thoroughly merged with the reptiles which
attacked them for punishment that the observer could not tell
which kind of being they had become; and finally the soul of
one, which had now become a brute, fled hissing along the valley. This canto, by an interesting coincidence, is immediately
preceded by one which refers prominently to Libya (the home of
Lamia) and its snakes, the most famous of which are enumer-
ated by name. Now it happens that on March 28, 1796, Coleridge had drawn from the Bristol Library the *Anthologia Hiber-
nica*, Volume I. Herein, on page 135, was a notice of a new volume of poems by the Rev. Henry Boyd, "translator of Dante's
celebrated poem called *Inferno*," and on page 418 was an extract from the translation. On June 23, 1796, Coleridge carried
off the two volumes of Boyd's Dante so far published (they had
appeared in 1785), and kept them until July 4. Southey had
already had them out in September and October, 1794.[10]

If any authority for Christabel's involuntary behavior is
necessary, here it is in the story of the American farmer[11] and in

---

[9] Another instance in which human beings are induced to hiss like serpents is related
by the fabulous Mandeville, when he tells how in Tracoda "thei eten Flesche of Serpentes; and thei eten but litelle, and thei speken nought; but thei hissen, as Serpentes
don" (*Voiage*, pp. 195–96).

[10] Kaufman, pp. 317–19.

[11] The real name of J. Hector St. John was Michel G. St. J. de Crèvecœur, and his
book, *Letters from an American Farmer*, had been published in London in 1782. If
Coleridge had become sufficiently interested to look up the whole work, he would have
found in this same chapter several other striking passages, though none which might
have contributed so directly to "Christabel" as the one cited. De Crèvecœur, an ama-
teur naturalist and observer with considerable narrative ability, described, for instance,
the blacksnake, admiring its beauty and stressing especially its power of fascination—
"the art of inticing birds by the power of its eyes". Later on he introduced a detailed

Dante. Moreover, so familiar to Coleridge that light echoes and heavy reverberations from it occurred in such disparate poems as "Kubla Khan", "Lewti", "Fears in Solitude", and "The Wanderings of Cain"[12] was one of the most popular and readable of all the contemporary works on America—William Bartram's *Travels through North & South Carolina, Georgia, East & West Florida* . . . . , which had first been published in Philadelphia in 1791 and had then been reprinted in London in 1794, the very year in which Coleridge's echoes from it began. Moreover, by the poet's own statement, he had been rereading the book late in 1797 or early in 1798.[13] William Bartram was at that time the leading American naturalist, whose accounts of his expeditions and field trips sounded like veritable tales of adventure and romance. The influence of his stories of alligators, snake-birds, tropical thunderstorms, and intermittent fountains on "Kubla Khan" has lost nothing through Lowes's retelling.

So far as "Christabel" is concerned, there is, for instance, Bartram's description of the rattlesnake when angry: ". . . . his tail by the rapidity of its motion appears like a vapour, making a quick tremulous sound, his whole body swells through rage, continually rising and falling as a bellows. . . . ."[14] So swells and falls the neck of Bracy's snake. Another of these passages from Bartram has already been cited[15] by E. H. C. as a close parallel to Bracy's entire dream of the snake and the dove: "I observed a large hawk on the ground, in the middle of the road; he seemed to be in distress, endeavouring to rise; when, coming up near him, I found him closely bound up by a very

---

and exciting account of a fight between a blacksnake and a water snake. And in between, with the artistic effectiveness of utter contrast, he drew a colorful picture of the flights and friendliness of the humming bird in his garden, with "Its little eyes . . . . like diamonds" (pp. 236–46; the passage quoted by *The Annual Register* occurs on p. 237). The beauty and innocence of the tiny bird, the treachery and fascination of the powerful snake—both were to be found within the compass of the American farmer's garden.

[12] Lowes, pp. 452–53, 513–16, 604*i*, 610, discusses this matter thoroughly.

[13] See his notes on "This Lime-Tree Bower My Prison," *Poems*, pp. 178–81, which would place this reading "some months" after June, 1797.

[14] Bartram, *Travels* (Philadelphia, 1791), p. 267.   [15] E.H.C., p. 91 n.

long coach-whip snake, that had wreathed himself several times round the hawk's body, who had but one of his wings at liberty. . . . . I suppose the hawk had been the aggressor . . . . and that the snake dextrously and luckily threw himself in coils round his body."[16]

This parallel, when narrowly analyzed, is obviously not very close. A pretty considerable transmutation would have had to take place in the poet's mind to turn a hawk, which had apparently attacked, into a dove, which had been attacked, and a "very long coach-whip snake" into a "bright green snake" small enough for Bracy to have failed to see it until he actually started to take the bird into his hand. However, if E. H. C. had looked farther, he would have discovered that Bartram had more of some pertinence to offer. Perhaps his account, a few pages earlier, of a peculiar species called a "glass snake" because its tail is brittle and breaks off easily may be slightly apropos, inasmuch as "the colour and texture of the whole animal is so exactly like bluish green glass. . . . ."[17] But this bottle green is, after all, not the brilliant, almost emerald green that Coleridge's description implies. Bartram, however, does limn a little snake which meets almost all the requirements, and he calls it the "green snake": "The green snake is a beautiful innocent creature; they are from two to three feet in length, but not so thick as a person's little finger, of the finest green colour. They are very abundant, commonly seen on the limbs of trees and shrubs: they prey upon insects and reptiles, particularly the little green chameleon; and the forked tailed hawk or kite feeds on both of them, snatching them off the boughs of the trees."[18] Here not only does the color match Coleridge's requirements, but the size and delicacy are correct. Moreover, the environment has changed. No longer are the hawk and the coach-whip snake struggling in the middle of a dusty road. We are now in a wood, as Bard Bracy was;[19] and everything is green, even to the tiny chameleon which the snake has captured.

[16] Bartram, pp. 218–19.   [17] *Ibid.*, pp. 195–96.   [18] *Ibid.*, p. 275.

[19] No one seems to have noticed that the wood in Bracy's dream in the second part of "Christabel" is described in a much later season of the year than the wood in the

There is only one alien element in this picture: the bird is killing the snake, rather than the snake the bird. But Coleridge's reading-list is not yet exhausted. In his letter to Thelwall he confessed his interest in science, some of which had certainly been derived from his study of *The Philosophical Transactions of the Royal Society of London*, a work with which he was familiar in both its complete and its abridged form. From April 23 to May 22, 1798, for instance, he had Volume LXXV of the main series out of the Bristol Library concurrently with Volume II of the *Manchester Memoirs*.[20] More significant than this, however, as Lowes has ingeniously proved by the use of the Gutch memorandum book, not long before this time he had been carefully reading the fifth volume of the abridgment of the *Philosophical Transactions* and making notes on the more striking and picturesque passages in it.[21] In this abridgment, within the space of less than twenty pages,[22] in addition to a communication from Cotton Mather to the Royal Society concerning his observations on New England rattlesnakes (especially on how they fascinate squirrels in trees), and an account of the belief in metempsychosis in India (which I shall revert to later), there is an extract from still a third work, entitled "Of the Ways of Catching Fowl and Deer in Ceilan, &c. by Mr. Strachan". And in this is another description of a green snake, closely paralleling that of Bartram but also including the missing element—the snake attacks the bird, and not the bird the snake. For, wrote Strachan, this creature "is green like a Leaf of a Tree, who winds himself, and climbs upon the Trees, and catches the Birds, lying still at the time, as if he had no Motion, until he sees a fit Op-

---

opening scene in the first part, though the tree under which he sees the dove and the snake appears to be the same ancient oak as the one at which Christabel met Geraldine. Such is clearly the implication of line 540: "Save the grass and green herbs underneath the old tree." But of course Bracy is seeing a vision, and Coleridge probably wrote this passage in September or October in Cumberland, not April in Somersetshire!

[20] Kaufman, p. 320.

[21] Lowes, pp. 38–42, 476–77. These bear especially on the lines in "The Ancient Mariner" concerning "The hornèd Moon, with one bright star/Within the nether tip."

[22] *The Philosophical Transactions (from the Year 1700, to the Year 1720) Abridg'd* .... (London, 1749), V, Part II, 162, 165–71, 180.

portunity to catch. He is above one half Inch Diameter, and a Yard long."

Since Coleridge had almost indubitably been reading all these passages during the general period when he was writing "Christabel", the cumulative effect of so many descriptions of birds and snakes could not have failed to leave an impression. If, moreover, one is looking for a source for the physical background of Bracy's dream, Strachan's picture seems much more pertinent than E. H. C.'s citation from Bartram.

So, perhaps, came suggestions for the hissing and the swelling, and the bright green snake and the dove—all details which help to make the character of Geraldine so strange and so fearsome. Yet two other matters have been only partially disposed of, both closely associated with these: the remarkable—almost supernatural—power of her eyes, and the repulsive appearance and touch of her bosom.

Few writers who have described or discussed snakes from the naturalist's or scientist's point of view have failed to dwell at some length on their alleged ability to fascinate their intended prey by looking fixedly upon it. De Crèvecœur, Bartram, and Mather all mentioned this subject at greater or less length and recited several anecdotes wherein such marvels occurred. Nor has Geraldine's power to do the same thing escaped the readers of "Christabel", as, for instance, Railo, who remarks: "Even as a fragment, *Christabel* is a masterpiece of the poetry of terror, and has enriched literature with an extremely effectual female demon, one endowed, moreover, with a terror-romantic feature of special interest, namely, the evil eye, the fascinating glance of the snake."[23] Oliver Wendell Holmes and E. H. C. have also been keenly impressed by this attribute and have commented upon it by searching for more or less similar stories in earlier literature.

The most notable of these, to which Holmes refers briefly, E. H. C. translates from the Latin of Mizaldus, as follows:[24] "When

[23] Railo, p. 263.

[24] *Elsie Venner*, chap. xvi; E.H.C., pp. 29–31, from *Mizaldus redivivus sive centuriae XII memorabilium: Memorabilium arcanorum VI* (Noribergae, 1681), p. 262.

Alexander the Great was in the East the King of Inde presented him with a damsel of singular beauty and comeliness. Fair though she was she had been reared and nourished on the poisonous wolf's bane, and mischief and treachery lurked in the gift. Now it chanced that Aristotle when he looked at the maiden perceived that one moment her eyes blazed and sparked, and then blinked and closed like the eyes of a snake. 'Have a care for yourself, my Lord Alexander,' said he, 'the damsel is steeped in venom. Destruction and death await you in her embrace.' Nor was Aristotle out in his rede, for as many as wooed the damsel were smitten of her poison and died. I give the story on the authority of Aristotle, of Averroes, of Galen and Avicenna, and many others."

E. H. C. suggests that Coleridge "may have found the story in one of his landlord's medical journals, or in Mizaldus or in some other ancient compiler of 'Tales of Wonder'. . . . ." Other possibilities may be added. Antonius Mizaldus was one of Robert Burton's favorite authors, and Coleridge's attention might have been engaged through Burton. Moreover, if Coleridge had met the tale in medical literature, he might have known it for many years, since his enthusiasm for reading Greek, Latin, and English books of medicine went back even to his childhood.[25]

This tale from Mizaldus seems to be patterned on the general model of Philostratus' tale about Lamia, for in both cases we have a philosopher detecting at a glance the true nature of a beautiful but perilous young woman and quickly saving his pupil from her death-dealing embrace. Here, however, it is especially the description of her eyes that is significant, though E. H. C. has considerably touched up the original "scintillantes et serpentum more nictantes oculos" when he states that at "one

[25] See above, p. 64 n. Oliver Wendell Holmes also alludes to another "memorabilium" of the same type, which Cardan derived from Avicenna. To these, Samuel Purchas has his quota to unload, for in his *Pilgrimage* he relates several tales of people "nourished with Poysons", so that snakes could not harm them, but they poisoned others (Purchas, p. 537). E.H.C. (pp. 30–31 n.) also reminds his readers that Hawthorne had anticipated Holmes by inventing a similar fable in "Rappaccini's Daughter". His footnote, however, is a good specimen of his inaccuracy, for he calls the story "The Daughter of Rapaccini [sic]" and says that it was afterward included in *Mosses of the Manse* [sic]—thus making three minor slips in two lines.

moment her eyes blazed and sparked, and then blinked and
closed like the eyes of a snake." But so, in a general way, did
Geraldine's eyes behave. First they were "large" and "bright"
as she turned them from Sir Leoline; then, suddenly, as she
quietly looked "askance" at Christabel, they became "dull and
shy", they "shrunk in her head". These two kinds of human
vision had always impressed, if not haunted, Coleridge, who
was extremely sensitive to such things. In his memorandum
book at this time, for example, he set down the following lines,
which at once reminded Brandl of Geraldine: "her eyes
sparkled, as if they had been cut out of a diamond quarry in
some Golconda of Faeryland—and cast such meaning glances,
as would have vitrified the Flint in a Murderer's blunder-
buss—"[26] Some ten years later, on the other hand, Coleridge
associated the opposite sight with the administration of some
belladonna to his son Derwent's eyes: "And a drop or two too
much, or too little diluted might make the pupil of his eye start
from its Holdings and shrink up like Geraldine's!"[27]

The eye—and especially the glittering eye—seems, in fact, to
follow the sensitive reader wherever he goes in Coleridge's early
poetry. It pursues him agitatingly through "The Rime of the
Ancient Mariner", "Christabel", "The Three Graves", and
Osorio. It is sometimes bound up with the power of the snake to
charm its prey, but this is only one phase of a much broader
topic that had enlisted the curiosity of Coleridge and many of
his contemporaries. Everywhere—through William Beckford's
Vathek, Matthew Gregory Lewis's The Monk, the verse narratives of Byron, and the outpourings of German romantic fiction
—the glittering eye and its effect on those within its range drew
the specialists in chills and shudders with an irresistible force.[28]
So pithy did the subject seem to be in relation to Coleridge, indeed, that Professor Lane Cooper many years ago wrote his
stimulating article, "The Power of the Eye in Coleridge", to
deal with it.[29]

[26] Archiv, p. 350.   [27] Letter to Southey, February, 1808, in Griggs, I, 395.

[28] See, e.g., Lowes, pp. 252–54.

[29] In Studies in Language and Literature in Celebration of the Seventieth Birthday of
James Morgan Hart   November 2, 1909 (New York, 1910), pp. 78–121.

Very pertinently, Cooper reminds us that the latter years of the eighteenth century had seen the volcanic rise to fame and world-wide acclamation of the Austrian mystic and physician, F. A. Mesmer, and the temporary acceptance of his theories of animal magnetism and hypnotic curing. Though his methods were based primarily upon occult "passes" and stroking with the hands, he used other means of fixing the attention, such as mirrors, lights, and music. The hypnotic glance was one of these, and many people became convinced that they possessed it. Coleridge's own eyes, according to the testimony of his friends, made an extraordinary impression on all who saw them. This peculiar power residing in some people's eyes, thinks Cooper, was clearly among those things which the poet described in his letter to Thelwall as " 'facts of mind,' that is, accounts of all the strange phantasms that ever possessed 'your philosophy'. . . . ." It is true that in his youth he was much more inclined to believe than when he became older, perhaps because from 1786 onward Mesmer himself and his disciples were in London, Bristol, etc., giving demonstrations and seances which cured some of his patients and threw others into fainting fits and convulsions. Coleridge would also have come across references to similar phenomena in Bryan Edwards's *West Indies* and Samuel Hearne's *Hudson's Bay*. Actually he once planned to write a book about mesmerism and animal magnetism; and as late as 1818 he was recommending that an article on the subject, though from a somewhat skeptical point of view, be included in the *Encyclopaedia Metropolitana*, in which he was interested.[30]

As for Coleridge's own use of ocular fascination, Cooper finds that it is largely limited to ideas of animal magnetism. The notion of "fixing", followed by a sudden release, continually recurs, associated with the naturally allied imputation of a good or evil will or purpose in the magnetizer himself. These conceptions appear dominantly in "The Three Graves", "The Rime", "Christabel", and much of *Osorio*. Mixed with the rest is enough conventional demonology of the Miltonic, Spenserian, and medieval types so that it is not clear whether Coleridge himself believed that fascination "is ever accomplished without demo-

[30] *Ibid.*, pp. 85–97; see also Lowes, pp. 153–54, 493, 546–47.

niac assistance. Let the reader who can at every point in the story say whether the Lady Geraldine is a witch, or 'an angel beautiful and bright' and yet 'a fiend', or a mere unsubstantial phantasm in the mind of Christabel, decide how Coleridge might have wished to settle this question. Presumably, in his effort to render the 'supernatural' more 'real', he failed to distinguish accurately for himself just when he believed and when he did not believe, in dubious or impossible phenomena; that is, he tried to steer a middle course between 'subjectivity' and 'objectivity'." To illustrate these bracing ideas, Cooper has analyzed Coleridge's early poems and has classified the allusions to the eye into ten types, only six of which are represented in "Christabel", though these are sufficient to bring together in the Coleridgean crucible the serpent's power of fascination, the witch's evil eye, and mesmeric ocular hypnotism.[31]

There is, to be sure, no Ancient Mariner in "Christabel", or no Wedding Guest either; but the force binding them together is nevertheless lurking in the background. In Lowes's words, the subject of animal magnetism "was working in Coleridge's mind —reinforced, as 'Christabel' irresistibly suggests, by who can tell what midnight delvings in occult Latin treatises on fascination."[32] Of course, no one can tell exactly; but Ferriar, who devotes some seven pages to a discussion of Mesmer's activities and theories, gives a few hints.[33] The work of Sennertus, *De fascinatione*, was well known; and Ferriar mentions it several times, notably as follows: "Thus, the atrophy of infants was long imputed to the power of *evil eyes*, and Sennertus has treated largely of this sort of fascination."[34] The blasting or shriveling of children by witches, however, was only one aspect of the larger power attributed to them—that of the "ligature", as it was often called, which meant a binding or inhibiting of the victim from performing his natural or desired actions. This power,

[31] Cooper, pp. 98–99, 102–18. Hanson (pp. 252–53, 481) also discusses the passage in "The Nightingale" in which Coleridge describes the glittering of unshed tears in little Hartley's eyes and which has its parallel in his notebook.

[32] Lowes, p. 254.

[33] *Manchester Memoirs*, III, 48, 49, 59, 61, 96–103, *et passim*.   [34] *Ibid.*, p. 59.

too, Geraldine possesses, for it is the very essence of the spell which she lays on Christabel at the end of the first canto, as she first "eyes the maid" and then takes her in her arms, saying:

> In the touch of this bosom there worketh a spell,
> Which is lord of thy utterance, Christabel!
> Thou knowest to-night, and wilt know to-morrow,
> This mark of my shame, this seal of my sorrow;
>> But vainly thou warrest,
>> For this is alone in
>> Thy power to declare,
>> That in the dim forest
>> Thou heard'st a low moaning,
> And found'st a bright lady, surpassingly fair;
> And didst bring her home with thee in love and in charity,
> To shield her and shelter her from the damp air.

This potent spell is so effective that throughout the second canto, whenever Christabel recalls the events of the preceding night and struggles to tell them, her mouth is closed once more by Geraldine's vindictive gaze.[35] Such a power of the "ligature" is described by Ferriar, with the announcement that the matter is treated at length by both Wier and Del Rio.[36] Thus, as man-

[35] Tuttle (pp. 472–73) finds an interesting parallel with this inhibition in Mary Robinson's novel, *Hubert de Sevrac, A Romance of the Eighteenth Century* (London, 1796), I, 247–48; II, 60–61. It is, however, a sacred oath and not a supernatural enchantment which prevents Sabina from telling her father of the danger which threatens him. Emily, in *The Mysteries of Udolpho*, also has a somewhat similar burden to conceal (Tuttle, p. 464).

[36] *Manchester Memoirs*, III, 61. Perhaps Coleridge once more verified his references in regard to fascination and binding; perhaps he was satisfied with what he already knew. There is evidence, however, in "The Ancient Mariner", that he was thinking of this power of the eye in terms of the old doctrine of magnetic, if not corpuscular, emanation, which, if also to be found among the eighteenth-century mesmerists, had been expressed over and over again many years earlier by such as Cornelius Agrippa. In the 1796 version of "The Ancient Mariner", as Lowes has pointed out (p. 253), the Wedding Guest is made to utter this speech:

> " 'Marinere! thou hast thy will:
> 'For that, which comes out of thine eye, doth make
> 'My body and soul to be still.' "

Coleridge later expunged this stanza and several others as an inappropriate interruption, but the quasi-scientific basis of his statement is clear. There is something sensible, perhaps even material, which is sent out from the eye.

Agrippa's doctrines were founded on the belief that the air "is a vitall spirit, passing through all Beings," and that therefore it is able to join things together, as if it were a "*Medium* or glew". In this fashion it transmits feelings and influences from one body to another, as in dreams, thought transference, and premonitions. Moreover, the ele-

kind has always believed with its heart, if not always with its mind, there are strange and imperfectly understood powers which are loose in the world, usually operating through the body of some animal or human being; and the eye, that bright and miraculous orb, is the center of some of the most incomprehensible of these.

Probably the chief reason for the mixed emotions which Geraldine arouses is contained in her speech at the end of the first canto, and particularly in the single line in which she alludes sadly and bitterly to her concealed physical blemish as "This mark of my shame, this seal of my sorrow." Something in her past which she now profoundly regrets and shudders at has left this indelible brand upon her. It is a sort of stamp or trademark which denotes her inescapable obligations to this power. With infinite artistry Coleridge refers to it again and again, sometimes directly, sometimes obliquely, hinting rather than describing, avoiding rather than stating. It was this subtlety of technique which prompted Hazlitt to his obscene charge of ob-

---

mental virtues in things attract or turn like to like. "If therefore we would obtain any property or Vertue, let us seek for such Animals, or such other things whatsoever, in which such a property, or Vertue is most vigorous." Among these animals, vipers and snakes are widely favored for the renewal of youth. This magical power of mutual attraction Agrippa makes a great deal of, sometimes referring to it under the Greek name of "συμπάθιαν", and remarking that if there is any disparity between its objects the inferior element is always drawn upward to the superior (Agrippa, pp. 14–15, 34–36, 74–75, 127–28).

Associated in his discussion with this power of mutual attraction is the related one of "binding". Through it, people, animals, and even objects may be prevented from performing certain actions, chiefly through the use of magic spells and potions but also often through the eye. In fact, he devotes one entire section to the subject "Of Fascination, and the Art Thereof". This particular variety of binding, he says, is accomplished by means of a sort of ray which emanates from the eye of the binder, passes through the air, strikes the eye of the victim, and from that aperture pierces to the heart, which controls the person's actions (ibid., pp. 78–79, 101–2). The indication that this was the orthodox conception of fascination during the Middle Ages and the Renaissance is proved by the fact that the monkish Malleus maleficarum, the notorious "Devil's Hammer" which the inquisitors used to beat their victims into submission, gives exactly the same sort of analysis and explanation of the means and results of ocular fascination. (Malleus maleficarum, pp. 12–13, 17. Montague Summers, the editor of this 1928 edition, attributes the authorship to Kramer and Sprenger; but Ferriar, who mentions the work in connection with Agrippa, makes the authors Kramer and Institor— see Manchester Memoirs, III, 42.) The doctrine is strangely like that underlying Coleridge's use of fascination in his poems written during this period.

scenity against "Christabel", not so much because of anything
that Coleridge had printed as because of the line which he had
left out: "Hideous, deformed, and pale of hue." As a matter of
fact, unless Hazlitt had seen some manuscript now lost (a contingency by no means impossible), the deleted line (as it now
stands in the extant manuscripts) had run: "Are lean and old
and foul of hue."[37] In either case, however, few sensible readers
would dissent from Coleridge's decision to drop the line entirely,
and break off with

> Behold! her bosom and half her side—
> A sight to dream of, not to tell!

In the second canto, nevertheless, he allowed himself to become slightly more explicit, in accordance with the principle of
both maintaining suspense and also partially allaying curiosity
by unraveling a mystery, skein by skein, or even thread by
thread. Now, as Sir Leoline embraced Geraldine with an emo-
tion which he probably assured himself was almost paternal,
Christabel experienced once more "The vision of fear, the touch,
the pain!" Still more specifically, however, immediately thereafter

> Again she saw that bosom old,
> Again she felt that bosom cold. . . .

And with these meager but suggestive details the direct clues to
his intention which Coleridge has left are exhausted.

Whether, somewhere in the back of his imagination, there
lurked a trace of the memory of the snakes which had been pur-
suing him all through this canto, there is little actual evidence
to go upon. Coldness, however, is always conventionally accepted as one of the attributes of a serpent's body. Moreover, if
the visions of the American rattlesnakes he had been reading
about were still flashing across his mind, as they seem to have
been, the foulness or discoloration of Geraldine's breast would
not be hard to account for. It should certainly be noted that the
next line after the foregoing description relates to the first of
Christabel's hissing fits. Consequently, it appears that, to Cole-

[37] E.H.C., p. 75 n.

ridge, Geraldine's bosom is closely associated with the thought of snakes.

But there is a much greater literature than this behind this one terrifying detail. Most earlier critics and interpreters, in fact, have pitched upon this item as embodying the one necessary key to the mystery of Geraldine's identity, and by so doing have so thoroughly simplified their problem that in the process they have destroyed much of the interest and originality of the character. That is, the commonest explanation of Geraldine is to call her, in a word of one syllable which will be understood even by a child in a nursery, nothing but a "witch".[38] The spot upon her bosom therefore becomes a plain, unadulterated "witch's mark", and every reader may easily finish the story from there for himself, either as Gillman did or with some facile variation.

In their hunt for the sources of Coleridge's inspiration, therefore, many scholars have raced too complacently to the most prominent and easily accessible example of such a type in English literature, and, arriving out of breath in their haste, have leveled their forefingers triumphantly at Spenser's *Faerie Queene*, simultaneously shouting: "Geraldine is Duessa! Christabel is Una! The problem is perfectly simple after all." There seems to be a little uncertainty as to who the Red Cross Knight becomes—whether he is transformed into Sir Leoline or Christabel's "lover that's far away" (though clearly destined to re-

[38] Coleridge's own attitude toward witchcraft when he was in a sober and reasoning frame of mind is discussed by Donald Davies, "Coleridge's Marginalia in Mather's *Magnalia*," *Huntington Library Quarterly*, II (January, 1939), 234–36. In the 1702 edition of Cotton Mather's *Magnalia Christi Americana*, now in the Huntington, Coleridge has jotted various derisive and scathing comments on Mather's credulity in the New England witchcraft epidemic of 1692. For instance, he tells ironically of how a "bewitched" girl, when reading a Quaker's book, was unable to pronounce the words "God" and "Christ" and had to omit the Lord's Prayer when reading the Church of England prayer-book. In the case of a man who accused a poor woman of bewitching him, Coleridge remarked: "In order to any rational Conviction of the miraculous nature of these quasi-*facts*, it would be a condition with me that a medical man of known science & philosophical temper, should have attended & examined & attested the case....." Davies does not speculate as to the date of Coleridge's ownership or use of the book, but the title-page bears the inscription: "Robert Southey. Nottingham. June 21. 1811."

turn before the end of the poem)—but obviously it is unwise to press parallels too closely.[39]

The general suggestion, therefore, may be briefly examined and dismissed. In the second canto of the first book of Spenser's poem, when the knight Fradubio, turned into a tree by the enchantress Duessa, tells the Red Cross Knight how he had seen her in her true form, he describes her as a "filthy foule old woman", with her "neather partes misshapen, monstrous. . . . ." Soon thereafter, when Duessa (as Fidessa) hears her story thus related, she pretends that she is overcome by the wonder of hearing a tree speak and seeing it bleed, and counterfeits a swoon, which distracts the Knight with anxiety at her weakness, until he is able to revive her. That is, her behavior superficially resembles that of Geraldine on her initial appearance. On the other hand, when Duessa is finally exposed, after Una brings Arthur to the rescue and he conquers the giant Orgoglio, her description is repeated with such a profusion of disgusting and exact details that the reader is more likely to vomit than shiver:

[39] The Germans have done the most speculating on this subject, most of it very weakly founded. Alois Brandl, in *Samuel Taylor Coleridge und die englische Romantik* (Berlin, 1886), translated into English as *Samuel Taylor Coleridge and the English Romantic School* (London, 1887), was perhaps the earliest to draw these parallels very definitely and (pp. 220–21 of the German edition) to let Sir Leoline substitute for the Red Cross Knight. Railo (p. 379) finds his suggestion "indeed striking". Eichler (p. 24) follows his master only partially, suggesting that the Red Cross Knight corresponds to Christabel's unnamed lover. But Professor Brandl also sees another "germ" for "Christabel", which Eichler (pp. 24–25) and E.H.C. (p. 13) both mention. This is the ballad of "The Marriage of Sir Gawayn", found in Percy's *Reliques*, which opens as follows (III, 23–24):

> "My father was an aged knighte,
>   And yet it chanced soe,
> He took to wife a false ladyè,
>   Which brought me to this woe.
>
> She witch'd mee, being a faire yonge maide,
>   In the green forèst to dwelle;
> And there to abide in lothlye shape,
>   Most like a fiend of helle."

This situation Brandl misstates so that it becomes parallel to the shifting in "Christabel" in which the father becomes the object of contention between the two women. Eichler also suggests that, just as Spenser has the magician Archimago assume the shape of the heroine's beloved, so Coleridge would have had the "demon" appear as Christabel's intended bridegroom (as, of course, Gillman did).

she is loathly, wrinkled, and old, like Geraldine's body, but her head is bald and scurfy; her dugs hang down like empty bladders; she has a fox's tail covered with filth; and one of her feet is like an eagle's claw, the other like the paw of a bear.[40] Such a description would be diametrically opposed to Coleridge's whole theory of dealing with the supernatural and the horrific; it was exactly the sort of technique for which he had criticized his friends Southey and Joseph Cottle.[41] If, therefore, Spenser's conception of Duessa influenced Coleridge in drawing Geraldine, it must have been because Coleridge sternly shut his eyes on the latter part of her history and refused to let himself picture her fully. There is actually more similarity with the story of Melusina at her bath of purification, because Melusina is presented compassionately in spite of the metamorphosis of the lower part of her body into that of a serpent,[42] than there is with the story of Duessa, because Duessa is consistently revolting and odious.[43]

The usual witch-mark of the Middle Ages, as it was actually regarded in the practical operations of the inquisitors, was a much simpler but far less obvious thing than Spenser made it. Father Sebastien Michaëlis, in his *Admirable Historie of the Possession and Conversion of a Penitent Woman. Seduced by a Magician That Made Her Become a Witch*, showed his thorough conversancy with the theory and application of these dreadful performances in his account of the examination, condemnation, and burning of the obviously innocent Gaufridy, who suffered death because of a hysterical and unbalanced woman and the zeal of a panel of sincere but misguided and sadistic clergy.

[40] *The Faerie Queene*, I, ii, stanzas xl–xli, and I, viii, stanzas xlvi–xlviii, in *The Works of Edmund Spenser A Variorum Edition* (Baltimore, 1932).

[41] *Letters*, I, 162; see also Lamb, *Letters*, I, 211–12.

[42] See above, pp. 99–100 n.

[43] Brandl and Eichler, apparently not being entirely convinced by their own parallels with *The Faerie Queene*, have another related suggestion to make, by which Geraldine becomes a species of "Proteus-Elfin", well known in medieval literature—a being most attractive when seen from in front or above, but most horribly unsightly when viewed from behind or beneath (Eichler, p. 24). This is much like the picture which Joseph Cottle draws of his witch in his *Alfred* (London, 1816), I, 42, in which he describes her as "Half red, half blue," with a footnote on the Scandinavian conception of Death: "The body of Hela is represented as one half blue, the other half of the colour of human flesh."

Michaëlis states the basic theory in a section of his *Pnevmology, or Discourse of Spirits*, on the subject of "Whether the Diuell Doth Marke Witches": "For experience doth demonstratively proue, that this kind of marke which they haue in their bodies is leprous, and deuoid of all sense; in so much (as we haue tried with a needle or a pinne) that if a man doth secretly and finely thrust up a pinne into the same, they feel it no more then if they were direct lepers." Consequently, after the examination had been ended, and the marks discovered as expected, the chief inquisitor announced in cold triumph that Revelation divinely stated that no Christian could bear such marks as had been discovered on the magician. Reminding his audience of God's promises and protection, he concluded: "As it is said in the same booke, he will not suffer his elect to carry the marke of the beast. ...." The mark of the beast! Again the inquisitor referred to it in his final condemnation of Gaufridy to be burned at the stake.[44] And up to Coleridge's own time this was the common phrase used to describe the so-called "witch's mark".

Whether or not the "Michaelis" which Coleridge and Southey drew from the Bristol Library early in June, 1795, each signing for a volume,[45] was the *Historie* and *Pnevmology*, or a work by another author of the same family name,[46] allusions to this brand or signature abound in the books which the former was reading about this time. There was, for instance, Dr. Thomas Burnet's massive and vivid *Telluris theoria sacra*, a grandiloquent and exciting attempt to devise a cosmology of the world which would reconcile science and religion. So popular and controversial did this volume prove that Burnet himself made an English translation and revision of it in 1684–90, as *The Theory of the Earth*. One or both of these versions Coleridge was so

---

[44] Michaëlis, *Historie* [and] .... *Pnevmology*, pp. 132–34, 375–78, 414–15.

[45] Kaufman, p. 319.

[46] The translation of J. D. Michaelis's *Introduction to the New Testament* by Herbert Marsh had been reviewed in *The British Critic* in June, 1794 (IV, 601–8), and J. B. Michaelis's *Sämmtliche poetische Werke* in four small volumes had been published at Vienna in 1791. Coleridge's interest in J. D. Michaelis is shown in his letter to Poole on May 6, 1796 (*Biographia Epistolaris. Being the Biographical Supplement of Coleridge's Biographia Literaria. With Additional Letters, etc.*, ed. A. Turnbull, London, 1911, I, 78).

struck with that his memorandum book and some of his writings of the period almost bristle with references, fragmentary quotations, and reminiscences; in fact, at one time, as the notebook reveals, he listed among his many projects which proved abortive a "theoria telluris translated into Blank Verse".[47] Book IV of Burnet's *Theory* is entitled "Concerning the New Heavens and New Earth, and concerning the Consummation of All Things"; and this book, particularly chapters iv and v, has a great deal to say about Revelation, 20:1-6, for this is the passage which, in Burnet's quotation, tells of the reward of those who "had not worshipped the beast, neither his image, neither had received his mark upon their fore-heads, or in their hands. . . . ."

One of the few strictly contemporary writers on witchcraft mentioned by Ferriar was the essayist and sentimental dramatist, Richard Cumberland, whom Ferriar classified among his fellow-Englishmen as follows: "The principal writers on spirits, of this country, are Aubrey, More, Glanville, Baxter, Beaumont, and professor Sinclair, of Glasgow, to whom we must add Mr. Cumberland a well-known living author, as the latest supporter of the doctrine amongst us, though he has produced only one history, and that of an old date."[48] In his collection of essays, *The Observer*, Cumberland had several times confessed his interest in the subject of witchcraft as a curious relic of old superstitions, and had even devoted two complete essays to a general discussion of it, in which he showed that he had consulted at least the more vulgar works about it.[49] Now, perhaps prompted by Ferriar's reference, perhaps of his own initiative, Coleridge had taken the first and the fifth volumes of *The Observer* from the Bristol Library on May 6, 1796, and had kept them out for a month.[50] In essay No. 34 of Volume I Cumberland took it upon himself not only to allude to the Mark but to explain some-

---

[47] Lowes, pp. 502-4, discusses the whole matter fully.

[48] *Manchester Memoirs*, III, 80.

[49] Cumberland's two essays are Nos. 33 and 34, though it is No. 71 to which Ferriar refers.

[50] Kaufman, p. 320.

thing of its nature and origin, according to the explanations of certain of the church fathers. Thus, he pointed out, the new adherent or disciple of the devil at once "proceeds to put some secret mark upon himself with the point of a needle, as the sign of the Beast or Antichrist, in which mark there is great potency, and in some cases, according to Irenaeus, it appears that the devil insists upon cauterizing his disciples in the upper membrane of the right ear; in others, according to Tertullian, in the forehead. . . . ."

Such specimens of the superstitions of the witch-mark could be extended almost infinitely. They could also be mingled with similar beliefs about other marks and signs, symbolizing the commission of a crime or some similar unforgivable deed. As Lowes has tentatively suggested in connection with the Ancient Mariner and his shadowy kinship with the Wandering Jew, there is the "brand of Cain", which God stamped upon the first murderer and which Coleridge must have met frequently in his exploratory researches for his poem on Cain. Bayle, for instance, discusses ten or a dozen possible explanations of this famous sign. So, too, there was the mark upon the Wandering Jew himself.[51] The world is full of such marks.

Thus the conventional witch-mark does not come physically so near to Geraldine's blemish as many preceding commentators have believed. Hers is not a spot which must be probed for with pins or needles, and even then is not visible to the ordinary eye. Hers does not appear only at certain seasons of the day or week, as does Duessa's or Melusina's, for it can be concealed only under her clothing and must always be patently revealed when she disrobes. She can never escape it or fully hide it, and it is continually weighing on her conscience. It is like a great shriveled scar or birthmark—old, chill, and discolored. Nevertheless, from the symbolical point of view her mark, like theirs, is a definite token of some transgression in her past.

Let us now reopen the Bible at Revelation, chapter 20. The passage concerns the first millennium, in which "the souls of them that were beheaded for the witness of Jesus, and for the

[51] Lowes, pp. 257–60, based partly upon Bayle, *Dictionary* (London, 1736), IV, 17 n.

word of God, which had not worshiped the beast, neither his image, neither had received his mark upon their fore-heads, or in their hands," were resurrected and "reigned with Christ a thousand years". These are the fortunate martyrs, whose reward for their sufferings shall long anticipate that of the rest of mankind. The apocalyptic events are foretold in the fourth verse. The first verse of the chapter, however, tells of the angel which came down from heaven with "the key of the bottomless pit and a great chain in his hand". And the second verse reads: "And he laid hold on the dragon, that old serpent, which is the Devil, and Satan, and bound him a thousand years." In other words (the third verse briefly adds a few details about "that old serpent's" fate), the passage in the Bible from which the famous "mark of the beast" was derived was intimately associated with the idea of snakes and dragons. What is more likely, then, than that Coleridge, in deciding to brand Geraldine with some mark symbolical of her sin, should have delineated it in terms of serpentry, and especially, perhaps, in terms of a snake preparing for rejuvenation and ready to shed its old skin for a new one?

V

THE TRANSMIGRATION OF SOULS

THERE is another, somewhat different and yet integrally related, way in which the puzzling circumstances of Geraldine's contradictory behavior may be regarded. As one pushes with fluctuating hope and despondence through the almost innumerable books of history, philosophy, religion, occultism, science, exploration, and literature which Coleridge left in a zigzag wake behind him, one is impressed more and more with the prevalence of certain themes and doctrines which run through a large portion of them. For beneath the credulous acceptance of the beliefs in vampires, demonology, reptilian transformations, and the rest lies one fundamental dogma, which permeated and honeycombed the thought of the ancient world in nearly all schools of philosophy and which was by no means eradicated when the great old civilizations of Greece and Rome lost their original vitality and power. Although the doctrine of metempsychosis is generally associated first of all with Pythagoras, it has never actually been confined to Greece. It had attracted the Persian wise men. It was the basis for much of the religion of India. Travelers reported that many of the Chinese and the Japanese held a similar creed. The later Jews shared it. Even in the little island of England, trembling on the western horizon like a mysterious outpost of humanity, the Druids had unfolded it to their devotees. And in this far-flung but affiliated field Coleridge was doing a vast amount of reading and research.

The Pythagorean principle of the transmigration of souls had naturally held much appeal for Plato, whose conceptions and explanations of the activities of the soul were really responsible for modifying and refining Pythagoras into a usable form. In the hands of the Neo-Platonists of all ages and countries, however, fancy and vaporings once more climbed completely into the saddle; and the rationalized whimsies of Paracelsus, for example, resulted. These men, it will be recalled, were Coleridge's "darling studies", and their roll extended all the way from "Thoth the Egyptian" (that is, Hermes Trismegistus) to "Taylor the English pagan", their modern translator. The little Neo-Platonic Bible, as Lowes calls it, which Thelwall had bought for his friend, contained, for instance, as announced in the combination title-page and table of contents:

> Iamblichvs de Mysteriis Aegyptiorvm, Chaldaeorum, Assyriorum.
> Proclvs in Platonicum Alcibiadem de Anima, atque Daemone.
> Idem de Sacrificio & Magia.
> Porphyrivs de Diuinis atq; Daemonib.
> Psellvs de Daemonibus.
> Mercvrii Trismegisti Pimander.
> Ejusdem Asclepius.[1]

Many of the earlier editions, edited and translated in Latin by Marsilius Ficinus in Venice, had contained other works by members of this school: "Synesius Platonicus de somniis", "Pythagorae philosophi aurea uerba", "Symbola Pithagorae philosophi", etc.

It may be supererogatory to feel that a direct connection must be established between these authors and Coleridge's knowledge of metempsychosis. One link should easily suffice. In the memorandum book stands a line in Greek from Plato's "Phaedo", which is again cited by Coleridge himself as authority for a passage which he wrote on September 20, 1796, in a sonnet on the birth of his son Hartley:

> .... and some have said
> We liv'd, ere yet this robe of flesh we wore.[2]

Below this Greek quotation in the notebook, obviously at the same or almost the same time, he set down: ". . . . and Synesius, the hyper-platonic Jargonist would have waved [sic] his claims to a Bishopric [rather] than allow his Soul to be younger than his Body." This is followed by a few Greek words from the second *Ennead* of Plotinus. The previous life of the soul and its

---

[1] *Iamblichvs de Mysteriis* . . . . (apud Ioannem Tornaesivm, 1607). Coleridge's copy was of this edition (E.H.C., p. 9).

[2] *Archiv*, p. 357; *Poems*, pp. 154–55.

rehabitation of earthly bodies were, then, subjects in which ⟨——
Coleridge was sufficiently interested in 1796 to make jottings on
them for his notes.

Specifically, what would he have found in his readings during
this period? Dupuis's *Origine de tous les cultes*, it has already
been shown, yielded high-grade ore in its symbolizing the serpent as the universal principle of evil; nor, in a work on universal religion, could Dupuis well overlook the almost equally general belief in the transmigration of souls. · So, quite naturally,
we find him asserting that the doctrine prevailed almost everywhere, from Persia and Greece to Japan, and quoting the theory
of such philosophers as Manes to the effect that the souls of
great sinners are sent into the bodies of inferior animals. And
here, again, appears Bishop Synesius, who "pretended, that
those, who had neglected to make their peace with God, would
by the law of fate be obliged to recommence a new mode of life,
the opposite of the preceding one, until they were repentant of
their sins."[3]

Similarly, the more formal historians of philosophy in the
eighteenth century, like the German Latinist Jacob Brucker
and his English epitomizer, William Enfield, could not escape
from the doctrine, and referred to it over and over in their *Historia critica philosophiae* and *The History of Philosophy*, respectively.[4] And in March and April, 1795, Coleridge was reading
Volume I of the Bristol Library's copy of Enfield; and during
March, April, and May, 1797, with apparently complete fear-
lessness of a fine for an overdue book, he kept its copy of the
original Brucker near him.[5] Yes, the Bristol Library was quite
serviceable to Coleridge, in spite of his high-and-mighty atti-

---

[3] Dupuis, pp. 356 ff.

[4] Iacobi Bruckeri, *Historia critica philosophiae* (Lipsiae, 1742), *passim*, and William
Enfield, *The History of Philosophy* (London, 1819), I, 93, 108, 397–98, 405; II, 63, *et
passim*.

[5] Kaufman, pp. 319–20. Coleridge also mentioned "Brücker" in a letter to Southey
early in 1800 (*Letters*, I, 330). Ferriar (*Manchester Memoirs*, III, 56) had also remarked,
in discussing modern references to witchcraft, that "Brucker mentions incidentally, in
his excellent Historia Critica Philosophiae, in 1766, that he thinks the question still
undecided. . . . ." (As for overdue books, letters in Griggs show that the library was
not willing to be quite so lenient as Coleridge thought he merited.)

tude toward it—after he had skimmed its cream and was complacently licking his chops afterward. It was there, indeed, that
he had to go in order to procure a copy of his friend Amos Cottle's translation of the *Edda*,[6] for seemingly it was only William
Wordsworth who was honored by being sent a presentation
copy; and in Cottle's prefatory dissertation one would have
found the same topic of metempsychosis touched briefly: "The
Druids believed in the transmigration of the soul. The Teutonic
nations, on the contrary, held that there was a fixed Elysium,
and a hell. . . . ."[7]

That great collector of religions, Samuel Purchas, one of Coleridge's favorites, was a witness to the widespread currency of
the notion throughout the world. Scarcely a religion which he
canvassed, ancient or modern, civilized or barbarian, but had
succumbed at one time or another to its allure. Most of the
sects of the Chinese, he learned, had long accepted the teachings
of the transmigrationists and had many "fables of men turned
into Dogs or Snakes, and againe metamorphosed into men."[8]
Still more significant is his review of the religious history of the
later Jews, especially the kabbalists, who carried their theories
of the exchange of souls to the most drastic lengths imaginable.
For example, to quote Purchas, "the Cabalisticall Authors,
sayth *Elias Leuita*, are of opinion that euery soule is three times
created, they meane, it rolleth or passeth thorow three mens
bodies. . . . . So they say the soules of Sinners passe into the
bodies of beasts; as if a man committed Sodomie, his soule passeth into a Hare, because that creature is sometimes Male, some-

---

[6] Kaufman, p. 320. In a letter to Poole (*Letters*, I, 270–71) Coleridge had written:
"The Bristol Library is a hum, and will do us little service. . . . ."

[7] Amos Cottle, *Icelandic Poetry, or The Edda of Saemund Translated into English
Verse* (Bristol, 1797), p. ix.

[8] Purchas, I, 462. These stories are somewhat reminiscent of the *Metamorphoses, or
The Golden Ass* of Apuleius. It is true that in this fabulous romance the hero is transformed directly into an ass by magical means, and without the necessity of having
first endured death; but the result of the incident is the same as if he had. This work
also contains the famous version of the tale of Cupid and Psyche. On November 4, 1796,
Coleridge drew the fifth volume of "*Apuleia Opera*" from the Bristol Library. (Lowes,
p. 604*e*, corrects Kaufman's error in dating this borrowing November 4, 1795.)

times Female: the soule of the Adulterer passeth into a cam-
ell."9

It was among the Hindus, however, that the belief in metempsychosis found the most complete modern adoption. Interest in the East had never died out in England since the days of
Mandeville, but much had been done to further it in a scholarly
and scientific fashion during the late eighteenth century by the
great orientalist, philologist, and jurist, Sir William Jones,
founder and first president of the Asiatic Society. In 1794, the
year of his death from overwork, he published the first of the
monumental series of studies in which he planned to digest all
the Mohammedan and Hindu law. This work, translated from
the Sanscrit and entitled *Institutes of Hindu Law: or, The Ordinances of Menu, According to the Gloss of Cullúca*, aroused the
public and the press, including *The British Critic*, to paeans and
hosannas of dignified praise. The preface to the 1797 volume of
The British Critic, for example, called the particular attention
of its readers to the review of the *Institutes* as one of the outstanding landmarks of the year.10 Consequently, no one will
wonder at finding this entry in Coleridge's memorandum book:
"Institutes of Hindoo Law—or the Ordinances of Minu. De-
brett."11 This was another tidbit which he could never pass by.

The last and most important chapter in Jones's work is entitled "On Transmigration and Final Beatitude". Here, in un-
relenting legalistic fashion, he analyzes and categorizes all the
Hindu tenets and laws, all the rewards and punishments, all the
causes and effects, contingent on the operation of the principle
of metempsychosis. A few specimen paragraphs will be pertinent here:

"40. Souls, endued with goodness, attain always the state of
deities; those filled with ambitious passions, the condition of

9 Purchas, p. 173.

10 *British Critic*, IX (1797), xi. It had been reviewing the work in sections, so as not
to slight any part of it; and it concluded its series in January (pp. 55–58), after continuing it from the preceding volume (p. 543).

11 *Archiv*, p. 372.

men; and those immersed in darkness, the nature of beasts: this is the triple order of transmigration.

"41. Each of those transmigrations, caused by the several qualities, must also be considered as threefold, the lowest, the mean, and the highest, according to as many distinctions of acts and of knowledge.

"42. Vegetable and mineral substances, worms, insects, and reptiles, some very minute, some rather larger, fish, snakes, tortoises, cattle, shakals [i.e., jackals], are the lowest forms, to which the dark quality leads. . . . .

"57. He, who steals the gold of a priest, shall pass a thousand times into the bodies of spiders, of snakes and cameleons, of *crocodiles and other* aquatick monsters, or of mischievous blood-sucking demons."[12]

The last is a dire threat indeed, and, it is to be hoped, saved their comfortable income undamaged for the good priests who needed its protection. It is mentioned now chiefly as a further instance of the association of transmigration with snakes and "bloodsucking demons", and not with the slightest intention of hinting that any of the characters of "Christabel" had committed, or even contemplated, the robbery of sacerdotal alms boxes.

Moreover, to very much the same effect was an excerpt from the abridgment of the *Philosophical Transactions* which Coleridge had been reading about the same time.[13] The complete article was entitled "An Account of the Bramins in the Indies, &c. by Mr. J. Marshal"—a well-informed exposition, the most interesting part of which is devoted to the Indians' belief in "*Pythagoras's* Transmigration or *Metempsychosis*, but in a grosser Sense" than his. This discussion would have been particularly well calculated to attract Coleridge's attention, for it not only explained the difference between the Brahman and the Greek conceptions, but it combined the transmigration of human souls into reptile bodies with a direct statement of the expiation motif: "For they believe that Mens Souls, that have not lived

[12] *The Works of Sir William Jones* (London, 1799), III, 448–51.
[13] See above, p. 113.

so well as they ought, go, as soon as the Body dies, not only into Birds and Beasts, but even into the basest Reptiles, Insects, and Plants, where they suffer a strong sort of Purgation to expiate their former Crimes. . . . ."[14]

Logically examined, vampirism itself, which lies at the base of much of the present study, is nothing but a phase of metempsychosis. Vampires simply possessed certain unpleasant habits which other reanimated bodies had escaped. Calmet, for instance, noted the belief in the ability of demons to quicken dead bodies and to keep them from disintegration for their own nefarious purposes: ". . . . some learned men have believed that the demon has power to restore life, and to preserve from corruption, for a time, certain bodies which he makes use of to delude mankind and frighten them, as it happens with the ghosts of Hungary. . . . ."[15] This ghostism, which apparently did not necessarily involve a human soul, but might do so, was also mentioned by Ferriar, with no connection with vampiric reanimation: "It is an opinion of considerable antiquity, that the bodies of deceased men were sometimes reanimated by demons."[16]

However, Dr. Ralph Cudworth, the Anglican Neo-Platonist, one of the leaders of the Cambridge group, saw the matter in another light, in his attempt to explain the origin and existence of demons or devils. Cudworth's *The True Intellectual System of the Universe* was never completed,[17] but it was the focal point of a philosophico-religious controversy which has still kept it alive for the braver kind of student. Ferriar referred to it frequently.[18] Coleridge had dared its difficulties at least twice, for he had drawn it from the library first on May 15, 1795, keeping it until June 6, and again on November 9, 1796, keeping it until Decem-

---

[14] *Philosophical Transactions . . . . Abridged,* V, Part II, 165–71.

[15] Calmet, II, 121.

[16] *Manchester Memoirs,* III, 84.

[17] The full title was *The True Intellectual System of the Universe: The First Part, Wherein All the Reason and Philosophy of Atheism Is Confuted and Its Impossibility Demonstrated* (London, 1678).

[18] In his article "Of Popular Illusions," *Manchester Memoirs,* III, 32, 41, 80, and also in his essay on Massinger and his "Observations on the Vital Principle".

ber 13.[19] He could therefore scarcely have missed Cudworth's chapter on "Apparitions, Miracles, and Prophecies", in which the author accepted the possibility, if not the probability, of all these things.[20]

On the authority of "*Sextus* the Philosopher", Democritus, and others he admitted the existence of "Idols or Spectres, that do often approach to men, some of which are Beneficent, and some Maleficent. . . . ." He admitted, too, the probable existence of "*Aerial* and *Aetherial Animals*", as well as "*Terrestrial*". He quoted Psellus to the effect that both angels and demons, or devils, "*are not altogether Incorporeal, but that they are Joyned to Bodies, and so converse with Bodies. . . . .*" Now having warmed to his task, he called on Josephus to testify as to the human origin of these demons: "*Josephus* declares it as his opinion, concerning the *Demons* or *Devils*, that they were . . . . *the Spirits or Souls of wicked men deceased, getting into the Bodies of the Living.*" These dangerous beings he named, by the terms of Josephus, "*Demoniacks* or *Energumeni*". Nor were these creatures confined to the past. "But that there is some Truth in this Opinion, and that at this very day, *Evil Spirits* or *Demons*, do sometimes really Act upon Bodies of men, and either Inflict or Augment bodily Distempers and Diseases, hath been the Judgment of two very experienced Physicians, *Sennertus* and *Fernelius*." Triumphantly concluding his demonstration, Cudworth cited references, quotations, and examples at imposing length, making especially much of the story in Psellus of the woman who spoke Armenian in her seizures, though she had never learned the language or knew it at any other time.

From the preceding rather miscellaneous list of authorities,[21] then, the belief would seem to be confirmed that the passage of souls from one person to another, and from a higher form of life to a lower, and vice versa, was authentic and normal. It was a sort of means of celestial justice, and punishments for sins were thus commonly visited upon the sinners.

---

[19] Kaufman, pp. 319-20.   [20] Cudworth, pp. 700-706.

[21] To them should be added Marshal's account of the Brahmans, discussed above, pp. 134-35.

But this basic theory was in some cases extended even farther, especially among the kabbalists. In anticipation of the modern psychoanalysts and their schizophrenias, the learned men of the Hebrews, seemingly in an effort to account for split personalities and instances of complex demoniac "possession", had assumed various powers for these demons. A couple of pages after his last quoted allusion to the revival of corpses, Calmet introduced the next phase of the topic: multiple reanimation or transmigration. Of this surprising phenomenon, he said: "We see by the Gospel that the Jews of the time of our Saviour believed that one man could be animated by several souls. Herod imagined that the spirit of John the Baptist, whom he had beheaded, had entered into Jesus Christ, and worked miracles in him. . . . ." To Calmet's mind, however, this was pure superstition, for such a thing would be contrary to "religion".[22]

Nevertheless, this mystical and panpsychic view of the world, and of the interrelationship of all things in it, would be well calculated to appeal to one of Coleridge's temperament. For he was much concerned at this time with the ideas of vengeance, retribution, and expiation. He had been reading intensively in the Bible and the Apocrypha, and marking passages for reflection. In his memorandum book he set down quotations such as this from Ecclesiasticus:[23] "There are spirits that are created to Vengeance in the time of Destruction they pour out their force and appease the Wrath of him that made them."[24] A less harsh and vindictive view, however, had just been re-expressed by his favorite Thomas Taylor, who had recently translated the "Phaedrus" of Plato, with commentary. Taylor's explanation of the Platonic theology, with its three orders or species of demons, is essentially one of expiation and amelioration. The Platonic classification called for three groupings of spirits: the first rational, the second both rational and irrational, and the third irrational. "And again of these the first is purely beneficent, but many among the other two species are malevolent

---

[22] Calmet, II, 123, 125 ff.   [23] *Archiv*, p. 355.

[24] Ecclesiasticus 39:28. The revised version of the Apocrypha, however, translates "spirits" as "winds".

and noxious to mankind; not indeed essentially malevolent (for there is nothing in the universe, the ample abode of all-bountiful Jove, essentially evil), but only so from the office which they are destined to perform: for nothing which operates naturally, operates as to itself evilly. But the Platonic Hermias, in his MS. Commentary on this dialogue, admirably observes on this passage as follows: 'The distribution of good and evil originates from the daemoniacal genus: for every genus, transcending that of daemons, uniformly possesses good. There are therefore certain genera of daemons, some of which adorn and administer certain parts of the world; but others certain species of animals. The daemon therefore, who is the inspective guardian of life, hastens souls into that condition, which he himself is allotted; as for instance, into injustice or intemperance, and continually mingles pleasure in them as a snare. But there are other daemons transcending these, who are the punishers of souls, converting them to a more pure and elevated life. And the first of these it is necessary to avoid; but the second sort we should render propitious. But there are other daemons more excellent than these, who distribute good, in a uniform manner.' "[25] This function of converting to a higher life Lowes perceives exemplified in the polar demon in "The Ancient Mariner".[26] It is surely a function which, embodied thus figuratively, was quite harmonious with Coleridge's philosophy.

In this welter of individual views on the life and alliance of soul and body it may seem at first that nothing can be made of an almost chaos in which each person of any independence of mind virtually invents his own cosmogony. Yet, if so many others before have done so, what is to prevent an author from trying to devise a new one of his own? Certain fundamental principles were at least accepted as to the existence of spirits and essences, benevolent and malevolent, which might invest a human body and endeavor to direct it for its own good or ill. There were reputed laws and ordinances through which a soul might achieve its own salvation or destruction.

[25] [Thomas Taylor,] *The Phaedrus of Plato* .... (London, 1792), p. 39 n.
[26] Lowes, p. 236.

Just what principles Coleridge intended to embody in Geraldine will probably never be known with absolute dogmatism. Apparently he was none too clear on the subject himself, or he would not have undergone the abortive agonies that he did to finish his story satisfactorily. Yet the paradoxes of her conduct all suggest that she was the victim of some such demonic possession as the believers in metempsychosis had described with such profusion. The alternating weakness and strength of Geraldine in the first canto, the internal contention which is always continuing within her, her sudden change of voice as she first echoes Christabel's prayer to her dead mother and then reminds the latter's invisible spirit that she has a mission to perform, her seemingly sincere remark that those "who live in the upper sky" love Christabel and that for their sake she too will try to requite the girl well, her attempt to pray before she lies down on the bed, her disgust at her own secret mark, her refreshment and beauty as she awakes from sleep—all these things and others imply clearly that she is at the mercy of contending forces struggling within her for mastery. Yet, as Christabel herself gasps out, clairvoyantly perceiving the outcome of the situation even in the midst of her own distraction and pain, "All will yet be well!"

Cornelius Agrippa went so far as to hold out hope that even some of the angels, or devils, who had been cast out of heaven with Lucifer might be redeemed. *"Origen's* opinion concerning the devils," he said in his *Three Books of Occult Philosophy,* "is: The spirits who out of their own free will, left the service of God with their Prince the devil; if they begun to repent a little, are clothed with humane flesh; That further by this repentance, after the resurrection, by the same means by which they came into the flesh, they might at the last return to the vision of God. . . . ."[27] If there is hope for the fallen angels themselves, through their taking human flesh upon them, there is surely hope for such an unwilling and contrite instrument of destiny as Geraldine.

[27] Agrippa, p. 401.

BOOK III

SUBSIDIARY ELEMENTS

I

THE GUARDIAN SPIRIT

IN THE cast of "Christabel", however, Geraldine is not the
only member who has ties with a world above and beyond,
or perhaps around and within, the human. This other
member is never given a specific name, nor does she ever actually appear so that she can be seen even in the imagination by the
reader. Nor does she utter a word which he can hear. Yet Geraldine, in a brief but ghostly interview, apparently both sees
and hears this spectral visitor, for she not only remonstrates
with her but also seems to ward off an attack by her. This
tenuous character is of course the dead mother of Christabel.
Undoubtedly, if Coleridge had redeemed the promise guaran-
teed in the first part of his own poem (and what writer of supernatural fiction of this type has ever dared to flout his own prophecies?), the mother's spirit would have somehow materialized
at the climax of the story, perhaps through a visible body, perhaps only through a voice, this time audible to all. But, whatever the means might have been, the reader would have known
that she had heard the castle bell strike twelve on her daughter's wedding day.[1]

This mother, however, is somehow more integrally bound up
with the situation and action. In awaiting the prophesied
event, she is not gruesomely confined to her grave, or immured
in purgatory, or even mewed up in a beatific heaven, in accordance with any of the commoner views of man's post-mortem
fate. Her spirit, in fact, has seemingly never completely left

[1] So, e.g., in Walpole's *The Castle of Otranto*, it is reported at the opening of the story
that Manfred is living in fear of the prophecy that "*the Castle and Lordship of* Otranto
*should pass from the present family whenever the real owner should be grown too large to
inhabit it.*" In the final chapter, of course, the prophecy is accomplished exactly,
since Manfred's son and daughter both die, the castle falls, and "the form of *Alphonso,*
dilated to an immense magnitude, appeared in the center of the ruins," and immediately afterward "ascended solemnly toward Heaven" (Walpole, *The Castle of Otranto
and The Mysterious Mother*, London, 1924).

the castle of Sir Leoline, as Geraldine's terrified protests indicate; at least, it has never permanently deserted the vicinity of the daughter for whose birth the mother's life was sacrificed. The mother, as Geraldine's speech announces, has become Christabel's "guardian spirit". At the same time, however, she is addressed as "wandering mother" and ordered to "Peak and pine!" Perhaps Coleridge's intention was to imply that the mother's commission was a sort of roving one—that on occasions of necessity and danger she was permitted to hasten to her daughter's side, but that at other times she remained in purgatory, where even the purest souls undergo the process of further purification suggested in the "Peak and pine!" and where Geraldine now wished her to return. Once more there seems to be in Coleridge's conceptions a conflict of pagan and Christian elements which makes for mystery and uncertainty.

The invention of a mother who has died in childbed is highly appropriate from the dramatic point of view, since it intensifies the childishness and helplessness of Christabel. There is nothing so extremely original in the situation as to demand that Coleridge get the idea from any particular source, and yet certain somewhat contradictory suggestions have been made. One of these has even implied that there was a personal, even autobiographical, background to it. In the *Anima Poetae*, a selection of passages from Coleridge's unpublished notebooks, Ernest Hartley Coleridge, its editor, included a note, dated 1810, which he headed "A Hint for *Christabel*". This reads: "My first cries mingled with my mother's death-groan, and she beheld the vision of glory ere I the earthly sun. When I first looked up to Heaven consciously, it was to look up after, or for, my mother."[2] At first glance, the parallel between this passage and the poem seems so striking as perfectly to justify E. H. C.'s heading. But then, one wonders, why did Coleridge wait until 1810 to set it down? One can assume, of course, such a thorough revision of the poem after 1810 as to allow the assimilation of the detail without harming the unity of the whole, but such an assumption is contrary to all the known evidence. Or one can assume—as

[2] *Anima Poetae. From the Unpublished Notebooks of Samuel Taylor Coleridge* (London, 1895), p. 223.

has been done too hastily[3]—that Coleridge had not copied the lines from any of his reading[4] but was really referring to himself and his own mother—a manifest impossibility, because she did not die until 1809, when he was thirty-seven years old!

This "Hint for *Christabel*", however, obviously did not impress even its presenter very seriously, for when E. H. C. brought out his elaborate edition of the poem in 1907 he failed to recall it. Instead, he had by this time found another parallel to advance, one which it cannot be denied bears a vague resemblance to the situation in Coleridge, but which is admissible largely because the work in which it occurs contains several other possible hints of a similar very general nature. In January, 1798 (Coleridge's copy is dated January 20), probably while he was at Shrewsbury, the poet bought a copy of the most talked-about play of the season—Matthew Gregory Lewis's *The Castle Spectre*.[5] The play and its popular reception so annoyed and aroused him that soon thereafter he wrote a long letter to Wordsworth, mostly in criticism of Lewis and public taste.[6] The only merit he could detect in this melodrama was "in its *situations*", which, although "all borrowed and all absolutely *pantomimical*", were at least "admirably managed for stage effect". Now one of these situations, as it happened (though he did not specify it in his letter), had to do with the rumor in the haunted castle that the ghost of the murdered Lady Evelina, Angela's mother, had been heard by many of the household playing a guitar and singing a lullaby. As Motley (who is, of course, the wise fool) put it: "Above all, they say that the spirit of the late Countess sits nightly in her Oratory, and sings her baby to sleep."[7] This regularity and exact localization of performance, obviously, are very different from the apparitional habits of Christabel's mother; but the fact that Lewis's melodrama, which

---

[3] Such is the clear implication of McElderry (*Studies in Philology*, XXXIII, 451 n.), when he introduces his quotation of the note by saying: "A note by Coleridge, dated 1810, and entitled 'A Hint for *Christabel*,' suggests that the emphasis of Christabel's mother was no accident....."

[4] I have not been able to locate their real source.

[5] E.H.C., pp. 13–14.   [6] *Letters*, I, 236–38.

[7] Lewis, *The Castle Spectre: A Drama* (London, 1798), p. 16.

Coleridge had been thinking seriously about at the time when he was writing "Christabel", has a dead mother who watches over her child is irrefutable. On the other hand, the fact that the Lady Evelina has been *murdered* a considerable time *after* the birth of her daughter is equally undeniable. The search for a ghostly mother who has died in childbed leads up a blind alley.

The trail of the mother as a "guardian spirit", however, may yield more profitable results. Such beings were, of course, familiar enough to Coleridge. He had put one into "The Ancient Mariner" in an incidental role and had twice referred to its custodianship of his ancient sinner. First, when the mariner's hard heart is melted by the sight of the life and beauty of the water snakes (for snakes form a vital element in this poem too), he attributes his repentance to this heavenly mentor:

> Sure my kind saint took pity on me,
> And I blessed them unaware.

Second, a few stanzas later, so that the mariner will not be alone in recognizing this otherworldly aid, Coleridge inserts a marginal gloss to explain the cause of the reanimation of the corpses of the dead crew: "But not by the souls of men, nor by daemons of earth or middle air, but by a blessed troop of angelic spirits, sent down by the invocation of the guardian saint."[8] In a somewhat similar fashion his friend Joseph Cottle, in his *Alfred*, had inducted another member of the genus into his story and had entitled one entire book "The Vision of the Guardian Angel". This helpful spirit had introduced himself to Alfred with the following explanatory speech:

> . . . . I am one
> Of the innumerable host, who throng
> This lower world; communicants of good.
> I am thy Guardian Angel! From the hour
> This world received thee, I have been thy friend,
> And ever near, commissioned by high Heaven
> To screen thee from the powers that roam abroad
> Hostile to human kind. . . . .[9]

[8] *Poems*, pp. 198, 200.   [9] Cottle, *Alfred*, II, 227.

Thus, both Cottle and Coleridge were accustomed to people their worlds with spirits benevolent and malevolent, contending for humankind.

Note, however, that there is a difference between the "guardian spirit" of "Christabel" and the "guardian saint" and "guardian angel" of "The Ancient Mariner" and *Alfred*. For the author of "Christabel" is by no means so good a medieval Christian as the authors of the other two works. In this matter of guardianship, the churchmen, the philosophers, and the demonologists found it as hard to agree as they did in most of the problems which they insisted on confronting. There was the Catholic point of view, and the Protestant; the pagan, and the Neo-Platonic. By the seventeenth century not many besides a few scholars knew how to differentiate among them, so much had they become entangled with one another; but, on the whole, the Catholic viewpoint was officially maintained with fair consistency and conviction. According to it, this celestial guardian is not a human being at all, and never has been. The proper term is "guardian angel". The creature thus belongs to another species than our own, though not far above it, since its position is in the very lowest order of the angelical hierarchy. This doctrine, it is true, admits the *Catholic Encyclopaedia* today, has never been made an article of faith, but it has always been accepted by the church as correct.[10] Coleridge could scarcely have been unacquainted with these opinions. If he had not met the controversy anywhere else, he could hardly have missed it in his reading of Pierre Bayle, for immediately after the latter's article on "Cain", which the poet had read for his projected poem, there was another on "Cainites", containing a long footnote on "Tutelar Angels" and allied matters.[11]

Thus Joseph Cottle was completely orthodox in his "Guardian Angel". In "The Rime of the Ancient Mariner", however, though the mariner himself was obviously a solid Catholic according to his lights, Coleridge did not make the status of his "guardian saint" as evident as he might; but at least, if originally human, it had undergone a process of beatification and was

[10] *Catholic Encyclopaedia* (New York, 1913), VII, 49–50.   [11] Bayle, II, 806–7.

therefore on a special plane of classification. It remained in heaven to intercede for the mariner and look out for his interests there. In "Christabel", on the contrary, it is simply a "guardian spirit"; and this description takes us back directly to paganism. Even among the Neo-Platonists these demons were accounted of a divine and spiritual order. So Iamblichus, the first of the authors in the little anthology Thelwall bought for Coleridge, would have told him in his discussion *De mysteriis Aegyptiorum, Chaldaeorum, Assyriorum.* Summoning Olympiodorus to his support, Iamblichus would have informed him that, even before "the soul descends to generation", these tutelar watchmen are assigned to it.[12] Since Christabel's mother died in bearing her, she could scarcely have qualified in this category.

Apuleius, however, was a thoroughly pagan member of the Neo-Platonic mystics, and his dissertation "De deo Socratis" was well known. Here Coleridge could, and probably did, find what is doubtless the most direct and lucid account of the various kinds of souls, or demons.[13] First is the human soul—the immortal "daemon" or "genius" which is generated with man. Next come the "lemures"—human souls which have not entered new bodies after the death of the old ones. These are divided into two classes—the familiar or domestic "lars", who, being assigned to guard their posterity, dwell quietly in men's houses; and the "larvae", "who, having no proper habitation, are punished with an uncertain wandering, as with a certain exile, on account of the evil deeds of their life, and become a vain terror to good, and are noxious to bad men. . . . ." Finally, there is a still "more sublime order of daemons", from which "Plato asserts that a peculiar daemon is allotted to every man, who is a witness and a guardian of his conduct in life. . . . ."[14] This exegesis of Apuleius upon Socrates, through Plato, is somewhere in the background of almost every later discussion of the subject, medieval, Renaissance, or modern.[15]

[12] See Thomas Taylor's translation of *Iamblichus on the Mysteries of the Egyptians, Chaldeans, and Assyrians* (Chiswick, 1821), pp. 321–23, 339–40.

[13] For Coleridge's reading of Apuleius, see above, p. 132, n. 8.

[14] Taylor's translation of *The Metamorphosis*, pp. 306–8.

[15] See, e.g., Lavater, pp. 2–5, who also cites St. Augustine, Festus, Macrobius, Porphyrius, Servius, and Apollonius—without clarifying the situation much further, however.

Additional material which bears directly on other aspects of Geraldine's spectral interview, lending precedent, if not inspiration, to Coleridge's treatment, may be found in John Beaumont's *An Historical, Physiological and Theological Treatise of Spirits*. In his fourth chapter, which he entitles *"What Perception some Persons have had of Genii, or Spirits by the Sense of seeing, when others present at the same time have seen nothing"*, Beaumont relates how these people are generally known as *"Second-Sighted Persons"*, gives various most remarkable tales of their experiences, and climaxes his revelations by admitting that he himself is one of this type and has seen and been plagued by hundreds of spirits, invisible to others, for months together. Such a thorough analyst as he, however, would not be satisfied to stop here, and so he devotes his second following chapter to *"What perception some Persons have had of Genii, or Spirits, and their Operations by the Sense of Hearing, when others present have heard nothing"*.[16] Thus Geraldine, who both sees and hears something that is denied to Christabel, is both second-sighted and second-eared; she is quite within the conventions of ghostly tradition, as is her spectral visitant.

If, then, something of the same process of assimilation and storage of the memory as Lowes has postulated for "The Ancient Mariner" and "Kubla Khan" may be assumed for "Christabel", Coleridge's creation of the character of Christabel's guardian spirit, her dead mother, came to pass in a devious way, piecing detail out with detail, sometimes incongruous or downright contradictory, but ending with a fabrication wholly harmonious with his purpose. Basically, Christabel's mother has in death become a "lar". Her soul has not entered into another body after her demise, but, undertaking the protection of her posterity, has settled down to abide in her own house, where she is found shortly after the story opens. On the other hand, Geraldine addresses her as "wandering spirit". But, according to Apuleius, Socrates, and the Neo-Platonics, it was not the

---

[16] John Beaumont, *An Historical, Physiological and Theological Treatise of Spirits, Apparitions, Witchcrafts, and Other Magical Practices* . . . . (London, 1705), pp. 82 ff. The phenomenon of "limited appearance" is, of course, conventional ghostly behavior. Eichler (p. 27) calls attention to the conduct of the ghosts in *Hamlet* and *Macbeth* in this respect.

"lar" but the "larva" which was doomed to wander as a punishment for its past life. Coleridge has, consequently, combined two mutually incompatible details, since the "lar" was a friendly spirit, the "larva" an unfriendly. His supernatural being is therefore essentially a pagan, not a Christian, conception, for she corresponds with neither the Catholic "guardian angel" nor the "guardian saint"; she does not belong to another order of creation, nor does she have any of the identifying features of the patron saint in "The Rime".

Yet perhaps it was a fleeting trace of Catholic doctrine in Coleridge's mind which may explain and reconcile the apparent contradiction; and this clue introduces, incidentally, still another feature in the brief episode. When Geraldine asserts her authority and commission, it will be recalled, she uses a very peculiar formula as part of her commands of dismissal:

> Off, wandering mother! Peak and pine!
> I have power to bid thee flee.

"Peak and pine!"—an attractive and memorable alliterative pair—seems to be a queer phrase in this connection. Did Coleridge make it up for his purpose? I believe that he did not. It was echoing in his mind from one of the most celebrated witch-passages in literature and was ready to fall unconsciously into its place. Here are the original significant lines:

> He shall live a man forbid.
> Weary sevennights nine times nine
> Shall he dwindle, peak, and pine.

The context is immaterial, for it concerns an intended revenge on a sailor whose wife has refused to share her chestnuts with the vindictive speaker. To Coleridge, all this unessential matter fell away as dross in the crucible. The essential link is that the words are those of the First Witch in *Macbeth* (Act I, scene iii, ll. 21–23) and that Geraldine, in addition to her other protean characteristics, has much of the witch in her. What more natural than to associate Shakespeare's phrase with her?

Yet "peak, and pine" as Shakespeare used the words meant simply "waste away". As Coleridge uses them, they plainly mean "vanish". Or can they mean something like "Go back to the place where you came from"? If so, we may perhaps perceive the association in Coleridge's mind and realize the process by which he combined the "lar" and the "larva" in a single person. If "Peak and pine!" was, strictly, a command to "waste away", it could not be obeyed until the hearer had returned to her proper place where wasting and languishing were appropriate. Now, a few months before Coleridge began "Christabel", he had been reading Dante, in the Reverend Henry Boyd's recent translation.[17] It is true that by this year Boyd had finished only the "Inferno", though he was to bring out the whole poem long before Coleridge's was published. Although Coleridge's knowledge of Italian cannot be dated definitely much before 1804,[18] there is no reason why he could not have had a general familiarity with the "Purgatorio" at the time he was reading the translation of the "Inferno".

And here in purgatory, of course (whether he had been imagining its lurid scenes through the stimulus of Dante or through other popular conceptions), the souls of those who are not damned undergo the refining process which will eventually admit them into paradise. Particularly vivid is Dante's description, in cantos 23 and 24, of the souls inhabiting certain of the circles near the top of the ascent. The figures of these persons are terribly emaciated, and their faces are drawn with hunger and thirst; yet they are grateful for their purgation. Shortly afterward (canto 27) Dante himself, with Virgil and Statius his guides, is forced to pass through the cleansing fire before he can enter the Garden of Eden. Perhaps this picture, or one similar to it, based on the conventional views of purgatory, was some-

[17] See p. 110.

[18] A note by Coleridge on his 1796 *Sonnets* (see James Dykes Campbell's edition of *The Poetical Works*, London, 1925, p. 542 n.) states that he "did not understand a word of Italian" at this time. In one of "Satyrane's Letters" in 1798 (*The Complete Works*, ed. W. G. Shedd, New York, 1884, III, 524), he quotes a simple Italian pun. Not until he takes his voyage to Malta in 1804, however, does he write to the Wordsworths about buying "Dante and a dictionary" (letter of February 8, 1804, *Letters*, II, 458). On April 16, 1804, he writes Southey that he has "done little else than read through the Italian Grammar" (*ibid.*, II, 474).

where in Coleridge's thoughts when he fetched his "guardian spirit" from some anonymous place to watch over her daughter, and then had Geraldine, temporary wielder of a superior force, bid her flee and return to her wasting away.[19]

[19] It should be noted, however, that the mother's spirit did not really obey Geraldine's command. At least, at the end of "The Conclusion to Part I", after Christabel's tranquillity returns to her in her sleep, Coleridge explains:

"No doubt, she hath a vision sweet.
What if her guardian spirit 'twere,
What if she knew her mother near?"

As a matter of fact, of course, Christabel had never known her mother.

II

MISCELLANEA, NATURAL AND SUPERNATURAL

AMONG the supernatural paraphernalia appropriated by Coleridge for "Christabel", there are many details which are purely incidental to the main plot and characters, but which enrich the background like an arabesque embroidery. Most of these, indeed, are so traditional that it would manifestly be labor lost to attempt to trace them to any individual source or even to suggest that Coleridge came upon them in any particular type of reading. To one or two of them, nevertheless, he has given such an original turn that some more specific fountainhead seems to be likely, though not necessarily to be found in books.

Certainly he has included several commonplaces of folklore and the supernatural, such as might be discovered in almost any fairy tale. Geraldine's appearance at the witching hour of midnight is, of course, a simple example of his compliance with tradition. Authority for this timing of her arrival might be found in plenty of the handbooks of witchcraft, such as F. M. Guazzo's *Compendium maleficarum* in 1608.[1] The behavior of the notorious "mastiff bitch" is a similar case in point, for this ancient animal moans angrily in her sleep while Geraldine glides past her kennel. Obviously the dog, even in her dreams, has some occult power which responds immediately and spontaneously to the presence of any demoniac or inimical element. Thus Lavater, in his dissertation *Of Ghostes and Spirites Walking by*

[1] Guazzo, *Compendium maleficarum* (ed. Montague Summers, London, 1929), pp. 35–36. See also Hyde, *Greek Religion*, pp. 136–37. Tuttle (pp. 453–54, 461) finds the original of this timing, as well as of practically all the details of the girls' trip through the dark, echoing hall of the castle, in a passage from *The Mysteries of Udolpho* which has nothing to do with the supernatural. Christabel's propensity to such midnight wanderings also finds an interesting parallel in *Udolpho*, where Emily contracts similar bad habits and often hears moaning sounds (usually the wind) in the distance (Tuttle, pp. 458–59).

Nyght, shivers while he explains: "Some mã walketh alone in his house, & behold a spirit apeereth in his sight, yea & sometimes ỹ dogs also perceue thẽ, & fal down at their masters fete, & wil by no means depart fro thẽ, for they ar sore afraid thẽselues too."[2] Because of the prevalence and vulgar acceptance of such old-wives' tales, Alois Brandl's attempt to trace the inspiration of this canine phenomenon, as well as the flickering of the flame in the fireplace when Geraldine passes, is as airy as most of his speculations concerning the poem.[3] Though the same combination of evidences of supernatural presence occurs in Monk Lewis's ballad "Alonzo the Brave, and Fair Imogine" in *Ambrosio or the Monk*, their recurrence in "Christabel" may be easily attributable to coincidence, just as may the stealthy entry of the two girls into the castle, which Brandl gleefully parallels with vaguely similar scenes in Ann Radcliffe's *The Romance of the Forest* and *The Mysteries of Udolpho*.[4] All of these passages, however, attest the existence of a widespread stereotype for such narratives.

In the same class falls the episode at the "little door" which Christabel opened "All in the middle of the gate" to bring her unexpected guest into the castle.[5] Here, on the very threshold,

---

[2] Lavater, p. 71.

[3] E.g., in his *Coleridge* (p. 211) he cites as authority for the dog's uneasiness the epilog speech of Robin Goodfellow in *A Midsummer Night's Dream*:

> "Now the hungry lion roars,
>   And the wolf behowls the moon;
> Whilst the heavy ploughman snores,
>   All with weary task fordone.
> Now the wasted brands do glow,
>   Whilst the screech-owl, screeching loud,
> Puts the wretch that lies in woe
>   In remembrance of a shroud.
> Now it is the time of night
>   That the graves, all gaping wide,
> Every one lets forth his sprite,
>   In the church-way paths to glide."

Even Eichler (p. 25) cannot understand the relevance of these lines. Obviously they would be more pertinent if the idea of a vampire had been in Brandl's mind, but in any case the parallel would remain extremely farfetched.

[4] Brandl, *Coleridge*, p. 212. Eichler (pp. 26–27) also quotes Brandl.

[5] Tuttle (p. 455) finds this door in some iron gates in *Udolpho*.

Geraldine sank down, "belike through pain," and the delicate Christabel was compelled to lift her and carry her inside. This incident, says Brandl, came "Auf dem alten Aberglauben"; and E. H. C. cites two or three similar remarks by modern writers.[6] The underlying theory, of course, is highly moral and symbolical: evil cannot attack one unless one allows it to enter by one's own act and permission. The principle is the same as that which Southey introduced into *Thalaba* shortly after his documented passage on vampires; in this scene Thalaba unwittingly binds himself with the golden thread of Maimuna, sister of Khawla, for in order that this thread may hold, a person must tie it himself. Interestingly enough, in Southey's story, Maimuna soon thereafter repents of her evil designs, reforms, and releases the young hero.[7]

One of the simplest and most vivid pictures in the whole poem, which consists of a series of vivid pictures, is the scene in Christabel's chaste and girlish bedchamber, with its rush-covered floor and its walls

> Carved with figures strange and sweet,
> All made out of the carver's brain,
> For a lady's chamber meet. . . . .[8]

Though "The moon shines dim in the open air", here not a moonbeam can enter. Yet the two girls, as they come in, do not need the moon's aid to see, for the room is lighted by a silver lamp, now burning "dead and dim". There is something unusual about this illumination. As Coleridge says,

> The lamp with twofold silver chain
> Is fastened to an angel's feet.

When Christabel has brought her guest into her boudoir, she turns to trim the lamp. After she has made the room bright and has inadvertently left the lamp swinging to and fro, she looks about at Geraldine, but to her surprise and consternation finds

[6] Brandl, p. 212; E.H.C., p. 70 n.

[7] Southey, *Poetical Works*, pp. 281, 291.

[8] E.H.C. (p. 15), echoed by Tuttle (p. 470 n.), finds the original of this chamber in the oratory "richly ornamented with carving" from Lewis's *The Castle Spectre* (Act III, scene iii).

that her new friend, "in wretched plight," has sunk "down upon the floor below" and must again be revived. Clearly the angel, and especially the wavering of its shadow about the room, have had the same effect upon Geraldine as her preserver's previous suggestion that they offer a prayer to the Virgin, "Who hath rescued thee from thy distress!" It is the same effect that, according to the instructions of the church and the demonologists, the sign of the Cross will have in warding off evil. Something of the same potency has been subtly transferred to the figure of the angel holding the lamp. How did this angel come to be in the picture? Was it really "All made out of the carver's brain", or had Coleridge's imagination, as usual, again been remolding the clay of his poetical accumulations nearer to his heart's desire?

After he had begun "Christabel" and had left it with only one canto written (and this probably not truly "finished"), he had put it aside and, with a party of friends, had gone to Germany. From there he had sent letters to various people in England, describing his experiences, his thoughts, and his studies. Some of these letters were naturally to his wife, for whom, in her loneliness and among her domestic responsibilities, he, with his fundamentally uxorious nature, felt some concern. On April 23, 1799, he was in the town of Göttingen, having come from Ratzeburg, which, like its fellows in Germany, had impressed him with some of its curious customs and institutions. The churches, especially, had challenged comparison with the churches of England, as they easily might in a man who had spent so much of his life in going in and out of them. The method of ringing bells, for instance, was quite different in the two nations, and he wrote his wife to that effect. Most amusing of all, however, was a strange part of the ritual of baptism, which he described to Mrs. Coleridge thus: "In the churches, what is a baptismal font in our churches is a great Angel with a bason in his hand; he draws up and down with a chain like a lamp. In a particular part of the ceremony down comes the great stone Angel with the bason, presenting it to the pastor, who, having taken *quant.*

suff., up flies my Angel to his old place in the ceiling—you cannot conceive how droll it looked."[9]

Here are all the essentials of the setting in Christabel's bedchamber, distorted and even comical, but easily recognizable. Here is the angel, large and made of stone (as apparently the carved angel in Christabel's chamber was), and probably very clumsy, but nevertheless an angel that moves, as the shadows do on Christabel's wall. Here are the chain and the lamp. The latter appears in two forms: first, in the pure comparison, "like a lamp," and second, as the transmogrified "bason", which is held in the German angel's hand, somewhat as the lamp is attached to the English angel's feet. The chain which draws the German angel up and down to the accomplishment of its pious mission has become the "twofold silver chain" holding the English lamp in its place, and allowing it to swing as the baptismal angel undoubtedly did on its return journey to its precarious perch among the church rafters, casting shadows on the walls as it went. It is even possible that the idea of the double strand and the feet to which it was fastened may have been unconsciously suggested by the sentence immediately preceding the two which I have quoted. For, in telling his wife about the German bell-ringers, Coleridge had written: "By the bye, the bells in Germany are not rung as ours, with ropes, but two men stand, one on each side of the bell, and each pushes the bell away from him with his foot." If it should be argued that he was not likely to associate in his memory two such separate pictures as these put into chance juxtaposition in his letter, I might suggest that, after all, people do reread their own letters, especially those describing their travels. There was nothing to prevent Coleridge from looking over his husbandly missives after his return to England. In fact, his recurrent fondness for them is attested by his printing some of them first in *The Friend* in 1809–10, again in the *Biographia Literaria* in 1817,

---

[9] *Letters*, I, 293. This passage has been immediately preceded by a long discussion of the superstitions of the German *Bauern*, especially among the Catholics. Coleridge's interest centered particularly on prayers and vows to the Virgin. "If any one dies before the performance of his vow, they believe that he hovers between heaven and *earth*, and at times hobgoblins his relations till they perform it for him" (*ibid.*, p. 291).

and also in the expanded *Friend* in 1818. And it was not long after his return that he began to work again on "Christabel".[10] The appearance of the angel in the first part, and not in the second, is good evidence that he did not leave the opening section intact after first composing it, as, with his untrustworthy memory for such facts, he has implied.[11]

One more detail of an otherworldly nature remains to be dealt with, or German scholarship will be offended. For it is the German scholars who, in their "detection" of remote or

[10] The silver lamp and the angel have bothered Tuttle considerably, since in Ann Radcliffe's Gothic novels he found plenty of ebony crucifixes, Etruscan lamps, silver tripods depending from silver chains, etc., but no angel (Tuttle, pp. 455, 456, 461 and n., 473–74). I am glad to be able to offer him the original.

[11] Further proof to the same effect is afforded by a note in Coleridge's own hand on the manuscript which E. H. C. prints in facsimile. On pp. 19 and 81 n. he calls special attention to this note, printed by him for the first time. The note reads: "Tairn or Tarn (derived by Lye from the Icelandic *Tiorn*, stagnum, palus) is rendered in our Dictionaries as synonymous with Mere or Lake; but it is properly a large Pool or Reservoir in the Mountains, commonly the Feeder of some Mere in the Valleys. Tarn Watling & Blellum Tarn, tho' on lower Ground than other Tarns, are yet not exceptions—for both are on elevations, and Blellum Tarn feeds the Wynander Mere." The "Lye" referred to is the Rev. Edward Lye, whose aid Percy acknowledged at the end of his opening preface to the *Reliques* as follows: "It is perhaps needless to name the Rev. Mr. Lye, editor of Junius's *Etymologicum*, and of the *Gothic Gospels*." The derivation mentioned is found under "Tarn" in *Francisci Junii . . . . Etymologicum Anglicanum. Ex autographo descripsit et accessionibus permultis auctum edidit Edwardus Lye . . . .* (Oxford, 1743). Since "tairn" is a North Country term, one would naturally expect it to be found in Part II of the poem, but such is not the case. Instead, it and its note occur as part of "The Conclusion to Part I", in the passage

> "By tairn and rill,
> The night-birds all that hour were still."

As E. H. C. suggests, the note must have been "designed for the instruction of South Country readers", and thus would appear to have been composed to explain a word which Coleridge had introduced after he had gone north. E. H. C. continues: "Blelham Tarn he had visited with Wordsworth in November 1799, but his knowledge of Tarn Watling, which lies above High Hesket on the road from Penrith to Carlisle, may have been derived from a map or guide-book or, in the first instance, from Percy's *Reliques* ('Marriage of Sir Gawaine,' part i, stanza 6). The spelling, Blellum for Blelham, and Wynander Mere, corresponds with entries in the journal of the tour in November 1799. In the first edition Windermere (line 344) is printed Wyn'dermere, evidently an abbreviation of Wynander Mere." The reference to "The Marriage of Sir Gawaine" is worth following further, for not only is "Tearne-Wadling" the site of the castle of the disrespectful giant who overcame King Arthur, but the name is also glossed thus by Percy (III, 24 n.): "*Tearne-Wadling* is the name of a small lake near Hesketh in Cumberland, on the road from Penrith to Carlisle. There is a tradition, that an old castle once stood near the lake, the remains of which were not long since visible. *Tearn*, in the dialect of that country, signifies a small lake, and is still in use." Incidentally, it should not be forgotten that this is the ballad in which appears that "lothlye ladye",

nonexistent parallels to "Christabel", have insisted most emphatically on Coleridge's influence by Gottfried Bürger's famous ballad of "Lenore", first published in the Göttingen *Musenalmanach* early in 1774. There is, of course, little doubt that Coleridge was acquainted with the German poem before he started to write "Christabel". If he had not met with it in its own language, he could scarcely have escaped it in the spate of translations which constituted a significant phenomenon in the gathering flood of English romanticism in the 1790's.[12]

---

with her "haires, like serpents," whom Gawaine loyally married in order to save the honor of his king, only to find when "they were in wed-bed laid" that she had turned into the "fairest flower" he had ever seen and that his marriage with her had released both her and her giant brother from the spell which her stepmother the witch had laid upon them.

[12] In the single month of July, 1796, for example, his attention must have been called to all of the four leading translations, or adaptations, that had been attempted up to that time. (Although Walter Scott's adaptation had been published in a very small private edition in the spring of 1796, the first public edition, in *The Chase and William and Helen*, was not made until the fall.) The most spirited and authentic of these four was that of William Taylor of Norwich, who had stirred his readers to an extraordinary pitch of enthusiasm. This admiration was shared by Charles Lamb, who could hardly contain himself until he had communicated his feeling to Coleridge. In a letter of July 6, Lamb wrote: "Have you read the Ballad called 'Leonora,' in the second Number of the 'Monthly Magazine'? If you have ! ! ! ! ! ! ! ! ! ! ! ! ! ! ! There is another fine song, from the same author (Berger), in the 3d No., of scarce inferior merit . . . . " (Lamb, *Letters*, I, 37. The "second Number" was that of March, 1796. Taylor later revised this version, which had actually been composed in 1790). In case Coleridge had not done this reading or did not respond to his friend's challenge immediately, he could scarcely have escaped coming into contact with Bürger's story in another way during this month or shortly after. One of the periodicals which he regularly read was *The Critical Review*; on September 27, for instance, he drew the May, 1796, number from the Bristol Library (Kaufman, p. 319). The June number contained a review of his own *Poems*, as well as another of Southey's *Joan of Arc*, one paragraph of which was devoted to the second book, which the critic pointed out had been composed mostly by Coleridge himself in a vindication of his theories of the preternatural (*Critical Review*, XVII, June, 1796, 188). And in the July number appeared a rather lengthy review of the three other translations of "Lenore" which had recently been made by J. T. Stanley, W. R. Spencer, and the poetaster laureate, H. J. Pye (*ibid.*, pp. 303–8). The method of the reviewer, who was by no means biased in favor of all these versions, was to support his criticisms by summarizing and excerpting the three poems so fully that the reader would carry away a pretty complete impression of both them and their original.

Did Coleridge know any of these versions or approaches to Bürger by 1797 or 1798? No one has questioned that he did. Certainly he was familiar with them a year or two later, for they form the subject of an interesting discussion and correspondence involving Taylor himself, Southey, Wordsworth, and Coleridge, after the return of the last from his German trip. In his remarks at this time Coleridge revealed himself as stopping far short of the unrestrained admiration of Lamb; it was an interest and a sympathy

Somewhere in this maze of German and Anglo-German balladry, according to several German scholars (Professor Alois Brandl in particular),[13] Coleridge is supposed to have obtained more of his material for "Christabel". Bürger's story (which many have intimated was suggested to him in part by the ballad "Sweet William's Ghost" in Percy's *Reliques*) concerns a wild midnight ride with Death, taken by the loyal but unsuspecting Lenore on the invitation of her lover William, who is actually a specter which turns into a skeleton just as the open grave in the churchyard is reached. In Bürger's rendition, the soldier Wilhelm had been killed in the Seven Years' War; in Taylor's he had become a knight of Richard Cœur de Lion and had fallen in the Holy Land.

Where, in this "spukhafte" tale, are Geraldine, Christabel, and the other figures in Coleridge's poem? Is it Christabel's "lover that's far away" (belike in the Crusades or almost anywhere else) that Brandl has in mind? It is nothing so definite or suggestive as this. Rather, it is the extravagant explanation of her presence that Geraldine offers Christabel under the ancient oak—her story of having been seized by a band of warriors, bound on a white horse, and carried away to an unknown destination. This tale, insists Brandl, Coleridge procured "for the most part" from Bürger, via Taylor. The horse, "as fleet as wind"; the girl, half-dead of fright; the nocturnal setting— all are there. Even the funeral procession met by Lenore and her ghastly lover has somehow become transformed into the "shade of night" which Geraldine asserts that her party crossed! If we waive the facts that Lenore went willingly, whereas Geraldine was kidnaped; that Wilhelm was alone, whereas Coleridge could not make up his mind whether to have three or five abductors (whom he styled "warriors" in some

---

that he expressed rather than a complete approbation. Lowes (pp. 578–80) discusses the question at large, correcting certain errors committed by Oliver Farrar Emerson in *The Earliest English Translations of Bürger's Lenore: A Study in English and German Romanticism* ("Western Reserve Studies," Vol. I, No. 1, May, 1915).

[13] Brandl, *Coleridge*, p. 211; also Eichler, p. 26. See also Brandl, "Lenore in England," in Erich Schmidt, *Charakteristiken* (Berlin, 1886), pp. 244–48.

versions, "ruffians" in others); that Wilhelm and Lenore were on the same horse, whereas Geraldine's captors "rode furiously behind" her; and that the German ride began and ended on the same night, whereas Geraldine's started in the morning and lasted through either one or two nights (Coleridge again could not make up his mind which he preferred) before the one on which Christabel found her—there remains this residuum of correspondency between the German and the English poems: a girl experiences a fearful nocturnal ride on horseback.

Such a residuum is obviously not sufficient to prove any direct indebtedness.[14] Perhaps Montague Summers overstates the situation slightly, but not much, when he says: "German critics have somewhat superfluously endeavoured to emphasize . . . . the influence of *Lenore*, since upon examination it would hardly seem that such is present even in the smallest degree."[15] It is at least not impossible that if Coleridge had seen the frontispiece of the 1778 edition of Bürger, or its copy in the 1796 edition of Spencer's free and moralized version, he might have retained a picture of Wilhelm, with Lenore behind him on the horse, galloping through the gates of Prague, surrounded and pursued by several figures of flying devils. This memory might have been reinforced by the presence of an Icelandic motto, taken from the Saemunda Edda, which Coleridge was interested in. If, however, this was the source of Geraldine's ride, it suffered an even greater sea-change than was usual in Coleridge's imaginative processes. Though Taylor's translation of Bürger's "Lenore" seems to have had its incidental contribution to make to "The Rime of the Ancient Mariner",[16] the part played by the German ballad in shaping "Christabel" was even more oblique and tenuous. The traditional features of

[14] Almost as good a case could be made out for the romantic tale of Thomas of Erceldoune, or Thomas the Rimer, whose journey to the other world with the Queen of Faerie was made under somewhat similar circumstances—except that there is little likelihood that Coleridge would have known the story before Scott published it in his *Minstrelsy of the Scottish Border* in 1804.

[15] Summers, *Vampire*, p. 276.

[16] Lowes, pp. 335-36, 545-46.

this type of romantic fiction would account for this episode, as they would for several other minor details of the poem.[17]

[17] The traditional nature of such an episode is conclusively, though unconsciously, proved by Tuttle (pp. 456–57, 460, 471) when he cites passages from *The Mysteries of Udolpho*, *The Romance of the Forest*, and *Hubert de Sevrac*, all of which Coleridge had been reading and all of which concern the abduction of a young girl by a band (of between three and five in number) who are invariably described as either "villains" or "ruffians" (the latter being Coleridge's term in some manuscripts), who bind her to a horse and who, in the last case at least, deposit her at the foot of a tree. Recall also the episode in Southey's *Thalaba*, discussed above, p. 73.

III

NAMES AND LOCAL HABITATIONS

ONE of the causes for the peculiar effectiveness of "The Rime of the Ancient Mariner" is that Coleridge has meticulously avoided the use of any specific names for either dramatis personae or settings. An atmosphere more or less out of time and place has thus been achieved—an atmosphere in which the laws of ordinary mundane phenomena no longer hold. In "Kubla Khan", however, the situation is different, since the poet was subconsciously composing under the express stimulus of Purchas. Even here, however, in the fifty-four lines which were completed, Kubla Khan himself is the only flesh-and-blood character that Coleridge has named; and the poetically distorted "Xanadu" and "Alph" for "Xamdu" and "Alpheus" are the only places. Moreover, in the prophecy of war which the Khan heard "from afar", it was "Ancestral voices" in the large that spoke to him, rather than the specific voice of any individual among that mighty race of conquerors.

"Christabel", however, is quite alien to both of its companions. The whole problem confronting Coleridge is completely unlike that in either of the others. The story, although dated somewhere in the distant past, is to be enveloped with a sense of immediacy and intimacy. The reader is to identify himself far more closely with the guileless heroine than would ever have been possible with the hard-bitten old mariner or the militant Khan. One cannot sympathize, except in an extremely abstract way, with a person who is nameless or whose experiences are conducted on a level quite separate from one's own. This poem is to be, par excellence, one concerning the simplest and most universal emotions; and its characters are to seem real and understandable, no matter how strange the situation involving them may be. For this reason they all demand names which will at once label them and simultaneously fit into the general atmosphere of the incidents.

Three courses were open to Coleridge in his choice-making: he could invent his own names to suit his need; he could cast about in his memory for names that were familiar and in more or less common use; or he could—as, consciously or unconsciously, he had done before with such good results in his general writing—let his books be his soothsayers and show him the way. A casual examination of the names which he selected for his five main characters (excluding Christabel's lover, who—except her mother—is the only important anonymous person, probably because he plays such a minor role in the completed cantos[1]) would likely lead to the conclusion that all three methods were

---

[1] It might also be noted here that two persons from Coleridge's own life have likewise been assimilated anonymously into the poem. One appears in the latest extant portion which is absolutely datable—"The Conclusion to Part II", beginning "A little child, a limber elf," and finished, with all but two or three minor variations, by May 6, 1801. On this date Coleridge, in a letter to Southey (*Letters*, I, 355–56), described his affection for his four-year-old son Hartley and inclosed these lines, styling them "a metaphysical account of fathers calling their children rogues, rascals, and little varlets, &c." The process by which Coleridge may have linked to his poem these apparently *disjecta membra* of an abortive third part finds its most plausible explanation in E.H.C., pp. 31–32, 96 n. The presence of line 674, "(O sorrow and shame should this be true!)", might also well be regarded as supporting his view, since the phrase "sorrow and shame" is quite evidently an echo of two earlier lines, 270 and 296. In the first of these, Geraldine exclaims over "This mark of my shame, this seal of my sorrow;" in the second, Coleridge himself, commenting on Christabel's troubled slumbers, cries: "O sorrow and shame!" Not so clear a bond, but one which has aroused my curiosity because it seems to have nothing to do with the rest of the passage and yet might easily be associated with something in Geraldine's past, is the couplet:

"To mutter and mock a broken charm,
To dally with wrong that does no harm. . . . ."

Perhaps some reader will be able to snap the links together.

The second person to appear anonymously is apparently Southey himself. At any rate, the famous passage in the second canto beginning "Alas! they had been friends in youth . . . .," is generally interpreted as Coleridge's generous apology to his friend for their breach over the pantisocracy squabble rather than as a reference to his temporary alienation from Lamb in 1798 because of some of Charles Lloyd's "tattle". E.H.C. (p. 27) and Hanson (pp. 353–55, 378 ff.) discuss the matter further. This seems to be a much better explanation of the passage than Tuttle's appropriation (pp. 449–50) of the family feud from the Percy ballad, "The Child of Elle," and the paralleling of the lines in "Alcanzor and Zayda" concerning how ancient wounds "Long have rent our house and thine" with Coleridge's "The cliffs that have been rent asunder".

It is also interesting to note than in 1810, according to a manuscript notebook of that date now in the possession of the Rev. G. H. B. Coleridge, Coleridge wrote that "C. Lloyd's mad & immoral & frantic ingratitude to me . . . . prevented my finishing the Christabel" (Hanson, p. 483). This excuse, however, seems far too easy.

used. But this conclusion would be premature and erroneous. It is, I believe, perfectly demonstrable that all five names— Christabel, Geraldine, Sir Leoline, Lord Roland de Vaux of Tryermaine, and Bracy—were picked in one way or another from books which Coleridge had been reading at or shortly before the first period of composition. Certain of these cases have already been proved by earlier students, but never have the antecedents of all five been pointed out conclusively.

The problem had perplexed Hall Caine and Dante Gabriel Rossetti, as Caine's remarks in his life of his friend indicate: "In a letter treating of other matters, Rossetti asked me if I thought 'Christabel' really existed as a medieval name, or existed at all earlier than Coleridge. I replied that I had not met with it earlier than the date of the poem. I thought Coleridge's granddaughter must have been the first person to bear the name. The other names in the poem appear to belong to another family of names,—names with a different origin and range of expression, —Leoline, Geraldine, Roland, and most of all Bracy." Caine then suggests that Coleridge may have invented the name, but thinks it more probable that he found it on his visit to Germany in 1798. Another conjecture that seemed to him reasonable "was that Coleridge evolved the name out of the incidents of the opening passages of the poem." Under the stimulus of these speculations, baseless as most of them were, Rossetti recollected that "in the grossly garbled ballad of *Syr Cauline*, in Percy's *Reliques*, there is a Ladye Chrystabelle, but as every stanza in which her name appears would seem to be certainly Percy's own work, I suspect him to be the inventor of the name, which is assuredly a much better invention than any of the stanzas; and from this wretched source Coleridge probably enriched the sphere of symbolic nomenclature. However, a genuine source may turn up, but the name does not sound to me like a real one."[2]

Rossetti was right. Apparently Coleridge did appropriate his heroine's lovely and appropriate name from Percy's re-written and "grossly garbled" (for Rossetti would naturally have an ear

[2] Caine, *Rossetti*, pp. 151–53.

for the true popular ballad note) version of "Sir Cauline". Not
only was the *Reliques* an indispensable part of his library, as
Lamb's sending it to Keswick after him in 1800 would prove,[3]
but he alluded to the ballad with great familiarity in his letter
to Wordsworth concerning *The Castle Spectre* in January, 1798,
when, in praising the language of a "pretty little ballad-song"
of Lewis's, he remarked: "The simplicity and naturalness is his
own, and not imitated; for it is made to subsist in congruity
with a language perfectly modern, the language of his own times,
in the same way that the language of the writer of 'Sir Cauline'
was the language of *his* own times. This, I think, a rare merit:
at least, I find, *I* cannot attain this innocent nakedness, except
by *assumption*. I resemble the Duchess of Kingston, who mas-
queraded in the character of 'Eve before the Fall' in flesh-col-
oured Silk."[4] Whatever the justice of Coleridge's modest comparison of himself with the somewhat tainted Duchess of Kingston, it is evident that he had been attempting to model himself in some ways after the ballad of "Sir Cauline", into which
Bishop Percy had introduced a heroine named Christabel, whose
lover Cauline is exiled in a far-off land, but returns unexpectedly
to die in saving both her and the king.[5]

Rossetti was thus completely correct in assigning the source
of the name Christabel to the medieval ballad;[6] but he was mistaken in expressing his even tentative suspicion that Percy had
invented it. E. H. C. in 1907 took the simple step that Caine
and Rossetti might easily have taken but for the fact that they
were "literary gentlemen" and not scholars: he traced the matter down in the complete *Bishop Percy's Folio Manuscript*,
which had been made perfectly available in 1868. Here he
found that in the original ballad, which Percy practically remade (even to the extent of giving the story an unhappy but
"artistic" ending), the heroine was nameless, being designated

[3] Lamb, *Letters*, I, 197.

[4] *Letters*, I, 237.

[5] Lowes (pp. 331–33) also shows the influence of "Sir Cauline" on the style and
language of the "Rime".

[6] Note, however, that Coleridge vacillated long between the spelling "Christabel"
and "Christobell". See above, p. 37.

simply as the "Lady".[7] But he found also that in the metrical
romance of "Eglamore" there was a heroine named "Christabell".[8] This romance, which was in Percy's possession, the
bishop did not print with the *Reliques*, although he alluded to
it in his accompanying essay "On the Ancient Metrical Romances, &c." as "Eglamour of Artas (or Artoys)".[9] Although
this poem had been printed in the black letter at Edinburgh in
1508, and subsequently at London,[10] there is no necessity for assuming that Coleridge had met it in this form—though he may
have done so. Percy, by neatly transferring the name of Christabel from one poem to another, had forestalled his needs. The
perfect appellation was waiting for him, and there was no cause
for invention. The probable reason why Coleridge was attracted to it will be discussed in the final chapter.[11]

When E. H. C. wrote his valuable introduction to the facsimile edition of "Christabel" in 1907, he rightfully made considerable use of William Hutchinson's *The History of the County of
Cumberland, and Some Places Adjacent . . . .*, for in it he found
the original of Sir Roland de Vaux of Tryermaine.[12] Hutchinson's
two ponderous tomes, the contents of which were not always so
forbidding as their exteriors would prophesy, were based partly
on his own observations and investigations and partly on similar
topographical and historical works by his predecessors. He was
especially fortunate in having at his disposal the previously unpublished notes of Denton, which he sometimes incorporated in
his text but generally reduced to a running fire of footnotes.
And through the whole first volume of Hutchinson, but particu-

---

[7] *Bishop Percy's Folio Manuscript*, III, 3–15. [9] *Reliques*, III, 370–71.

[8] *Ibid.*, II, 341–89; E.H.C., pp. 12–13 n. [10] *Folio Manuscript*, II, 338.

[11] The similarities between "Christabel" and the fourteenth-century romance, "Syr
Eglamoure of Artoys," are discussed by E. H. W. Meyerstein, in the London *Times
Literary Supplement*, April 6, 1933, p. 248. Although he brings out some interesting
resemblances, Meyerstein was unfamiliar with the discussions of both E. H. C. and
Caine concerning the relation between "Christabel" and "Sir Cauline"; otherwise he
would probably have withheld his speculations, which are nevertheless worth the ex-
amination of the curious, since there is no proof that Coleridge had *not* read "Syr
Eglamoure".

[12] E.H.C., pp. 21, 23–27. I think that Tuttle's mention of Lord Vaux's poem
"Cupid's Assault", in Percy, may be safely passed over as a "source".

larly in certain of Denton's notes, the name of the ancient Cumberland family of De Vaux, or De Vaulx, draws the eye like a refrain in a poem. In one lengthy note especially, Denton recalled his detailed findings on the fee of Tryermaine, which he spelled "Triermaine", and Hutchinson called "Tryermain, or Treverman".[13]

According to Denton, at the time of the Norman Conquest Tryermaine was a fee of Gilsland, whose lord, Gilandos, stood against the invader, but whose son, Gilamor, later made his peace with the Earl of Cumberland. After the death of this son, Tryermaine passed down in the Vaux family through a succession of Ranulphs, Roberts, Rolands, and Alexanders until finally "they were named Rolands successively that were lords thereof until the reign of Edward IV. . . . ." Roland was, therefore, a favorite name of the Vaux gens, and Coleridge would have had plenty of individual representatives to select from. Very likely, however, he had in mind the particular Sir Roland de Vaux (that is, "de Vallibus"—"of the Valleys") who was honored by being buried in a special tomb in the transept of Lanercost Priory and whose stone effigy, fragments of which were recovered and rehabilitated in the nineteenth century, indicates that he lived in the latter part of the fourteenth century.[14] In any case, it was undoubtedly the following obituary verses in Hutchinson which caught Coleridge's eye, no matter which Sir Roland they were intended to elegize:

"*In Ecclesia Parochali de Lanercost.*
"SIR ROWLAND VAUX, that sometime was the Lord of Triermaine,
"Is dead, his body clad in lead, and ligs law under this stane;
"Evin as we, evin so was he, on earth a levand man;
"Evin as he, evin so moun we, for all the craft we can."[15]

---

[13] William Hutchinson, *The History of the County of Cumberland, and Some Places Adjacent, from the Earliest Accounts to the Present Time* . . . . (Carlisle, 1794–97), I, 99–100. The name Vaux is also prominent in the accounts of Gilsland (*ibid.*, pp. 46 ff.) and of Lanercost Abbey (*ibid.*, p. 55).

[14] E.H.C., p. 25 n., quotes from H. Whitehead and G. Baldwin Brown, *Lanercost Priory* (1896), pp. 18 ff., and gives a photograph of the remains of the tomb. He believes, however, that the tomb probably belongs to a later Sir Roland than the effigy.

[15] "*Milbourn's Adds. to Denton's MS.—Ex MS. Antiq. penes F. W. Arm.*," in Hutchinson, I, 55 n. E.H.C., p. 25 n., prints a slightly different version, in which the name is "Sir Rowland de Vaux".

Such a bravely resigned *memento mori* must surely have appealed to Coleridge's sense of the fitness of style and matter.[16]

It is apparently E. H. C.'s opinion that Hutchinson's book came to Coleridge's attention first in 1800, after he had moved to Cumberland and had embarked on the second part of the troublesome poem, with its locale now settled in the Lake District. At any rate, he points out that, whereas in the first part Geraldine's hypothetical father is vaguely described as "noble" and dismissed without a name, early in the second part all the hitherto lacking details are supplied as applying to the new Sir Roland. Moreover, in recalling that the fragment entitled "A Thought Suggested by a View of Saddleback in Cumberland" is in the meter of "Christabel", he asserts that the first two lines are adapted from the opening of a poem by the Lake poet Isaac Ritson, which Coleridge found in Hutchinson's *Cumberland*, "one of the County histories which slumbered on his landlord's shelves. . . . ."[17] Where E. H. C. got such exact information about the location of the particular copy of Hutchinson which Coleridge read, he does not state; but if he himself had done what he insists his grandfather did—"read the two volumes from

---

[16] This is probably the same Sir Roland de Vaux of Triermain whom Scott made his hero in "The Bridal of Triermain", published in 1813. Since Scott's poem thus appeared three years before Coleridge's, *Blackwood's* for April, 1817, promptly accused Coleridge of plagiarism. As a matter of fact, of course, the influence was in the other direction, as the following summary of Scott's poem will indicate: The young Sir Roland first sees a vision of the beautiful Gyneth, daughter of King Arthur and a sort of fairy creature named Guendolen. He falls in love with this apparition, and endures the usual dangers in his quest to wake her from the sleep which she has endured in the Valley of St. John for five hundred years. It seems that Merlin had enchanted her as a punishment for her heartlessness in letting Arthur's knights slaughter each other in a tournament for her hand. The description of the maiden who will be a suitable match for Roland (canto I, stanza 1) is much like that of Christabel. Roland also sends his page on a journey to a Druid prophet, much as Bracy goes on his mission, and through the same country. In the end, of course, De Vaux survives all his terrible tests, wins through to the sleeping maiden, now purified from her pride, and awakens her with a chaste kiss on her soft hand, while the walls of the enchanted castle crash and fall about them. In several respects Scott's poem is thus somewhat suggestive of V.'s "Christobell".

[17] E.H.C., pp. 21–23; Coleridge, *Poems*, p. 347 and n. Coleridge wrote Poole on August 14, 1800 (*Letters*, I, 335–36), that his landlord, "who resides next door in this twofold house [at Keswick]," has "as large a library as yours,—and perhaps much larger—well stored with encyclopaedias, dictionaries, and histories, etc., all modern." He also expects to "have free access to the magnificent library of Sir Gilfred Lawson".

end to end"[18]—he would have found some cause to doubt his conclusion that this contact was first made in Cumberland, though it may well have been renewed there.[19]

The first volume of Hutchinson's work was issued at Carlisle in 1794 and was well received, though it took a little time to attract public attention. For instance, it was not until June, 1797, that *The British Critic* reviewed it, but with a great deal of praise and hospitality.[20] At the end of the August number the magazine printed the following announcement: "*Hutchinson's History of Cumberland*, is now completely printed, and will soon be delivered to the subscribers. It forms two large Volumes in Quarto."[21] Finally, the November number led off with a very flattering eleven-page review of the second volume, which had just come out.[22] In other words, both volumes were available by the latter part of 1797, and both had received much favorable publicity by that time. The first volume, however, had been in print since 1794—and, in spite of E. H. C., I have come across no evidence to indicate that Coleridge ever read more than that volume; but I have found plenty of evidence which establishes his reading of this one by 1797 or 1798.

For not only did S. T. C. get his Sir Roland from Hutchinson —he also got his Geraldine and his Sir Leoline, both of whose names appear so conspicuously in the first canto that it would have been virtually impossible for the poet to weave them into its texture later without re-writing it.[23] As for Geraldine's descent, E. H. C. made an excellent guess. "Geraldine," he stated dogmatically, "was called after Surrey's disdainful lady-love,"[24] but how Coleridge came to know Surrey and his story he did not trouble to show. Yet he was essentially right. The

---

[18] E.H.C., p. 23.

[19] Lowes, p. 604*k*, follows E. H. C. in placing the reading of Hutchinson in 1800.

[20] *British Critic*, X (1797), 69–73. [22] *Ibid.*, pp. 461–72.

[21] *Ibid.*, p. 220. [24] E.H.C., p. 13.

[23] Tuttle (pp. 446, 454 n.) finds some occult significance in the fact that "Leoline" (probably) rimes with "Cauline", and "Geraldine" with "Barnardine" (in *The Mysteries of Udolpho*). He might with equal cogency have pointed out that both rime (perhaps) with "Emmeline" in "The Child of Elle".

Geraldine of "Christabel" was also the Geraldine of Surrey, but she had made her entrance into the poem not directly through Surrey's sonnets but by the roundabout way of the county of Cumberland as its history was revealed by Hutchinson.

In a long and prominent footnote toward the end of the first volume—so long, indeed, that it far overshadows the main text for several pages—Hutchinson has placed an account of the famous Howard family. As part of this discussion he naturally devotes considerable space to Henry Howard, Earl of Surrey, in the course of which he indulges in some amusingly innocent but pardonable bragging over his "discovery" of the identity of Surrey's sweetheart, the mysterious Geraldine.[25] For, being far more than a mere genealogist and archeologist, as his fondness for quoting from the poets on all occasions would suggest, Hutchinson had long owned a copy of the earl's "elegant and tender sonnets. . . . . In imitation of Laura, our Earl had his Geraldine. . . . . I flatter myself, I have at length discovered who this fair lady was: here is the Earl's description." He then quotes at length from the poem, outstanding lines of which are: "From Tuscan came my ladie's worthy race;" "Bright is her hewe, and Geraldine she hight;" "Happy is he that can obtain her love." Following his theory that "I am inclined to think, that her poetical appellation was her real name, as every one of the circumstances tally [sic]," he makes her the daughter (probably Elizabeth) of Gerald Fitzgerald, Earl of Kildare, and his second wife, Margaret. Moreover, she is not merely "Geraldine" to him; more frequently she is, as to Surrey, "the fair Geraldine". Even in the family tree which he constructs, he labels her prominently on his page as "Elizabeth, the Fair Geraldine," and he quotes from Pope's "Windsor Forest" concerning Surrey and his epitaph, lines including the following: ". . . . Fair Geraldine, bright object of his vow. . . . ." So Coleridge twice describes his "maid forlorn"; she too is "fair Geraldine".[26] Of course, the epithet is a conventional one and could be paralleled in dozens of places; but when it occurs in a book Coleridge

[25] Hutchinson, I, 373–75 n.   [26] See ll. 105, 449.

was perusing, and this book contains the only use (certainly the only signal use) of the name Geraldine which I have noted in all my retracing of his reading during this period, then its appearance seems obviously to be more than a simple coincidence. It is Coleridge once more assimilating what may be of value to him.

This artless Geraldine, it is true, might at first remind the reader more of Christabel than of her namesake. Yet there is another element in Hutchinson's footnote which may have established the opposite connection in Coleridge's mind. After correcting his rival Drayton (who, he found later, had made the same identification) on a few historical points, Hutchinson goes on to more vulnerable quarry: "Anthony Wood, vol. I, p. 68. was still more mistaken, for he thinks she was born at Florence; he says, that Surry travelling to the emperor's court, grew acquainted with Cornelius Agrippa, famous for natural magic, who shewed him the image of his Geraldine in a glass, sick, and weeping on her bed, and resolved all into devout religion for the absence of her Lord. . . . ." This Italian Geraldine is still Coleridge's Christabel, with her piety, her thoughts of her absent lover, and her sufferings, but her name has now become associated with that of the world-famed magician, Cornelius Agrippa, whom the poet had been meeting in his other studies. Somewhat as the First Witch of *Macbeth* became the link between Geraldine and her "Peak and pine!" addressed to the spirit of Christabel's mother, so might the sorcerer Agrippa have acted as a bridge between Geraldine the innocent and Geraldine the guilty, with all her occult powers. The tendrils of memory, in reaching out to recreate their contacts, had slipped slightly and awakened the wrong, though allied, image.

Coleridge, then, would have come upon his "fair Geraldine" first on page 373 of the initial volume of Hutchinson. He would have met De Vaux first on page 46 of the same volume, but especially on pages 99–100. He would not have had to turn half that many pages, however, before his eye would have struck the name which he was to adopt for Christabel's beloved but deluded father. Leoline, like Christabel, at first looks as if it might be a fabricated name, but actually it was not uncommon among the English aristocracy. Sir Leoline Walden, for instance, was the father-in-law of the economist Charles Davenant in the seventeenth century.[27] Consequently, Coleridge might well have picked the name up from life. This contingency is extremely unlikely, however, when the name is found on page 17 of the book which was also to furnish him with Sir Roland and Geraldine, as well as certain scenery and place names which will soon be discussed. For on this page, in the midst of an introductory history of the past of Cumberland, Hutchinson quotes from the 1695 translation of William Camden as follows: "King Edmund, with the assistance of Leoline, King of Wales, spoiled Cumberland of all its riches; and having put out the eyes of Dunmaile, king of that country, granted that kingdom to Malcolm, King of Scots. . . . ." This Leoline, it is true, was king of Wales; but Coleridge was living not far from Wales when he began to write "Christabel". And Malcolm is the son of the murdered Duncan who is hailed as king of Scotland at the end of *Macbeth*. These connections, together with the romantic euphony of the name, would have been sufficient to fix it in Coleridge's mind.[28]

Of course, it is just possible that the suggestion came from Camden in the direct line—a suspicion that might be momentarily strengthened when one recalls that, when Coleridge published his "Introduction to the Tale of the Dark Ladie" (later retitled "Love") in *The Morning Post* for December 21, 1799, his prefatory letter to the editor began with these words: "The following Poem is the Introduction to a somewhat longer one, for which I shall solicit insertion on your next open day. The use of the Old Ballad word, *Ladie*, for Lady, is the only piece of

[27] Leslie Hotson, *The Commonwealth and Restoration Stage* (Cambridge, 1928), p. 236.

[28] If it were only possible to eat my cake and have it too, I should like to make something of the fact that not far from Grasmere and Keswick, where Wordsworth and Coleridge were living in 1800, was the Cumberland pass called Dunmail Raise, which Wordsworth introduced with such good descriptive effect into "Michael". But to use Dunmail as a means of rooting Leoline in Coleridge's memory would be to push his first acquaintance with Hutchinson forward into the year 1800, a conclusion which I hope I have already shown to be erroneous.

obsoleteness in it; and as it is professedly a tale of ancient times, I trust, that 'the affectionate lovers of venerable antiquity' (as Camden says) will grant me their pardon, and perhaps may be induced to admit a force and propriety in it."[29] The poet, then, had pretty definitely added William Camden to his already staggering reading-list. Suppose, however, that he had started out to check his references. What would he have found?

If he had consulted the most recent translation of the *Britannia*, that edited by Richard Gough in 1789, Christabel would never have had a sire named Leoline; for Gough's scholarship informed him that this was only a Latinism and that the proper native designation was "Lewellin" (i.e., Llewellyn): "But when the Saxon government was subverted by the Danish wars, it had princes of its own, styled kings of Cumberland, till the year 946, at which time, as Matthew of Westminster informs us, 'king Edmund, assisted by Lewellin king of Demetia, plundered Cumberland of all its wealth, and having put out the eyes of the two sons of Dunmail king of that province, gave the kingdom to Malcolm king of Scotland. . . . .'"[30] A "Sir Llewellyn" would have been quite out of place in Coleridge's cast! But suppose that he had consulted the translation from which Hutchinson himself claimed to be quoting—that made and edited by Edmund Gibson "of Queens-College in Oxford" in 1695. Here is what he would have found was really there: ". . . . *At which time* (as *Florilegus* tells us) *King* Edmund, *by the assistance of* Leolin *King of South-Wales, spoil'd Cumberland of all its riches, and having put out the eyes of the two sons of* Dunmail *King of that County* [sic] *granted that Kingdom to* Malcolm *King of Scots.* . . . ."[31] The name is now easily recognizable, but it is

---

[29] *Poems*, pp. 330–31, 550. The poem, according to E. H. C.'s notes, was probably written, for the most part, during the preceding month.

[30] I quote from the second edition: *Britannia: or, A Chorographical Description of the Flourishing Kingdoms of England, Scotland, and Ireland, and the Islands Adjacent; from the Earliest Antiquity* (London, 1806), III, 430. Immediately before the quoted passage (pp. 429–30) occur references to Gillesland, Irthing, Trederman, Lanercost Priory, "founded by R. de *Vaulx*, lord of Gillesland," and a brief history of the De Vaulx family, but these are by no means so specific or graphic as Hutchinson's.

[31] *Camden's Britannia, Newly Translated into English: with Large Additions and Improvements* (London, 1695), p. 836.

Leolin, not Leoline; it could never rime satisfactorily with Geraldine, whether she was "divine" or simply of "sober mien". Finally, however, suppose that Coleridge went with scholarly zeal and thoroughness to Camden's original Latin. Here is the pivotal phrase: ". . . . (vt inquit Florilegus Westmonasteriensis) *Rex Edmuudus* [*sic*], *adiutorio Leolini regis Demetiae fretus.* . . . ."[32] There is no help here as to "Leolin" or "Leoline". The evidence is therefore conclusive: only in Hutchinson would Coleridge have found the form of the name which he adopted. Even though he had been reading Camden during this period, he did not pilfer him to find a father for his heroine.

Thus, only one more character remains to be located, and here again E. H. C. has been before me, though in a rather sketchy fashion.[33] When, early on the night of September 14, 1800, Sarah Coleridge was delivered of her third son, her doting husband precipitately set the following entry down in his journal: "Sunday night ½ past 10 a boy born. ?Bracy."[34] His first hasty and enthusiastic intentions, however, met a check somewhere, perhaps from his wife, perhaps from his own new local pride. The boy was not destined to be named Bracy after all. In fact, for a time it appeared as if the name given him would not matter, since he seemed unlikely to survive to bear it, though he eventually recovered. On September 27 his father sorrowfully scribbled: "The child being very ill was baptized by the name of Derwent."[35] Thus, just at the time that Bard Bracy makes his appearance in the second part of "Christabel", the name Bracy makes an ephemeral bid for inclusion in the Coleridge family tree, and then as quickly vanishes. Where it went to, and why, no one has been able to say; but more can be said about where it perhaps came from.

---

[32] *Britannia sive Florentissimorvm regnorvm, Angliae, Scotiae, Hiberniae, et insvlarvm adiacentivm ex intima antiquitate chorographica descriptio. Authore Gvilielmo Camdeno* . . . . (London, 1587), p. 530.

[33] E.H.C., pp. 28–29, 38.   [34] *Ibid.*, p. 38; and *Letters*, I, 338 n.

[35] *Letters*, I, 338 n. By October 9 Coleridge was able to write his friend Humphry Davy and tell him that he had named his baby Derwent "from the river, for, fronting our house, the Greta runs into the Derwent" (*ibid.*, pp. 338–39).

From August 25 to October 13, 1797, Coleridge had borrowed from the Bristol Library its two volumes of T. R. Nash's *Collections for the History of Worcestershire*, first published in 1782.[36] In the second volume of this work, E. H. C. discovered this sentence, in a short account of the "very ancient family of the *Bracys*", who had lived in the town of Madersfeld in the deanery of Powick, on the Severn: "William Bracy (7 Henry VI) was returned into the exchequer as an esquire to attend the king into France."[37] Here E. H. C. stops. Farther on, however, the same event is again referred to, with the same name.[38] But this is by no means the only mention of the Bracy family or families in Nash's book. A William and a Robert de Bracy are also alluded to frequently,[39] and in an appendix to the second volume the arms of two Bracy families are illustrated and discussed.[40] Most significant of all, in the first volume there occurs a name which Coleridge's eye could not have escaped being drawn to, because of its similarity to his own—the town of Cotheridge. And in the very midst of the three-page account of Cotheridge, not only does a "Francis Brace" appear but also on the same page a branch of the Vaulx family of Northumberland is cited.[41] What a combination that is: Cotheridge, with its echo of Coleridge; Brace (undoubtedly pronounced Bracy); and De Vaux, the family to one of whose representatives the "merry bard" Bracy was to be sent by his master Sir Leoline![42] Perhaps from this point of view Coleridge was more right than has been believed when he insisted that he had planned the whole of "Christabel" in his head from the beginning. Certainly the names of the entire cast were available to him before he set pen to paper, and

36 Kaufman, p. 320.

37 The statement occurs on p. 117 of Vol. I of the second edition of the work (London, 1799).

38 *Ibid.*, p. 452.

39 *Ibid.*, pp. 203, 291; II, 295, 299, 318.

40 *Ibid.*, II, lxxxv.   41 *Ibid.*, I, 258.

42 Tuttle, however, believes (p. 450) that the combination of a "sir Bracy" and a minstrel, John of Rampayne, mentioned by Percy in his essay in the *Reliques* (I, 345 ff.), is far more likely than Nash to have produced "Bard Bracy".

there seems to be no good reason why he could not have called them up afterward as he needed them.[43]

Thus a Bracy, rooted in the soil of Worcestershire, found himself somewhat unexpectedly transported into Cumberland and metamorphosed into a poet there. Fortunately, in this new situation a guide had been provided for him, so that he did not need to fear becoming lost among the crags and mountain passes which he must traverse to accomplish the dangerous mission which would take him from Langdale Hall to Tryermaine. For Bard Bracy, introduced at the very beginning of the second canto, is the chief geographical authority in the poem and the center of all the place names and local legends. When in the morning he hears the Sacristan tolling the memorial knell,

> Which not a soul can choose but hear
> From Bratha Head to Wyndermere,

[43] Nash's history of Worcestershire also suggests another way in which Coleridge might have met the name Bracy and been sufficiently attracted to it to consider using it for his son, and then, rejecting it there for one with greater sentimental associations, to apply it to the minstrel in his own versified romance. In the church of St. Mary at Malvern, only some fifty or so miles from Nether Stowey, there were, or had been, according to Nash, three elaborate windows containing representations of the figures of a William Bracy and his family, as well as several inscriptions concerning them. The name, usually spelled "Braci", recurs many times in a lengthy analysis and description of the stained glass, most of which, Nash sadly admitted, was now broken, though a complete report of it was extant from the time of Charles I (Nash, II, 131–32). It is certainly not impossible that Coleridge in his travels about the west of England had come upon the church itself and all its associations with the Bracys, and had carried their memory away, to store in his mind with the rest of his copious collection. Nevertheless, the nearest I have been able to bring him to Malvern is on the trip which he undertook in January and February, 1796, in order to procure subscriptions from the benevolent and well-intentioned for his projected magazine, *The Watchman*. As he describes this disheartening experience in the *Biographia Literaria* (in *Works*, New York, 1884, III, 278), "I set off on a tour to the north, from Bristol to Sheffield, for the purpose of procuring customers, preaching by the way in most great towns, as a *hireless* volunteer, in a blue coat and white waistcoat. . . . ." His course brought him, one night late in January, 1796, to the home of "Mr. Barr of Worcester" (*Letters*, I, 154). Now the line of towns and villages known as Malvern, lying along the beautiful Malvern Hills, is only a few miles from Worcester, and, in fact, might almost be regarded as a sort of suburb to the larger city. With the famous hills and the celebrated architecture of the priory to attract him, there is every reason to believe that the itinerant poet-preacher-editor would have strayed from the direct path of duty and sought consolation and diversion in the church of St. Mary. Certainly the Malvern district was a favorite and well-known one in his circle, as his reference to Joseph Cottle's poem on "Malvern Hill", in a letter to Southey in 1801, would indicate (*ibid.*, p. 358).

he remarks, "So let it knell!" and adds that the ghostly echoes,
set in motion by the spirits of "Three sinful sextons", will come
back redoubled from Langdale Pike, Witch's Lair, Dungeon-
ghyll, and Borrodale.[44] Later, as he is to set out northward from
Langdale Hall, Sir Leoline sees him, in his mind's eye, hastening
over the mountains and along the valley road, clad in his minstrel's costume to avoid attack by "wandering folk, that are
abroad. . . . ."

> And when he has crossed the Irthing flood,
> My merry bard! he hastes, he hastes
> Up Knorren Moor, through Halegarth Wood,
> And reaches soon that castle good
> Which stands and threatens Scotland's wastes.

Bratha Head, Langdale Pike, Wyndermere, and Borrodale
are easy and obvious. Anyone going up into the Lake District
today would hear all about them within the first twenty-four
hours; and Coleridge's friends and informants when he joined
the Wordsworths there were not likely to have been less gar-
rulous and proud of their scenery than are the inhabitants of
the region in the twentieth century. Witch's Lair and Dungeon-
ghyll, thinks E. H. C., were the occasion of a penciled description in Coleridge's notebook when, in July, 1800, and probably
with Wordsworth as his guide, the newcomer had explored the
rocks and waterfalls of Great Langdale.[45] Langdale Hall is almost as simple. Though the Hall itself seems to be fictitious,
there were plenty of other "halls" near by, such as Rydal Hall,
Coniston Hall, or even the newly built Greta Hall; and Langdale was a palpable name to apply to the invented home of Sir

---

[44] The strange story of these sextons' ghosts, with their "ropes of rock and bells of
air", probably has its source in some local legend which has escaped my researches.
Ernest Morris's *Legends o' the Bells* (London, n.d.) contains nothing resembling it.
However, it is worth noting that Hutchinson (II, 183–89) devotes several pages to a
description of the echoes around Keswick and tells of various experiments made in
that neighborhood with cannons, bells, etc. Moreover, when Coleridge ascended the
Brocken in 1799, he tells of visiting a cave filled with stalactites, one of which, "on
being struck, gave perfectly the sound of a death-bell. I was behind, and heard it repeatedly at some distance, and the effect was very much in the fairy kind,—gnomes,
and things unseen, that toll mock death-bells for mock-funerals" (Coleridge, "Fragment of a Journey over the Brocken, &c. in 1799," in Gillman, pp. 130–32, 135).

[45] E.H.C., p. 22.

Leoline.[46] The landmarks of Bracy's projected journey, however, are in a distinctly different category.

Fortunately for the bard, an alien in the Cumberland country, a guidebook had been provided for his use. It was Hutchinson's history of Cumberland, which had already furnished Coleridge with the names of three of his characters and was now to yield him certain details and topographical features which probably not even the shepherds of the district would have been able to recall, since they had last been noted by the surveyors who had examined and described the *"Manerium de Tradermayne"* for an "inquisition" made at the command of Queen Elizabeth. Here are some extracts from that inquisition, as quoted by Hutchinson: "Item, there be divers and sundry groves and places of wood within the said manner, viz. Willparke, Halegarth Wood, Dundell Wood, etc. Item, there are divers commons of heath and moor grounds belonging to the manner, viz.—Torthoy Dundell, ... Knorren Moor and others. . . . . Item, the bounder of the said manner beginneth at the foot of Knorren, and up Knorren to the foot of Cragg Burne, ... from thence to Irdinge, from Irdinge to Brudessolle . . . . and from thence to the Stone Cross, and from thence to the foot of Knorren, where this bounder first began."[47] Irdinge, or Irthing, which

---

[46] As a matter of fact, E.H.C. (p. 22) considers the actual locale of the beginning of Christabel's midnight adventure to be "Holford Wood hard by to Alfoxden in Somersetshire". In Dorothy Wordsworth's *Journals* during the spring of 1798 may be traced possible suggestions for the "huge, broad-breasted, old oak tree", with its "one red leaf, the last of its clan", the green moss, the night-birds (or owls), the moon and the clouds, the baying of the dog, etc. In his footnotes E. H. C. points out several of these passages, some of which have their clear echoes in Coleridge's notebook (*Archiv*, pp. 340, 358). Others could easily be added (*Journals*, I, 3-18, *passim*). Certainly these scenes are more likely to have been remembered by Coleridge than the descriptive passages in the Gothic romances cited by Tuttle (pp. 447, 450, 458, 459). Of course, it should not be assumed too hastily that it was Dorothy Wordsworth who put these pictures and words into the minds of Coleridge and her brother. It is just as likely that they were a sort of communal composition, or even that her reiteration of them in her diary represents her desire to set down for preservation the remarks which she had heard the others make, with some additions of her own. So believe Lowes (p. 512), Hanson (pp. 257-59), and Ernest de Selincourt (*Dorothy Wordsworth*, Oxford, 1933, pp. 82-83). These correspondencies between "Christabel" and the *Journals* suggest irresistibly that it was actually "the month before the month of May" when the events attending the arrival of the sinister Geraldine at Langdale Hall began to take form in the poet's mind.

[47] Hutchinson, I, 99-100.

Coleridge designates as a "flood", is of course the Irthing River, which, still under that name, flows through Lanercost and Gilsland some fifty miles or so from Windermere. But Halegarth, or Hallguards, Wood and Knorren Moor, or Fell, as E. H. C. asserts, "are place-names which none but inquisitors or surveyors would have in remembrance."[48] They were landmarks of the ancient Tryermaine which Coleridge would never have noticed or heard of even if he had himself followed the northern route which he assigned to Bracy, and there is no definite evidence that at this time he had made such a trip.

In fact, his description of the "castle good" which was the home of his Sir Roland would prove conclusively that he had never examined its ruins or site, but had taken over without question the picture and situation given by Queen Elizabeth's surveyors. According to them, the "scite of the said manner of Tradermayne was sometimes a fair castle, called Tradermayne Castle, a house of great strength and of good receipt: it stood and was built opposite to the wasts of Scotland and Tyndell, and about vi miles from Lydderesedell, and was a very convenient place, both for annoying of the enemie and defending the country thereabouts; but now the said castle is utterly decayed."[49] Thus Coleridge draws it as

> that castle good
> Which stands and threatens Scotland's wastes.

Yet in the eighteenth century the site of Tryermaine was a good twenty miles from the Scotch border—a very different picture from that which Coleridge's lines summon up, of a great, menacing stronghold looking directly down into Scotland itself. Just what Elizabeth's inquisitors meant when they stated that it was "built opposite to the wasts of Scotland" is not clear unless, as E. H. C. suggests, "Spade Adam Waste" to the northeast of the castle was at that time considered part of Scotland.[50] Moreover, if S. T. C. had been creating from life, after he had personally inspected the remains of Tryermaine, he would scarcely have given the place the aura of a citadel, for in his

[48] E.H.C., pp. 26–27.   [49] Hutchinson, I, 99–100.   [50] E.H.C., pp. 24, 89 n.

day, though not quite "utterly decayed", all that survived was a section of masonry, probably part of the wall of a tower, capping a relatively small plot of ground. In E. H. C.'s words, "A 'fair castle' and of 'good strength' it may have been, but in its palmiest days it must have been but a 'castlet' compared with Naworth, or even with its neighbours Thirlwall and Bewcastle."

Thus it is obvious that Coleridge, searching for names for his dramatis personae and, in the second canto, for a definite geographical setting where his events might befall, indulged in his usual process of creation: words and lines and paragraphs from books—in this case, Percy's *Reliques*, Nash's *Worcestershire*, and, most important, Hutchinson's *Cumberland*—stood out in bold relief in his mind and beckoned to him.[51] So clear was their call that, like his own Wedding Guest, he could not choose but hear.[52]

[51] In addition to the passage in Hutchinson already cited, Denton's notes describing the boundaries of Cumberland also mention many of the names of Bard Bracy's journey (I, 43–44).

[52] Another name, or rather exclamation, in the poem which has aroused considerable speculation is the "Jesu, Maria" (in some manuscripts "Jesu Maria") with which the poet twice begs celestial aid to shield Christabel (ll. 54, 582; E.H.C., pp. 65 and n., 92). This double-barreled adjuration aroused much merriment among the parodists and was frequently introduced into their burlesques with what they thought was a perfectly devastating effect. E.H.C. (p. 15 and n.) has speculated about the provenience of this phrase and has pointed out that Lewis has used it in Act III, scene iii, of *The Castle Spectre* (p. 57), which Coleridge was reading with marked interest in 1798. In this scene, Alice, the maid, exclaims at one point: "Jesu Maria! the devil! the devil! the devil!" Moreover, he notes that one of the vessels in which Captain George Shelvocke sailed around the world was named the *Jesu Maria*; and at this time Coleridge had been using Shelvocke's *A Voyage round the World by Way of the Great South Sea, Performed in the Years 1719, 20, 21, 22, in the Speedwell of London . . . .* (London, 1726) to good effect in parts of "The Ancient Mariner" (Lowes, pp. 530–32, etc.). To these two forerunners I can add a third. In August, 1750, Thomas Gray wrote a sort of burlesque poem which he entitled "A Long Story" and which was printed in *Six Poems by Thomas Gray* in 1753. Here, in the third from the last stanza, occur the lines:

> "Jesu-Maria! Madam Bridget,
> Why, what can the Viscountess mean?"
> —*The Poetical Works of Gray and Collins* (Oxford ed., 1919), p. 108

One of Coleridge's ambitions was the same as that of the Oxford Press: to edit Gray and Collins; and so he set it down in his notebook as one of his multifarious projects (*Archiv*, p. 354). So "Jesu, Maria" was well established in English literature before Coleridge perceived its usefulness to his purpose and gave it its most famous context.

BOOK IV

THE INTERPRETATION

A "ROMANCE" OF THE "PRETERNATURAL"

TO SUMMARIZE: the retracing of the course of Coleridge's reading so far as it seems to apply to the main problems in "Christabel" has resulted in a rather well-defined pattern for the poem. The figure of the fascinating villainness, Geraldine, betrays a clear affiliation with the behavior and motivation of the vampire, as this being had been discussed and described down the ages. But, like Geraldine, the vampire, though horrible, is also to be pitied, because it is not always responsible for its condition. The lamia, a variety of vampire, is also to be pitied, when its antecedents are known; moreover, the lamia, because of the serpent characteristics which have been attached to it by legend, indicates an even closer relationship with Geraldine, a sort of serpent-woman. Her amazingly contradictory aspects, with her strange vacillation between sinister and kindly impulses, may well derive from the widely accepted doctrines of metempsychosis, which posited sin and expiation as the basis for its transformations; for the brand of some undivulged sin in her past disfigures her body ineffaceably, to her shame and disgust. She seems, likewise, to be under the control of some spirit power from the other world, and has a mission to carry out, though she is apparently not completely reconciled to it herself. She is demon, witch, snake, vampire, and appealing woman by turns and sometimes at the same moment. All these details may be paralleled in Coleridge's reading during the 1790's.

These gleanings from his books all went into the caldron of his imagination, to be mixed and blended and seasoned with a few choice extracts from his daily life. Yet his witch's brew, like that of the hags in *Macbeth*, could scarcely have been concocted at haphazard, with no recipe or formula behind it. In the toad's venom, the fillet of the fenny snake, the eye of newt and toe of frog, the scale of dragon and the root of hemlock "digg'd i' the dark", there were specific virtues, and all were to be mingled in their due proportions. Surely there must have been some guiding principle, some shaping agency, behind the elements which Coleridge wished to fuse in "Christabel". He had scarcely—as Dryden had once said of Abraham Cowley—"swept like a drag-net, great and small", for his mind and memory were selective as well as assimilative.

Coleridge's taste in reading had been formed early. In the series of autobiographical letters which he wrote to Thomas Poole in October, 1797, at the latter's solicitation, he analyzed his own temperament and formative period: "At six years old I remember to have read Belisarius, Robinson Crusoe, and Philip Quarles; and then I found the Arabian Nights' Entertainments, one tale of which (the tale of a man who was compelled to seek for a pure virgin) made so deep an impression on me (I had read it in the evening when my mother was mending stockings), that I was haunted by spectres, whenever I was in the dark: and I distinctly remember the anxious and fearful eagerness with which I used to watch the window in which the books lay, and whenever the sun lay upon them, I would seize it, carry it by the wall, and bask and read. My father found out the effect which these books had produced, and burnt them."[1] The Reverend John Coleridge's pedagogical methods seem to have been somewhat drastic; but the harm had been done before his interference, and his young son's inclination toward this kind of literature could not be eradicated. As the next letter to Poole confessed, these works—ill-adapted, as many thought them, to the juvenile mind—were, in Coleridge's older and reasoned opinion, essential to the full and proper development of a child. "For from my early reading of fairy tales and genii, etc., etc., my mind had been habituated to *the Vast*, and I never regarded *my senses* in any way as the criteria of my belief. I regulated all my creeds by my conceptions, not by my *sight*, even at that age. Should children be permitted to read romances, and relations of giants and magicians, and genii? I know all that has been said

[1] *Letters*, I, 12.

against it; but I have formed my faith in the affirmative. I know no other way of giving the mind a love of the Whole and the Great. . . . ."[2]

As for the particular tales and romances here cited, there is no evidence that they had any specific contribution to make to "Christabel"; yet their influence on his fancy and general lofty and unrestrained cast of thought is obvious. Many years later, when in a letter to Dr. Gillman in October, 1825, he reviewed the contest between Mind and Nature which goes on in every alert adolescent, he recurred to these very stories, at the same time inadvertently confessing the association which they had in his thoughts with both "Christabel" and "The Rime of the Ancient Mariner": "In youth and early manhood the mind and nature are, as it were, two rival artists both potent magicians, and engaged, like the King's daughter and the rebel genii in the Arabian Nights' Entertainments, in a sharp conflict of conjuration. . . . . For a while the mind seems to have the better in the contest, and makes of Nature what it likes, takes her lichens and weather-stains for types and printer's ink, and prints maps and facsimiles of Arabic and Sanscrit MSS. on her rocks; . . . . transforms her summer gales into harps and harpers, lover's sighs and sighing lovers, and her winter blasts into Pindaric odes, Christabels, and Ancient Mariners set to music by Beethoven. . . . ." Yet by 1825 he was forced to make an admission that he would never have considered in 1797; that in the long run Nature gets the better of Mind.[3] But in 1825 the abortive "Christabel" was still associated in his memory with winter and with the grave spiritual harmonies of Beethoven.

Just a few months before his confidences to Poole—in January of the same year, to be exact—Coleridge had received a letter from Charles Lamb which must have set him thinking about his future course of writing. Lamb was ambitious for his friend, but, having already read the secret of the other's procrastinatory character, was privately fearful of his staying powers. Consequently he attempted to encourage his friend to great projects: "Coleridge, I want you to write an Epic poem.

---

[2] *Ibid.*, p. 16.   [3] *Ibid.*, II, 742–43.

Nothing short of it can satisfy the vast capacity of true poetic genius. Having one great End to direct all your poetical faculties to, and on which to lay out your hopes, your ambition, will shew you to what you are equal. By the sacred energies of Milton, by the dainty sweet and soothing phantasies of honeytongued Spenser, I adjure you to attempt the Epic. Or do something more ample than writing an occasional brief ode or sonnet; something 'to make yourself for ever known,—to make the age to come your own.' . . . . You have learning, you have fancy, you have enthusiasm—you have strength and amplitude of wing enow for flights like those I recommend. In the vast and unexplored regions of fairyland, there is ground enough unfound and uncultivated; search there, and realize your favourite Susquehana [sic] scheme."[4]

There was nothing epic, of course, in Coleridge's makeup. The epic was a form which he was wise to leave to his industrious colleague Southey. Yet there were suggestions in Lamb's letter more consonant with his own temperament and genius— suggestions that might make the age to come his own far more successfully than was ever granted to Lamb's "poet, very dear to me,—the now out-of-fashion Cowley." The "vast and unexplored regions of fairyland", at least, must have stirred Coleridge into responsiveness; and the "dainty sweet and soothing phantasies of honeytongued Spenser", with his underlying moral allegory, could scarcely have failed to arouse his attention, for his own inclinations were also moral and allegorical.

Moreover, during the last three or four years he had been thoroughly immersed in another, though closely allied, type of literature. The Gothic romance had not only engaged his rather shamefaced interest, as it had that of most of the reading public of the day, but he had actually been engaged in reviewing several of these horrendous books for the magazines.[5] The clues

---

[4] Lamb, *Letters*, I, 85.

[5] This fact has of course been known, but Garland Greever was the first who seriously tried to recover the reviews themselves, which, according to the journalistic custom of the day, had been printed anonymously. Greever's valuable discoveries are explained and reprinted in the appendix to his book on William Lisle Bowles, *A Wiltshire Parson and His Friends* (Boston and New York, 1926). Tuttle, in his "*Christabel*

are, as usual, found in the correspondence between him and various of his friends at the time. The earliest suggestion of such a journalistic occupation occurs in the letter which Lamb wrote him on July 6, 1796, inquiring whether his friend was not connected with *The Critical Review*.[6] Coleridge's reply has not been preserved; but on December 12 he remarked to Poole, on the same topic, "I receive about forty guineas yearly from the 'Critical Review' and the new 'Monthly Magazine.' "[7] Most concrete of all, however, is his letter to William Lisle Bowles in March, 1797, apropos of his own projected play, *Osorio:* "The plan I have sketched for my tragedy is too chaotic to be transmitted at present—but immediately I understand it myself, I will submit it to you: and feel greatly obliged to you for your permission to do it. It is 'romantic and wild and somewhat terrible'—and I shall have Siddons and Kemble in my mind. But indeed I am most weary of the terrible, having been an hireling in the Critical Review for these last six or eight months. I have been lately reviewing the Monk, the Italian, Hubert de Sevrac, &c., &c., in all of which dungeons, and old castles, and solitary Houses by the Sea Side, and Caverns, and Woods, and extraordinary characters, and all the tribe of Horror and Mystery, have crowded on me—even to surfeiting."[8] Coleridge's optimism concerning the casting of Siddons and Kemble in his play proved chimerical; but the reviews which he mentioned, as well as others included in the "&c., &c.," were all published and may be summoned to the witness stand.

Mrs. Ann Radcliffe was his favorite and became the standard by which he measured all members of the school. He could be very contemptuous when either she or her imitators failed to live up to what, in his opinion, were her best canons. Thus, although he had conducted a correspondence with Mrs. Mary ("Perdita") Robinson and in general spoke highly of her and

---

Sources", has built largely on this material, but has unfortunately confined his attention entirely to an attempt to find factual parallels in the novels themselves, and has therefore completely overlooked the basic importance of the theories involved.

[6] Lamb, *Letters*, I, 36.

[7] Coleridge, *Letters*, I, 185.   [8] Greever, pp. 29–31.

her work, especially her poetry,[9] he reviewed her *Hubert de Sevrac. A Romance, of the 18th Century* pretty scathingly in August, 1798: "The character of Mrs. Robinson's novels being generally known, it is perhaps sufficient to say, that Hubert de Sevrac is inferior to her former productions. It is an imitation of Mrs. Radcliffe's romances, but without any resemblance that may not be attained by a common pen. There are detached parts, however, of which we may speak with approbation; and, during the prevalence of the present taste for romances, the whole may afford amusement to the supporters of circulating libraries. But it may be necessary to apprise novel-writers, in general, that this taste is declining, and that real life and manners will soon assert their claims."[10] The discussions of the theoreticians of the *Lyrical Ballads* are here amusingly in evidence, insinuating their propaganda into the rival field of fiction; and the general viewpoint is that which Coleridge had expressed to Wordsworth in his criticism of *The Castle Spectre* in January of the same year: "Passion—horror! agonizing pangs of conscience! Dreams full of hell, serpents, and skeletons; starts and attempted murders, etc., but positively, not *one* line that marks even a superficial knowledge of human feelings could I discover."[11]

Coleridge's remarks on Mrs. Radcliffe herself go back at least to August, 1794, when *The Critical Review* published his opinions of *The Mysteries of Udolpho, A Romance*, which had just come out. He began by comparing it with her earlier story, *The Romance of the Forest*, which for some strange (but possibly later explicable) reason seems to have been his favorite—a book which proved that she had the key to "unlock the gates . . . . of horror, that and thrilling fears." In the new book, "The same powers of description are displayed, the same predilection is discovered for the wonderful and the gloomy—the same mysterious terrors are continually exciting in the mind the idea of a

[9] Earl Leslie Griggs discusses their friendship in "Coleridge and Mrs. Mary Robinson," *Modern Language Notes*, XLV (February, 1930), 90–95.

[10] *Critical Review*, XXIII (August, 1798), 472; or Greever, p. 190.

[11] *Letters*, I, 237.

supernatural appearance, keeping us, as it were, upon the very
edge and confines of the world of spirits, and yet are ingeniously
explained by familiar causes; curiosity is kept upon the stretch
from page to page, and from volume to volume, and the secret,
which the reader thinks himself every instant upon the point of
penetrating, flies like a phantom before him, and eludes his
eagerness till the very last moment of protracted explanation."
Yet, the reviewer was careful to point out, "This method is,
however, liable to the following inconvenience, that in the
search for what is new, an author is likely to forget what is
natural; and, in rejecting the more obvious conclusions, to take
those which are less satisfactory." Thus he was driven to the
conclusion that *Udolpho* was inferior to *The Romance of the Forest:* "Curiosity is raised oftener than it is gratified; or rather, it
is raised so high that no adequate gratification can be given it;
the interest is completely dissolved when once the adventure is
finished, and the reader, when he is got to the end of the work,
looks about in vain for the spell which had bound him so strongly to it." In spite of these faults, and others which he cites, the
reviewer finishes by quoting two excerpts, one describing Emily's discovery of the corpse behind the curtain in the torture
chamber, as a "specimen of one of those picturesque scenes of
terror, which the author knows so well to work up," and the
other the poem "The Sea Nymph", as a specimen of Radcliffe's
"pleasing" verse.[12]

The problems here raised might almost seem to be anticipa-
tions of those with which Coleridge was himself confronted when
he began to write "Christabel" some four years later. Horace
Walpole, too, had perceived and considered them many years
earlier in the preface to the second edition of *The Castle of
Otranto*, the progenitor of the original and rival Gothic school.
In his excursus on the old and the new types of romance, he had
examined the different techniques and had defended his own
practice in these terms: "It was an attempt to blend the two

[12] *Critical Review*, XI (August, 1794), 361-74; or Greever, pp. 168-84. This prose
quotation is the one which, in Tuttle's opinion (pp. 453 ff.), furnished Coleridge with
the greatest number of his borrowings.

kinds of Romance, the ancient and the modern. In the former, all was imagination and improbability: in the latter, nature is always intended to be, and sometimes has been, copied with success. . . . . The author of the following pages thought it possible to reconcile the two kinds. Desirous of leaving the powers of fancy at liberty to expatiate through the boundless realms of invention, and thence of creating more interesting situations, he wished to conduct the mortal agents in his drama according to the rules of probability; in short, to make them think, speak, and act, as it might be supposed mere men and women would do in extraordinary positions. He had observed, that, in all inspired writings, the personages under the dispensation of miracles, and witnesses to the most stupendous phenomena, never lose sight of their known character: whereas in the romantic story, an improbable event never fails to be attended by an absurd dialogue."[13]

The principle of verisimilitude, of "truth to nature", was, then, as much a part of Walpole's credo as it was of Mrs. Radcliffe's and of Coleridge's. Mrs. Radcliffe, however, allowed herself no supernatural explanations of her extraordinary events; Walpole indulged himself to the saturation-point with the supernatural, but, theoretically, applied the realistic principle of "nature" to the behavior and language of his characters. Thus, once more, has an identical measuring-rod in terminology been applied in perfect good faith to works of the most widely divergent techniques.

In June, 1798, Coleridge continued the same critical line of thought in his review of Mrs. Radcliffe's *The Italian; or, The Confessional of the Black Penitents. A Romance* (later known as *The Sicilian*), and gloated a bit over the realization of his earlier prophecy: "It was not difficult to foresee that the *modern romance*, even supported by the skill of the most ingenious of its votaries, would soon experience the fate of every attempt to please by what is unnatural, and by a departure from that observance of real life, which has placed the works of Fielding, Smollett, and some other writers, among the permanent sources

[13] Walpole, pp. 13–14.

of amusement. It might for a time afford an acceptable variety to persons whose reading is confined to works of fiction, and who would, perhaps, be glad to exchange dullness for extravagance; but it was probable that, as its constitution (if we may so speak) was maintained only by the passion of terror, and that excited by trick, and as it was not conversant in incidents and characters of a natural complexion, it would degenerate into repetition, and would disappoint curiosity. So many cries 'that the wolf is coming,' must at last lose their effect." Consequently, Coleridge believed that *The Italian* fell short of *Udolpho*, just as *Udolpho* fell short of *The Romance of the Forest*, and for the same cause—repetition. He admitted that it contained a few scenes that "powerfully seize the imagination, and interest the passions," but called the sensational chapter describing the examination of Vivaldi, the hero, before the Inquisition "so improbable, that we should rather have attributed it to one of Mrs. Radcliffe's numerous imitators."[14]

Nature, probability, and originality seem thus far to be Coleridge's chief criteria for judging this type of fiction. But in his elaborate review of Lewis's *The Monk* in February, 1797,[15] he had added other elements in his evaluation of the "romance", as *The Critical Review* always carefully classified such works. He began with his customary warning: "The horrible and the preternatural have usually seized on the popular taste, at the rise and decline of literature. Most powerful stimulants, they can never be required except by the torpor of an unawakened, or the languor of an exhausted appetite. The same phaenomenon, therefore, which we hail as a favorable omen in the belles lettres of Germany, impresses a degree of gloom in the compositions of our countrymen. We trust, however, that satiety will banish what good sense should have prevented; and that, wearied with fiends, incomprehensible characters, with shrieks, murders, and subterraneous dungeons, the public will learn, by the multitude of the manufacturers, with how little expense of

[14] *Critical Review*, XXIII (June, 1798), 166–69; or Greever, pp. 185–89.

[15] *Critical Review*, XIX (February, 1797), 194–200; or Greever, pp. 191–200.

thought or imagination this species of composition is manu-
factured."

Nevertheless, while feeling that this sensationalism marked
a period of decline in English literature though simultaneously
announcing a renaissance in German art, Coleridge admitted
that, "cheaply as we estimate romances in general, we acknowledge, in the work before us, the offspring of no common genius."
Pointing out first the basic similarity of Lewis's story to that
of the temptation and downfall of the holy man, Santon Bar-
sisa, retold in the one hundred and forty-eighth *Guardian* from
The Turkish Tales, he selected for special commendation the
"truly terrific" inner "tale of the bleeding nun", together with
the bold and happy conception of the "burning cross on the
forehead of the wandering Jew (a mysterious character, which,
though copied as to its more prominent features from Schiller's
incomprehensible Armenian, does, nevertheless, display great
vigour of fancy)." This selection is highly interesting for several
reasons. Least of these is Coleridge's own use of criminal and
witch-marks. More arresting is the fact that in the story of the
bleeding nun the hero, Raymond, to his speechless horror discovers his midnight visitor, the nun, to be "an animated corse",
and remains in the power of this specter "a whole long hour,"
just as Christabel did with Geraldine.[16] Capping all, however,
is Coleridge's mention, immediately afterward, of the character
of Mathilda, the lovely and enchanting villainess-heroine and
"the chief agent in the seduction" of Ambrosio the monk—a
portrait which reminds us at once of Geraldine in its general
effect if not in its details. To Coleridge, Mathilda was "the
author's master-piece", and was "exquisitely imagined and as
exquisitely supported".[17]

[16] Tuttle (pp. 468–70) discusses this comparison.

[17] The description of Geraldine, Tuttle (pp. 466–68), following and expanding E.H.C.
(p. 70), believes to have been "compounded of three characters" from *The Monk*—
not to mention additional details drawn from "Mathilda's master, the fallen angel
Lucifer." Here is Coleridge's first picture of Geraldine, with the details italicized by
Tuttle:

> "There she sees a damsel bright,
> *Drest in a* silken *robe of white,*

These matters are not new; they do, however, confirm former statements. The most significant points, as regards Coleridge's critical theory, are to be found in his analysis of the defects of *The Monk*, which to his mind far outweighed its merits. The first bears on the question of incidents and their impression. Since in such a work the author may change the order of nature almost at will and all events may thus seem almost equally probable, the reader will derive little pleasure from the "perception of *difficulty surmounted*. The writer may make us wonder, but he cannot surprise us." This business of the author's domination over plot without regard to nature leads, however, to a vastly more important defect. "For the same reasons a

> *That* shadowy in the moonlight *shone:*
> *The neck that made that white robe wan,*
> *Her stately neck, and arms were bare;*
> *Her* blue-veined *feet* unsandal'd were,
> *And wildly glittered here and there*
> *The gems entangled in her hair.*
> I guess, *'twas frightful there to see*
> *A lady so richly clad* as she—
> *Beautiful exceedingly!*"

With this check the following descriptions of the innocent Antonia, again with Tuttle's italicization:

". . . . Her features were hidden by a thick veil; but struggling through the crowd had deranged it sufficiently to *discover a neck which for symmetry and beauty might have vied with the Medicean Venus. It was of the most dazzling whiteness,* and received additional charms from being shaded by the tresses of *her* long *fair hair. . . . .* Her dress was white; it . . . . just permitted to peep out from under it a little *foot* of the most delicate proportions."

". . . . *her neck was full and beautiful in the extreme; her hand and arm were formed with the most perfect symmetry.*"

"Antonia *arrayed in* bridal *white. . . . .*"

Supplement these details with the following ones concerning two women appearing "in a religious procession at a festival":

". . . . reclined the most beautiful form that eyes ever witnessed. It was a damsel representing St. Claire: *her dress was of inestimable price, and round her head a wreath of diamonds formed an artificial glory: but all these yielded to the lustre of her charms.*"

". . . . *was robed in white, and her brow was ornamented with a sparkling diadem.*"

Add to these the description of Mathilda herself:

". . . . She had quitted her religious habit: she was now clothed in a long sable robe, on which was traced in gold embroidery a variety of unknown characters: it was fastened by a girdle of precious stones, in which was fixed a poniard. *Her neck and arms were uncovered;* in her hand she bore a golden wand; *her hair was loose,* and flowed wildly upon her shoulders; her eyes sparkled with terrific expression; *and her whole demeanor was calculated to inspire the beholder with awe and admiration.*"

And conclude with this picture of Lucifer himself:

". . . . *his silken locks were confined by a band of many-coloured fires, which played*

romance is incapable of exemplifying a moral truth," dogma-
tized Coleridge, adding that no proud man would be made more
humble by reading a tale about how the devil once seduced a
presumptuous monk. The struggle is too unequal, for man, no
matter how prudent and sagacious, has no sufficient defense
against the "power and cunning of supernatural beings". Considered beside this moral inadequacy, the failure of such a book
to give genuine pleasure palls to insignificance. Such frightful
and unbearable sufferings as those described shatter the illusion and force the reader to charge such an author with a peculiar species of brutality in apparently deriving a personal
pleasure in such wanton imaginings. "The merit of a novelist,"

---

*round his head, formed themselves into a variety of figures, and shone with brilliance far
surpassing that of precious stones."*

This eclectic method of selection of random details, all supposedly coalescing into
one unified and coherent picture, is to my mind one of the most dangerous sins of
modern scholarship. For these details are chosen from widely separated passages
(Tuttle's references to the London, 1800, edition of *Ambrosio or the Monk* run as follows: I, 5–6, 11, 40, for Antonia; III, 135, 133, for the anonymous women in the procession; II, 271–72, for Mathilda; and II, 276, for Lucifer). Moreover, only one of the
characters involved, Mathilda, bears any fundamental resemblance to Geraldine, the
other women being much more like Christabel, and Lucifer, of course, being totally
unlike either. It seems to me, too, that at least some attention ought to be devoted
to the *un*italicized details. If they are studied with any care, it will be realized at once
that they constitute entirely discordant elements, especially in the case of Mathilda,
who is clothed in black and gold and bears a golden wand. The other descriptions of
dresses simply prove the obvious: that women, especially when they are preparing
for a marriage ceremony or are in a religious procession, are prone to clothe themselves
in white. It is a commonplace of romantic fiction for women to have well-proportioned
arms and necks of dazzling whiteness—but note that Antonia's, which are thus described, are not really bare like Geraldine's; it is only Mathilda's, which are *not* thus
described, which are "uncovered". Naturally, women have feet—which is about all
that is said of Antonia's; Geraldine's, however, are both "blue-veined" and "un-
sandal'd". As for the "gems entangled in her hair", I admit that Coleridge's eye might
well have been attracted to the comparison of the "wreath of diamonds" to "an artificial glory" (see above, p. 59); on the other hand, Geraldine's precious stones "wildly
glittered here and there"—there was no formality of a diadem in her adornments. In
other words, the two women who, like Geraldine, have disarranged hair have no jewels
in it, whereas the two who wear tiaras have clearly prepared their hair in a most
fastidious fashion—though it must be admitted that Mathilda wears "a girdle of
precious stones, in which was fixed a poniard." Perhaps these stones have been dis-
persed, raised from her waist, and scattered through Geraldine's hair!

For such reasons as these, although one cannot deny Tuttle's claim that Coleridge
in his description of Geraldine "could have taken nearly every detail from *The Monk*",
I should like to express my extreme doubt that he *did* do so. I had examined all these
passages and rejected the possibility some time before his article came out.

insisted the critic, "is in proportion (not simply to the effect, but) to the *pleasurable* effect which he produces." On this subject he waxed eloquent indeed: "To trace the nice boundaries, beyond which terror and sympathy are deserted by the pleasurable emotions,—to reach those limits, yet never to pass them,— *hic labor, hic opus est.* Figures that shock the imagination, and narratives that mangle the feelings, rarely discover *genius,* and always display a low and vulgar *taste."* How grieved he must have been twenty years afterward to see himself being accused of the very sins that he had attacked so earnestly in his youth!

Thus it was the moral weakness and even viciousness of *The Monk* that to Coleridge constituted its greatest defect. In the character of Ambrosio he felt that Lewis had manifested a complete "ignorance of the human heart". Such a high-minded and righteous person would be incapable of degenerating so rapidly and thoroughly as Ambrosio did. "The romance-writer possesses an unlimited power over situations; but he must scrupulously make his characters act in congruity with them. Let him work physical wonders only, and we will be content to *dream* with him for a while; but the first *moral* miracle which he attempts, he disgusts and awakens us." So Ambrosio's behavior after the diabolic revelations seems "not improbable, but impossible; not preternatural, but contrary to nature. The extent of the powers that may exist, we can never ascertain; and therefore we feel no great difficulty in yielding a temporary belief to any, the strangest, situation of *things.* But that situation once conceived, how beings like ourselves would feel and act in it, our own feelings sufficiently instruct us; and we instantly reject the clumsy fiction that does not harmonise with them."

Is there not here a foreshadowing of that "willing suspension of disbelief for the moment which constitutes poetic faith"? Coleridge freely admits the supremacy of the Gothic fictionist over the realm of matter, because man has not yet plumbed its secret mysteries and probably never will completely do so; it is in the domain of the human soul, which he professes it is within the power of man to understand and predict, that the writer of prose romances has no control. Here the romance writer is sinning against the Holy Ghost when he gives rein to his depraved and distorted imagination.

The Monk, therefore, Coleridge characterized as "a romance, which if a parent saw in the hands of a son or daughter, he might reasonably turn pale. . . . . though the tale is indeed a tale of horror, yet the most painful impression which the work left on our minds was that of great acquirements and splendid genius employed to furnish a *mormo* for children, a poison for youth, and a provocative for the debauchee. Tales of enchantments and witchcraft can never be *useful:* our author has contrived to make them pernicious, by blending with an irreverent negligence, all that is most awfully true in religion with all that is most ridiculously absurd in superstition." Lewis's blasphemy against Christianity and the Bible were to Coleridge unbearable. Even the excellent poetry scattered throughout the volume, tender and heart-touching as most of it was, could not atone for the moral disintegration of the story.

In the light of these reviews, presented at this length and as largely as possible in Coleridge's own words because of their vital bearing on the problem, it becomes easy to understand why he was at first so reticent and even embarrassed about his poem "Christabel". For it is obvious that, in spite of what he said to Bowles about being surfeited with such horrific but trivial fare, he was himself composing what was essentially a "romance". The chief perceptible difference was that his romance was in verse, whereas the stories of Lewis, Radcliffe, Robinson, *et al.*, were in prose. He too was commandeering old castles, woods, serpents, dreams full of hell, extraordinary and incomprehensible characters, mysterious terrors upon the very edge and confines of the world of spirits, and was turning them into the outward fabric of his poem. His leading character, so "exquisitely imagined", yet so sinister, might also be regarded as "a *mormo* for children"—and Mormo, be it remembered, was a female demon of the lamia genus. He too was relating a tale of enchantment and witchcraft, which, if he had harkened to his own categorical generalization, could "never be *useful*". There was a patent inconsistency between his publicly reiterated theories and the fascinating project that had perversely germinated from these seeds and was now beckoning him on.

On the other hand, the fact that his romance was to be poetry, and not a mere novel, might have made all the difference in his mind.   A poetical romance, if it did not stretch the bounds of "nature" too far and was careful not to pass the "nice boundaries, beyond which terror and sympathy are deserted by the pleasurable emotions," might also be capable of "exemplifying a moral truth". He definitely did not want his tale to belong to the supernatural school of Walpole and Lewis; the more natural and rational school of Radcliffe pleased him better. And this is probably the reason why he was so fond of *The Romance of the Forest*, inferior as it strikes one as being today: it possesses even less of an atmosphere of supernaturalism—even counterfeit supernaturalism—than any of Mrs. Radcliffe's other books. Yet he could not sacrifice this element entirely, or the interest in the kind of story he was impelled to present would utterly evaporate.

Perhaps one of the words which Coleridge used prominently in his critique of *The Monk* has lodged in the reader's memory as it did in mine. It is a word which I should like to offer as at least a partial solution to the problem, which, after all, is not completely inscrutable. It is a word which Coleridge, without being any too explicit and clear-cut in his distinctions, evidently opposed to the supernatural, on the one hand, and the natural, on the other. The word is "preternatural". "The horrible and the preternatural" were the first words in his review and were clearly intended to apply to two distinct but related realms. Later, Ambrosio's behavior impressed him as "not improbable, but impossible; not preternatural, but contrary to nature." That there was some special significance to this word in its relation to "Christabel" is manifest when two of his most regrettably uncompleted projects are recalled.

At the end of the thirteenth chapter of the *Biographia Lit-*

eraria he announced a critical essay "on the uses of the Supernatural in Poetry", to be prefixed to a future edition of "The Ancient Mariner". He had already informed Byron of the same plan on March 30, 1815.[18] How far he got with this exciting scheme there is no telling, though he had made a start some years before[19] and was still toying with the idea in 1817 when he was preparing the prospectus for his course of lectures, given the next year but never printed. According to Gillman, the eleventh and the twelfth sections were to consist as follows: "XI. On the Arabian Nights Entertainments, and on the *romantic* use of the supernatural in Poetry, and in works of fiction not poetical. On the conditions and regulations under which such Books may be employed advantageously in the earlier Periods of Education. XII. On tales of witches, apparitions, &c. as distinguished from the magic and magicians of asiatic origin. The probable sources of the former, and of the belief in them in certain ages and classes of men. Criteria by which mistaken and exaggerated facts may be distinguished from absolute falsehood and imposture. Lastly, the causes of the terror and interest which stories of ghosts and witches inspire, in early life at least, whether believed or not."[20] Here, in the case of the supernatural at any rate, Coleridge seems to have imagined some distinction between its use in poetry "and in works of fiction not poetical".

To balance this unsubstantial treatise, many years earlier he had privately announced an even more baffling work—and in such forthright terms that the finished manuscript seemed to be already in his hand. On March 16, 1801, he had written to Thomas Poole as follows: "I shall therefore, as I said, immediately publish my 'Christabel,' with two essays annexed to it, on the 'Preternatural' and on 'Metre.' "[21] Could any more tantalizing mystery be piled on the other tantalizing mysteries al-

---

[18] Griggs, II, 133.

[19] In a letter to J. H. Green on December 13, 1817 (*Letters*, II, 683–84), he refers to a sentence of his own in "a fragment of an Essay on the Supernatural many years ago, viz. that the presence of a ghost is the terror, not what he *does*. . . . ."

[20] Gillman, p. 334.   [21] *Letters*, I, 349.

ready accumulated for "Christabel"? For of course neither of
the essays promised is extant, though perhaps a fragment of the
second is preserved in the last paragraph of the preface to the
poem when it was printed in 1816. Is it possible to recover what
Coleridge meant by "preternatural" and to apply the results to
the poem which was once to have carried them as an introduction? For obviously, in his mind, "Christabel" was to exemplify
the "preternatural" just as "The Rime of the Ancient Mariner"
exemplified the "supernatural".[22] Fortunately, here again he
has left behind him a trail, somewhat obliterated and indistinct,
for those who will look.

Early in 1796 Robert Southey published his *Joan of Arc, an
Epic Poem*, which was printed at Bristol under the auspices of
Joseph Cottle. In his preface Southey announced that approx-
imately the first four hundred and fifty lines of the second book
were not by himself, but by his friend Coleridge.[23] In June,
1796, *The Critical Review*, for which Coleridge himself was already a "hireling", published its review of the epic, as well
as one of Coleridge's own *Poems*.[24] In the criticism of *Joan of
Arc* the reviewer included these remarks: "In the part composed by Mr. Coleridge, which is almost all the 450 lines of the
second book, preternatural agency is introduced and vindicated.
This subject is treated too obscurely, perhaps, for epic poetry,
and without leaving probably on our minds the impression that
the Maid was under any such influence. It may, however, be
thought by many, that the poem required some such contriv-
ance, together with dreams and magic, to supply the want of
angels, daemons, and gods, the machinery that form the
θαυμαστον of an heroic poem, the *dignus vindice nodus*."

What had apparently happened was this: Since 1793 Southey
had been at work on his epic, but before he published it in
1796 he had changed and renovated it very thoroughly. In the
meantime Coleridge too had become sufficiently interested in

---

[22] Hanson (p. 257) casually notes this point, but fails to follow it up.

[23] Southey, *Joan of Arc, an Epic Poem* (Bristol, 1796), p. vi.

[24] *Critical Review*, XVII (June, 1796), 188, 209–12. Incidentally, on September 27,
1796, Coleridge drew the May number from the Bristol Library (Kaufman, p. 320).

the Maid to project and begin a poem of his own, which he thought of under a variety of titles, such as *The Progress of Liberty*, *The Vision of the Maid of Orleans*, *Visions of the Maid of Orleans*, *Visions of the Maid of Arc*, and *The Vision of the Patriot Maiden*.[25] Eventually, what he had composed was published among the *Sibylline Leaves* in 1817 under a totally different title, "The Destiny of Nations," which he also described as "A Vision". In the meantime, however, he agreed to insert in Southey's epic the most important passage of what he had written, seemingly because it contained what he regarded as at least a semi-reasonable explanation of those famous visions which turned Joan from a common peasant girl into the savior of France. These lines were described in the "Argument" to the second book as dealing with "Preternatural agency". The fact that certain essential parts of this passage were later omitted from "The Destiny of Nations" may account for the failure of Lowes and others to realize their importance.[26]

Freed from the incumbrances of lengthy footnotes on the theories of the aether as held by Sir Isaac Newton, David Hartley, and Andrew Baxter, and rid of turgid rhetorical and metaphysical disquisitions on Fancy, Reason, and the Universe, the significant aspects of Coleridge's suggestions on the preternatural may be disentangled thus. He first inveighs against those foolish scientists who

> deem themselves most free
> When they within this gross and visible sphere
> Chain down the winged thought, scoffing ascent[,]
> Proud in their meanness. . . . .

For those people, he insists, are merely cheating themselves

> With noisy emptiness of learned phrase,
> Their subtle fluids, impacts, essences,
> Self-working Tools, uncaus'd Effects, and all
> Those blind Omniscients, those Almighty Slaves,
> Untenanting Creation of its God.

[25] See Coleridge, *Poems*, p. 131 n.

[26] Cf. Lowes, pp. 77, 483, *et passim*. Hanson (pp. 147–48, 189, 297–98) recognizes the importance of this passage in general, but does not see its application to "Christabel".

Coleridge is emphatically no mechanist; he cannot believe that "Properties are God".[27]

But there is a bolder group of thinkers, who argue on the analogy that, since any body of matter is composed of innumerable atoms, so one "all-conscious Spirit" may be made up of "Infinite myriads of self-conscious minds". This Spirit directs

> With absolute ubiquity of thought
> All his component monads, that yet seem
> With various province and apt agency
> Each to pursue its own self-centering end.
> Some nurse the infant diamond in the mine;
> Some roll the genial juices thro' the oak;
> Some drive the mutinous clouds to clash in air;
> And rushing on the storm with whirlwind speed
> Yoke the red lightning to their vollying car.
> Thus these pursue their never-varying course,
> No eddy in their stream. Others more wild,
> With complex interests weaving human fates,
> Duteous or proud, alike obedient all,
> Evolve the process of eternal good.

This is evidently a reflection of Leibnitz's theory of monads, probably through the medium of Hartley, who at this time was still high in Coleridge's favor; but it is also an echo of the cosmology of Paracelsus, which Coleridge found provocative in explaining not only the physical but also the moral universe. It could likewise be used to solve the presence and use of evil in the world:

> And what if some rebellious, o'er dark realms
> Arrogate power? yet these train up to God,
> And on the rude eye unconfirm'd for day
> Flash meteor lights better than total gloom.[28]

The Laplander, with all his wizards and prodigies, is still fortunate, since by the power of his fancy he is taking the first step which "unsensualizes the dark mind" and, by peopling the air,

> By obscure fears of Beings invisible
> Emancipates it from the grosser thrall
> Of the present impulse, teaching self controul
> 'Till Superstition with unconscious hand
> Seat Reason on her throne.[29]

---

[27] *Joan*, pp. 40–41.   [28] *Ibid.*, p. 43.   [29] *Ibid.*, p. 45.

These speculations lead Coleridge directly to his hypothesis of the preternatural, which he advances, though tentatively, to explain the visions and mission of Joan. In its theory of the reason for the existence of evil it has a strongly Miltonic cast; but after all, from the theological point of view, what theory is more reasonable? So Coleridge wrote:

> If there be Beings of higher class than Man,
> I deem no nobler province they possess
> Than by disposal of apt circumstance
> To rear some realm with patient discipline,
> Aye bidding PAIN, dark ERROR's uncouth child,
> Blameless Parenticide! his snakey scourge
> Lift fierce against his Mother! Thus they make
> Of transient Evil ever-during Good
> Themselves probationary, and denied
> Confess'd to view by preternatural deed
> To o'erwhelm the will, save on some fated day
> Headstrong, or with petition'd might from God.
>
> And such perhaps the guardian Power whose ken
> Still dwelt on France. He from the Invisible World
> Burst on the MAIDEN's eye, impregning Air
> With Voices and strange Shapes, illusions apt,
> Shadowy of Truth. . . . .[30]

In the later version the last fourteen lines, the pivotal part of the passage, were altered completely and became nothing more than an apology for the choice of such a humble person as Joan for the subject of an epic poem.

This, it must be admitted, is all none too clear. The Delphic author might well have appended to some of these lines the same candid commentary that he later set down opposite another disjoined fragment in "The Destiny of Nations": "These are very fine Lines, tho' I say it, that should not: but, hang me, if I know or ever did know the meaning of them, tho' my own composition."[31] Yet, if I understand them at all, they may be paraphrased somewhat in this fashion: There may be in the universe some kind of being, more divine than man, which is commissioned to care for the welfare of men and kingdoms. Pain may sometimes be necessary to dispel error, but permanent

[30] *Ibid.*, pp. 47–48.   [31] *Poems*, p. 140 n.

good will come from transitory evil. These beings are themselves probationers (that is, they are undergoing a period of
trial—a common theological sense). They are usually invisible;
but, when their efforts are withstood, they may, in order to
overcome the stubborn or ignorant human will, become visible
"by preternatural deed", either through their own headstrong
nature or through their pleading with God himself. Thus a
guardian spirit was watching over France, and, coming from
the invisible world, made Joan of Arc his instrument, in spite
of her initial fear and unwillingness.

Thus, "preternatural" to Coleridge would seem to have a
somewhat different meaning from that usually attached to it.
It referred not only to phenomena of a remarkable nature beyond the normal course of events but also to matters on another plane of existence. Preternatural occurrences, according
to his use of the term in his review of *The Monk*, would be
improbable occurrences, but not impossible—not completely
contrary to nature; the horrible he also distinguished on this
basis from the preternatural. Divergences from the known, the
normal, he therefore, in *Joan*, suggested might be explained by
the interference of beings from another world, themselves subject to regularly established laws. These beings, however, were
essentially moral beings, or at least were allowed to operate only
for an ultimately moral purpose, which might be reached only
through their inflicting of suffering or pain. It is obvious that
such a doctrine really comes very close to supernaturalism,
since the manifestations of such phenomena would appear miraculous to man. In the proper sense of the word, Mrs. Radcliffe's romances dealt with the preternatural, since only in
their initial outward show were her events beyond the natural,
and their explanation was finally found. In *Joan of Arc* (which,
it may be worth noting, preceded his review of *The Monk*)
Coleridge sought this explanation in another world and, having
thus found it, labeled the agency no longer supernatural but
preternatural.

Though these distinctions may seem pretty metaphysical and
not completely satisfactory, it is nevertheless clear that Cole-

ridge once conceived of "Christabel" as illustrating his theory of the preternatural. Moreover, to him it also fell into the "vision" category, for he had confessed in his preface that the "very first conception of the tale" had come to his mind "with the wholeness, no less than the liveliness of a vision. . . . ."[32] And so he continued to look at it, for, as Gillman says, "When in health he sometimes said, 'This poem comes upon me with all the loveliness of a vision;' and he declared, that though contrary to the advice of his friends, he should finish it: At other times when his bodily powers failed him, he would then say, 'I am reserved for other works than making verse.' "[33]

If it is, then, a vision of the preternatural, how do its characters and incidents harmonize with what he has said on the subject in the above-mentioned sources? From this point of view Derwent Coleridge's interpretation, which has been generally rejected or doubted, seems substantially justified. It is vital enough to bear repeating: "The sufferings of Christabel were to have been represented as vicarious, endured for her 'lover far away;' and Geraldine, no witch or goblin, or malignant being of any kind, but a spirit, executing her appointed task with the best good will, as she herself says:—

> All they, who live in the upper sky,
> Do love you, holy Christabel, &c."

Moreover, it will be remembered that Geraldine reminds the spirit of Christabel's mother that she has been delegated special power for the time of her mission. Lastly, it is even possible to explain Geraldine's past on the "probationary" basis. Whatever she is or has done, she is now suffering in expiation of her sin, the brand or symbol of which is still visible on her body (recall here the use of the expiation motif in the doctrine of metempsychosis),[34] and her future depends on the successful accomplishment of her repugnant duty. This interpretation should satisfy E. H. C.'s half-doubts about Derwent Coleridge's reliability, when he concludes that the latter's theory "must be

---

[32] E.H.C., p. 57 n.

[33] Gillman, p. 281.   [34] As discussed on pp. 129–39, *et passim.*

received with respect, but it does not add much to the interpretation of the poem as a whole."[35] On the other hand, it un-
equivocally confutes Gillman, who insisted that Geraldine was
intended to represent the power of evil, and nothing else.[36]

So much for the center of the mystery—fair Geraldine. In
this framework, just how does Christabel function? The main
clues, such as they are, include her relationship with her absent lover, her name, and her association in her creator's mind
with St. Teresa. She herself appears to be a maiden of perfect
innocence and piety. But all is not so well with her absent
lover. Both Derwent Coleridge and Gillman agree that in the
remainder of the story this lover was to have been saved from
his temptations and sins by her unmerited sufferings. Obviously, if these two are to be trusted (and there are none more
likely than they to have heard the truth from S. T. C.'s own
lips, especially since this time they agree on the point), the
poem was to have been founded on the doctrine of vicarious
atonement, and in this way would have established its moral
justification. Was it only because of its euphony and beauty
that Coleridge was attracted to the name Christabel? Was it
not also because of its echo of the word Christ itself?[37] For Christ
was the supreme exemplar of this doctrine. He was the sacrificial
lamb, whose sufferings were supposed to have washed man clean
of sin. He was the dove, the exemplification of goodness. And
Sir Leoline had called his favorite dove—"That gentle bird,
whom thou dost love," as Bracy had put it—by his daughter's
name. Bracy, it is true, had seen this dove fluttering within

---

[35] E.H.C., p. 52 n.

[36] Gillman, p. 283. It also confutes Tuttle, who, with McElderry, sets himself solidly
against any didactic interpretation when he says (p. 468 n.): "In view of the fact that
Christabel is a versified Gothic romance, it seems unnecessary to develop an elaborate
theory about the intended moral significance of Christabel's sufferings. (See McElderry,
op. cit., p. 452.) The heroine's duty was to suffer, faint, and at last be rescued. Her
wanderings in the forest, seizures by ruffians [but when was Christabel seized by
ruffians?], and eventual happiness were essentials of the plot taken for granted by both
authors and readers." Nego!

[37] Cf. Caine, Rossetti, p. 152: "The beautiful thing, not more from its beauty than
its suggestiveness, suited his purpose exactly."

the coils of the green snake, the traditional representation of evil; but Bracy's powers of vision were limited to the obviously supernatural, and the purposes of the preternatural were closed to him. At the end of Oliver Wendell Holmes's *Elsie Venner*, one may recall, all of Elsie's serpent characteristics disappeared, and she was left a sympathetic and pitiful woman.

With these suggestions accepted, Coleridge's statement to Allsop that certain lines in Crashaw's poem on St. Teresa were always present in his mind while he was writing the second part of "Christabel", "if, indeed, by some subtle process of the mind they did not suggest the first thought of the whole poem,"[38] no longer retains its enigmatic quality. The passage which Allsop quotes as having been cited to him by Coleridge runs thus:

> Since 'tis not to be had at home,
> She'l travail to a ma[r]tyrdome.
> No home for her confesses she,
> But where she may a martyr be.
> She'l to the Moores, and trade with them
> For this invalued diadem,
> She offers them her dearest breath
> With Christ's name in 't, in change for death.
> She'll bargain with them, and will give
> Them God, and teach them how to live
> In Him, or if they this deny,
> For Him she'll teach them how to die.
> So shall she leave amongst them sown,
> The Lord's blood, or, at least, her own.
> Farewell then, all the world—adieu,
> Teresa is no more for you:
> Farewell all pleasures, sports, and joys,
> Never till now esteemed toys—
> Farewell whatever dear'st may be,
> Mother's arms or father's knee;
> Farewell house, and farewell home,
> She's for the Moores and martyrdom.

Here, and through the entire poem, the idea of martyrdom is stressed. And the martyr idea is definitely an aspect of vicarious atonement, and a vastly important one. The earliest title of Crashaw's poem stressed this element, for it read: "In Memory of the Vertuous and Learned Lady Madre de Teresa That

[38] Allsop, I, 195–96.

Sought an Early Martyrdome"; only later was the title changed
to "A Hymn to the Name and Honor of the Admirable Sainte
Teresa. . . . ."[39] Moreover, certain of the lines preceding those
which Coleridge quoted should be noticed in view of Christabel's
night spent in Geraldine's vampirical embrace. Crashaw speaks
thus of the childish Teresa, whose small body as yet contains
scarcely enough blood to make "A guilty sword blush for her
sake":

> She never undertook to know
> What death with love should have to doe;
> Nor has she e're yet understood
> Why to show love, she should shed blood. . . . .[40]

Nor did Coleridge rely wholly on Crashaw for his knowledge
of Teresa. For the following four lines in the conclusion to the
first part of "Christabel" are not, as E. H. C. incautiously intimates,[41] attributable to Crashaw's portrait of Teresa:

> Yea, she doth smile, and she doth weep,
> Like a youthful hermitess,
> Beauteous in a wilderness,
> Who, praying always, prays in sleep.

There is nothing at all in the "Hymn" about hermits or her-
mitesses. Nor are they mentioned in Crashaw's other poems on
the same subject—"An Apologie for the Fore-Going Hym" and
"The Flaming Heart: Upon the Book and Picture of the Se-
raphicall Saint Teresa. . . . ."[42] But the pertinent passages on her
life, or rather her childhood, are all to be found in the various
English translations of her autobiography from the Spanish,
or in their abridgments. The thing that struck Crashaw and
Coleridge most was her precocious saintliness. For when she
was still only a child, she and her little brother loved to play
hermit, and build hermitages in the garden. They also read
books of martyrdoms and laid their plans to go to Barbary to
labor among the Moors, and, if necessary, to lose their lives
there, "for our Lord." This desire to seek a Moorish martrydom
was quite common and typical of her day, as she referred to it

---

[39] Crashaw, *Poems* (Cambridge, 1904), pp. 383, 266.

[40] *Ibid.*, p. 267.   [41] E.H.C., pp. 18–19.   [42] Crashaw, *Poems*, pp. 272–77.

at least twice more, after she had entered the nunnery and taken the veil.[43] Whether Coleridge owned or had consulted one of these lives I cannot say, but he did own a copy of the 1675 edition of *The Works of the Holy Mother St. Teresa of Jesus, Foundress of the Reformation of the Discalced Carmelites . . . . ,* though I do not know when he bought it. At any rate, in 1812 he made extensive and interesting notes in it, reflecting astutely upon her life and character and speculating upon the nature of her visions and the cause of her ever present sense of sin.[44] Moreover, in *Remorse*, his revision of *Osorio*, he renamed his character Maria and called her Teresa; and in his letter to Byron on March 30, 1815, announced that he intended to re-write this character for the projected collected edition of his works.[45] Thus Coleridge's abiding interest in Teresa, both the person and the name, is demonstrated.

Fortunately Teresa never found it necessary to seek her martyrdom in Barbary. Instead, she found it at home, with her visions and her constant praying and suffering for the sins of herself and mankind. Thus, in all likelihood, Christabel would have found hers, in an abbreviated but concentrated form, at her father's castle of Langdale Hall. Teresa's love was to be a spiritual one, though expressed in earthly terms by Crashaw:

> THOU art love's victime; & must dy
> A death more mysticall & high.
> Into love's armes thou shalt let fall
> A still-surviving funerall.[46]

Christabel's fate was, so far as can be hazarded, to lie in the consummation of her earthly love; her marriage was to be with her lover, not with Christ. Yet her name—"With Christ's name

[43] See, e.g., "M.T.," *The Flaming Heart or the Life of the Glorious S. Teresa. . . . . This History of Her Life, Was Written by the Saint Her Selfe, in Spanish, and Is Newly, Now, Translated into English, in the Yeare of Our Lord God, 1642* (Antwerp, 1642), pp. 3, 14, *et passim;* and *The Life of the Holy Mother St. Teresa . . . .* (London, 1758), pp. 2–3, 308, 318.

[44] *Notes, Theological, Political, and Miscellaneous* (ed. Derwent Coleridge, London, 1853), pp. 91–97.

[45] Griggs, II, 133.   [46] Crashaw, *Poems*, p. 269.

in 't", as in Teresa's "dearest breath"—was to stand for vicarious atonement and suffering for the sake of others, just as was the saint's.

But, if the theme is so simple and straightforward as this, the skeptic may well ask: Why all of Coleridge's sweatings and agonizings to finish the story, which eventually expired in complete though grudging failure? Since I am already so well embarked on the treacherous sea of speculation, it can do no harm to offer a few more theories for the benevolent reader to consider.

In the first place, it is one thing to conceive a theme, and another to invent suitable persons and incidents to embody it in flesh and blood. These persons and incidents, moreover, are likely to get out of hand, as all writers know, and insist on leading lives of their own, irrespective of what their creators planned for them. Such an independent spirit and uncontrolled existence are especially likely to develop in the case of an inspirational and intuitive poet like Coleridge, who gladly surrenders the reins of reason into the obliging hands of imagination. His impotent endeavors to escape from the intricate and bewitching byways where his teeming fancy had led him are probably represented not only in his struggles in composition but also in those tantalizing excisions and revisions, so many traces of which remain. Recall that the extant poem totals only 677 lines; that in October, 1800, he announced that it was running up to 1,400 lines; that after 1800 he admitted that he had written part of a third book; that in 1804 he apparently had added still more; and that in 1807 Dorothy Wordsworth had news from him that "he had been going on with *Christabel*, and had written almost as much as we have already seen. . . . . "[47] What further mysteries and complications these portions would have contributed to the problem, I for one prefer not to consider, though they would undoubtedly have also furnished new confirmation of his main purpose. Even in the extant 677 lines

[47] See above, pp. 12–14.

he has been unable to resist the temptations of all the strange figures and bookish superstitions which were thronging his mind, and as a consequence let himself be inveigled into adding embroidering touches and motives which he obviously found it impossible to reconcile and explain in spite of the liberality of his theory of the preternatural. The supernatural was encroaching inexorably on the other domain, and he did not have the power or will to banish it.[48] Geraldine's malignant characteristics were getting the upper hand over her altruistic ones. Probably his intentions altered from time to time, and, although he might maintain that he had seen the whole plan before him from the beginning, he might actually and easily have forgotten the glowing fantasies of his youth as his imagination cooled and hardened into the metaphysical casts of his age. In other words, either Gillman might have failed to grasp or retain the real significance of the design that was unfolded to him, or else his informant's own constantly shifting memory was betraying him. The character which Schedoni, the villain-monk in Coleridge's favorite Ann Radcliffe's *The Italian*, draws of Vivaldi, the hero, may be very appropriately applied to Coleridge himself:

" 'And what do you term my prevailing weakness?' said Vivaldi, blushing.

" 'A susceptibility which renders you especially liable to superstition,' replied Schedoni. . . . . 'Have you forgotten a conversation which I once held with you on invisible spirits?' . . . .

" 'I have not forgotten the conversation to which you allude,' replied Vivaldi, 'and I do not recollect that I then disclosed any opinion that may justify your assertion.'

" 'The opinions you avowed were rational,' said Schedoni, 'but the ardour of your imagination was apparent, and what ardent imagination ever was contented to trust to plain reasoning, or to the evidence of the senses? It may not willingly confine itself to the dull truths of this earth, but, eager to expand its faculties, to fill its capacity, and to experience its own pe-

[48] With this view compare that of Lane Cooper, discussed above, p. 118.

culiar delights, soars after new wonders into a world of its own!' "[49]

It was in 1838, four years after Coleridge's death, that John Wilson, who had played a contradictory and slightly unsavory part in the critical reception of "Christabel" in 1816, wrote for *Blackwood's* his devastating review of Martin Farquhar Tupper's *Geraldine*. In this review he avowed his actual and final opinion of "Christabel" and his content to accept and admire it as a miraculous fragment of genius even in preference to having the whole completed. Enthusiastically he said:

"Coleridge's Christabel is the most exquisite of all his inspirations; and, incomplete as it is, affects the imagination more magically than any other poem concerning the preternatural. . . . .

"Coleridge *could* not complete Christabel. The idea of the poem, no doubt, dwelt always in his imagination—but the poet knew that power was not given him to robe it in words. The Written rose up between him and the Unwritten; and seeing that it was 'beautiful exceedingly,' his soul was satisfied, and shunned the labour—though a labour of love—of a new creation.

"Therefore 'tis a Fragment—and for the sake of all that is most wild and beautiful, let it remain so for ever."[50]

In the face of this warning, and many others like it, I fully realize my temerity and even recklessness in having attempted to pick my way along the road to Tryermaine after so many years have weathered and defaced its never too well-marked outlines. Professor Lowes wisely did not try to predict the course of "Kubla Khan", for Coleridge obviously has provided little more than an atmosphere to work from. But in "Christabel" he has dotted in so many points in his design that it is hard to resist drawing the connecting lines in order to see what sort of picture may result. Moreover, the process is not exactly like the scientific one of reconstructing, let us say, the pterodactyl from the lucky recovery of a single wing-finger. It

[49] Radcliffe, *The Italian*, II, 267.   [50] *Blackwood's*, XLIV (December, 1836), 835.

is more of an *ex pede Herculem* affair—or the sketching of a unicorn from a shard of hoof, a shoulder blade, and a piece of corkscrewed horn. For the pterodactyl once actually lived, beat the groaning air with its leathery wings, and staggered clumsily along the earth. Hercules and the unicorn, on the contrary, were pure figments of the human imagination. Who can say what they really looked like, since they never existed? Each man has a right to his own opinion and may see in his mind's eye what he desires. I believe that by some good luck my eye has caught a glimpse of the glow, the illumination, which was in a poet's mind. This fortune is reward enough in itself. I shall therefore feel more than compensated if my adventures among the vampires, lamias, serpents, and demons of the air should afford any other persons a similar insight into the ever elusive but always provocative imagination of Samuel Taylor Coleridge.

INDEX

INDEX

The following index, when used in combination with the footnotes, is designed to take the place of the usual bibliography. Each work referred to in the book is fully described in a footnote on its first appearance, and thereafter is alluded to only in abbreviated form. Titles are listed under authors' names whenever possible. Figures in roman type refer to the main text; those in italics refer to the footnotes.

Since the volume of "Studies in Honor of George McLean Harper", edited by Earl Leslie Griggs and entitled *Wordsworth and Coleridge* (Princeton, 1939), did not reach me until after my own study was in page proof, I now insert brief references to three articles therein which have some bearing on the present book. In "Coleridge's 'Preface' to *Christabel*", B. R. McElderry, Jr. (*op. cit.*, pp. 166–72), discusses the apparent growth of the preface from two of Coleridge's own earlier letters: one answering the anonymous offer in 1811 "to review W. Scott's poems to his injury" and concerning Coleridge's views on critics who see only debts to preceding authors in any new work (cf. also T. M. Raysor, *Coleridge's Literary Criticism*, Harvard, 1930, II, 231–39); and the other to Byron on October 22, 1815, concerning the circumstances surrounding the composition of "Christabel" (see pp. 15, 17, and 21 of the present study). He also quotes Byron's assurance that he had written "The Siege of Corinth" before he knew anything about "Christabel" (see n. 45, p. 79, of the present study). In "An Early Defense of *Christabel*" (*op. cit.*, pp. 173–91) Griggs believes, with no new proof, that the two reviews of the poem in *The Edinburgh Review* and *The Examiner* were "almost certainly the work of William Hazlitt" and were written in a fit of "cantankerous and unjustifiable malignity" (see pp. 28 ff. of the present study). The main part of the article consists of a recently discovered, unpublished review of "Christabel", which is apparently in the handwriting of John J. Morgan, "who with his wife and sister-in-law, looked after Coleridge during the four or five years prior to the publication of *Christabel*," and which, Griggs speculates, was very likely inspired or even dictated in part by Coleridge himself as a reply to Hazlitt. In the profuse summary of the poem Geraldine is referred to consistently as merely a "supernatural and malignant being" (see n. 32, p. 40, of the present study). There is, however, no real evidence that this view represents Coleridge's own opinion. In "Samuel Taylor Coleridge Discovers the Lake Country", the Rev. G. H. B. Coleridge contributes two hitherto unpublished Coleridge journals (*op. cit.*, pp. 135–65). The first (p. 140) shows that Coleridge passed Blelham Tarn on November 3, 1799 (see n. 11, p. 158, of the present study); he also mentions "Wynandermere" and other tarns on p. 141. Coleridge's reading of Hutchinson (see p. 159 of the present study) is shown by his entry early in August, 1802 (p. 153): ". . . . had read in the History of Cumberland that there was an 'excellent Library' [at St. Bees]"; but it proved to be worthless. "Men who write Tours and County Histories I have by woeful experience found out to be *damned Liars*, harsh words, but true!" Although much of the 1802 tour was in the Wastdale district, he makes no reference to Tryermaine (see pp. 180–81 of the present study).

⟦ PRINTED IN U·S·A ⟧